Monetary and Financial Integration in West Africa

Monetary and Financial Integration in West Africa details the progress, challenges faced, and potential of the project intended to create a West African Monetary Zone (WAMZ) between The Gambia, Ghana, Guinea, Nigeria and Sierra Leone. Given the trend towards regionalization of economic ties across the world, especially after the launch of the euro, a detailed analysis of the WAMZ is needed. As this is the first book on monetary and financial integration in Gambia, Ghana, Guinea, Nigeria and Sierra Leone, it is an essential read for anyone interested in economic development in West Africa, and indeed in Africa as a whole.

This book is extremely well-researched, with detail on virtually all aspects of economic integration in the region; with issues ranging from the institutional details of integration, trade and financial market integration, to progress on convergence of macroeconomic fundamentals to the required payments system infrastructure. The book deploys solid empirical facts and sophisticated analyses to thoroughly defend its assertions. This collection is a valuable contribution and an excellent companion book for monetary economics or international economics classes as well as African development literature. It will provide students and researchers with an exciting chance to apply concepts of, for example, optimum currency areas, central bank structure or monetary policy approaches, to a real-world case of potential monetary union.

Dr. Temitope W. Oshikoya and his collaborators have written the authoritative book on the subject of monetary union in the West African Monetary Zone. As is evident in the level of detail of the book, Dr. Oshikoya brings rich field experience from his role as Director General and CEO of the West African Monetary Institute. This book will be of interest to postgraduates and researchers in development economics; as well as policy-makers, monetary authorities and development practitioners.

Temitope W. Oshikoya is the Director General and Chief Executive Officer of West African Monetary Institute.

Routledge studies in development economics

Monetary and Financial Integration in West Africa

Edited by Temitope W. Oshikoya

 Routledge
Taylor & Francis Group

LONDON AND NEW YORK

First published 2010
by Routledge
2 Park Square, Milton Park, Abingdon, Oxon OX14 4RN

Simultaneously published in the USA and Canada
by Routledge
270 Madison Avenue, New York, NY 10016

Routledge is an imprint of the Taylor & Francis Group, an informa business

© 2010 Selection and editorial matter Temitope W. Oshikoya, individual
chapters; the contributors

Typeset in Times by Wearset Ltd, Boldon, Type and Wear
Printed and bound in Great Britain by TJI Digital, Padstow, Cornwall

British Library Cataloguing in Publication Data
A catalogue record for this book is available from the British Library

Library of Congress Cataloging in Publication Data
Monetary and financial integration in West Africa/edited by Temitope W.
Oshikoya.
p. cm.
Includes bibliographical references and index.

1. Africa, West–Economic integration. 2. Monetary unions–Africa, West.
I. Oshikoya, Temitope Waheed,
HC1000.M66 2010
332′.0420966–dc22

2010004110

ISBN13: 978-0-415-58008-3 (hbk)
ISBN13: 978-0-203-84658-2 (ebk)

Contents

Illustrations

Figures

Tables

Boxes

Appendices

Contributors

Emmanuel Adamgbe is Principal Economist, Financial Integration Department, West African Monetary Institute.

Abdoulaye Barry is Director, Financial Integration Department, West African Monetary Institute.

Mohamed Conte is Senior Economist, Research and Statistics Department, West African Monetary Institute.

Cyprian K. Eboh (PhD) is Principal Manager, Operations and Regional Integration Department, West African Monetary Institute.

Lanto Harding (PhD) is Chief, Operations and Regional Integration Department, West African Monetary Institute.

Lamin Jarju is Senior Economist, Operations and Regional Integration Department, West African Monetary Institute.

Hilton Jarrett is Economist, Multilateral Surveillance Department, West African Monetary Institute.

Adeniyi Karunwi is Director, Finance and Administration Department, West African Monetary Institute.

Rohey Khan is Senior Economist, Multilateral Surveillance Department, West African Monetary Institute.

Gladys Kufour is Chief Counsel, Legal Department, West African Monetary Institute.

Tajudeen Nasiru is Senior Economist, Payment Systems and ICT Department, West African Monetary Institute.

Chris Odiaka is Director, Payment Systems and ICT Department, West African Monetary Institute.

Twum Ohene-Obeng is Deputy Director, Payments Systems and ICT Department, West African Monetary Institute.

Linda Omolehinwa is Chief Finance Officer, Finance and Administration Department, West African Monetary Institute.

Emmanuel Onwiodoukit is Deputy Director, Financial Integration Department, West African Monetary Institute.

Temitope W. Oshikoya (PhD, FCIB) is Director General, West African Monetary Institute.

Momodu Sissoho is Principal Economist, Research and Statistics Department, West African Monetary Institute.

Tidiane Syllah is Senior Economist, Multilateral Surveillance Department, West African Monetary Institute.

Abu Bakarr Tarawalie (PhD) is Director, Research and Statistics Department, West African Monetary Institute.

John H. Tei Kitcher is Director, Multilateral Surveillance Department, West African Monetary Institute.

Hussein Thomasi is Director, Legal Department, West African Monetary Institute.

Emmanuel Ukeje is Policy Advisor, West African Monetary Institute.

Jibrin Yakubu is Economist, Multilateral Surveillance Department, West African Monetary Institute.

Preface

In the past decade, there has been a growing interest in monetary and financial integration in West Africa. The region has witnessed rapid expansion of cross-border financial activities, and these have been fostered both by private sector initiatives and by the regulatory authorities. Since 2001, The Gambia, Ghana, Guinea, Nigeria and Sierra Leone, the member countries of the West African Monetary Zone, have also taken a number of initiatives towards establishing a single currency and monetary union.

This book examines the process, progress, prospects and challenges of forming a monetary union and of the ongoing financial integration among these five West African states. The book has adopted a comprehensive and multi-dimensional approach, both in the treatment of the various subjects of interest and in viewing monetary union and financial integration as part of a wider process of community-building within West Africa, which is itself part of a greater regional integration within Africa. The subjects treated include: macroeconomic and structural convergence; fiscal sustainability; trade and financial market integration; payments system infrastructure; and the operational, legal and institutional frameworks required for a successful monetary and financial integration.

The book would not have been possible without the contributions of several people. It is a product of collaborative efforts among the staff of the West African Monetary Institute, which has been at the centre of making the technical preparations for monetary union and financial integration in the West African Monetary Zone. The book has benefited from comments on earlier drafts by the staff of central banks and various finance and trade ministries in member countries of the West African Monetary Zone. Omotunde Johnson, Chidozie Emenuga, A.F. Gokel and Osita Ogbu have also provided suggestions on the technical aspects of the book. The contributions of anonymous reviewers are also recognized. In addition, the book gained from the editorial assistance of Richard Synge. I would also like to thank Yemah Woobay and Endurance Adjei for secretarial assistance in producing this book

Temitope W. Oshikoya
Director General
West African Monetary Institute
January 2010

Acronyms

AACB	Association of African Central Bank
ACH	Automated Clearing House
ACP	automated cheque processing
ADF	Augmented Dickey–Fuller
AEC	African Economic Community
AfDB	African Development Bank
AfDF	African Development Fund
AMU	Arab Maghreb Union
ATM	Automated Teller Machines
AU	African Union
BAP	Banjul Action Plan
BCEAO	Central Bank of West African States
BCPs	Basel Core Principles
BCS	Brown Card Scheme
BIS	Bank for International Settlement
BOFIA	Banking and Other Financial Institutions Act
BOG	Bank of Ghana
BOP	balance of payments
BPM	Balance of Payments Manual
BRIC	Brazil, Russia, India and China
BRVM	Bourse Regionale des Valeurs Mobilieres
BSL	Bank of Sierra Leone
CAC	Corporate Affairs Commission
CAR	capital adequacy ratio
CAT	Continuous Auction Trading
CBG	Central Bank of The Gambia
CBN	Central Bank of Nigeria
CBS	Central Bank Survey
CCI	Certificate of Capital Importation
CDS	central depository system
CEMAC	Economic Community of Central African States
CEPS	Customs, Excise and Preventive Service
CET	common external tariff

CFA franc	franc de la Communauté Financière de l'Afrique
CIFTS	CBN Inter-bank Funds Transfer System
COICOP	Classification of Individual Consumption by Purpose
COMESA	Common Market of Eastern and Southern Africa
COSSE	Committee of SADC Stock Exchanges
CPI	Consumer Price Index
CPIA	Country Policy and Institutional Assessment
CRMS	Credit Risk Management System
CSD	Central Securities depository system
DCS	Depository Corporation Survey
DFIs	development finance institutions
DHs	discount houses
DMBs	deposit money banks
DSA	Debt Sustainability Analysis
EAC	East African Community
EC	European Commission
ECA	Economic Commission for Africa
ECB	European Central Bank
ECCAS	Economic Community of Central African States
ECOWAS	Economic Community of West African States
ECSC	European Coal and Steel Community
ECU	European Currency Unit
EEC	European Economic Community
e-FASS	Electronic Financial Analysis and Surveillance System
EFTA	European Free Trade Association
EMCF	European Monetary Cooperation Fund
EMCP	ECOWAS Monetary Cooperation Programme
EMI	European Monetary Institute
EMS	European Monetary System
EMU	European Monetary Union
ERM	Exchange Rate Mechanism
ERP	Economic Recovery Programme
ESCB	European System of Central Banks
ETI	Ecobank Transnational Incorporated
ETLS	ECOWAS Trade Liberalization Scheme
EU	European Union
FAL	Final Act of Lagos
FCs	finance companies
FCS	Financial Corporation Survey
FDI	foreign direct investment
FINSSP	Financial Sector Strategic Plan
FSAP	Financial Sector Assessment Programme
FSDP	Financial Sector Development Programme
FSS	Financial System Strategy
FTA	Free Trade Area

GCC	Gulf Cooperation Council
GCNet	Ghana Community Network
GDP	Gross Domestic Product
GFCI	Global Financial Centre Index
GFS	Government Finance Statistics
GIPC	Ghana Investment Promotion Centre
GSE	Ghana Stock Exchange
HHI	Herfindahl–Hirchman Index
HICP	Harmonized Index of Consumer Prices
HIPC	Heavily Indebted Poor Countries
HS	Harmonized System
IDA	International Development Association
IFC	International Financial Centre
IFRS	International Financial Reporting Standards
IMF	International Monetary Fund
ISIC	International Standard Industrial Classification
ISRT	Inter-State Road Transit
JSE	Johannesburg Stock Exchange
LAFTA	Latin American Free Trade Association
LFC	Lekki International Financial Corridor
LICs	Low Income Countries
LPA	Lagos Plan of Action
MAP	Millennium Partnership for the African Recovery Programme
MDRI	Multilateral Debt Reduction Initiative
MFBs	microfinance banks
MFIs	micro finance institutions
MITAF	Microfinance Investment and Technical Assistance Facility
MMOU	Multilateral Memorandum of Understanding
MOU	Memorandum of Understanding
MPC	Monetary Policy Committee
MPR	Monetary Policy Rate
MRR	Minimum Rediscount Rate
MSG	Meteorological Satellite Second Generation
NAI	New African Initiative
NAICOM	National Insurance Commission
NASSIT	National Social Security and Insurance Trust
NATO	North Atlantic Treaty Organization
NBFI	Non-Bank Financial Institutions
NCBs	national central banks
NDIC	Nigerian Deposit Insurance Corporation
NEPAD	New Partnership for Africa's Development
NIPC	Nigerian Investment Promotion Commission
NIS	National Insurance Commission
NPG	Non-Ponzi Game
NPL	non-performing loans

NPV	Net Present Value
NSE	Nigeria Stock Exchange
OAU	Organization of African Unity
OCA	Optimum Currency Area
ODCS	Other Depository Corporation Survey
OMO	open market operation
OSFIC	Office of the Superintendent of Financial Institutions of Canada
PAP	Pan-African Parliament
PMIs	primary mortgage institutions
PP	Phillips–Perron
PPP	Purchasing Power Parity
PTA	Preferential Trade Agreements
PVBC	Present Value Budget Constraint
RBS	Risk-based supervision
RECs	Regional Economic Communities in Africa
RER	real exchange rates
ROA	return on assets
RTFC	Road Transit Facilitation Committees
RTGS	Real Time Gross Settlement
SADC	Southern African Development Community
SAP	Structural Adjustment Programme
SCF	Stabilization and Cooperation Fund
SDRs	Special Drawing Rights
SEA	Single European Act
SEC	Securities and Exchange Commission
SETC	Sierra Leone Stock Exchange Technical Committee
SIC	State Insurance Company Ghana Limited
SME	small and medium enterprises
SOEs	State-owned Enterprises
SPS	sanitary and phyto-sanitary
SRO	Self Regulatory Organization
SSS	Scriptless Securities Settlement
TARGET	Trans-European Automated Real-Time Gross Settlement Express Transfer
TC	Trade complementarity
TIB	Terminos Internet Banking
TOT	Technical Obstacles to Trade
TPD	Transactional Pricing Database
UEMOA	Union economique et monetaire ouest-africaine
UN	United Nations
UNECA	United Nations Economic Commission for Africa
VAR	Vector Auto-regression
VAT	value added tax
VISACAs	village savings and credit associations
WACB	West African Central Bank

WAEMU	West African Economic and Monetary Union
WAFSA	West African Financial Supervisory Authority
WAMI	West African Monetary Institute
WAMU	West African Monetary Union
WAMZ	West African Monetary Zone
WAN	Wide Area Network
WIFTS	WAMZ Inter-bank Funds Transfer System
WTO	World Trade Organization

1 Introduction

Temitope W. Oshikoya

Monetary union has been on the African political and economic agenda for a long time. It has been regarded as an important development strategy and thus considered to be crucial in attaining economic development, promoting regional stability and guaranteeing African influence in international negotiations. Essentially, it has been motivated by the desire to counteract the perceived economic and political weakness of individual countries. The small size of most of the economies in the region is often regarded as growth-retarding and thus, a combination of these countries in the context of an appropriate regional integration scheme would bring about a sufficiently large market size to generate lower production cost that might enable the integrated region to compete better with the rest of the world. In the same vein, a grouping of several small countries into a regional bloc could help Africa negotiate more effectively either bilaterally or multilaterally.

Monetary union will also be a major step in the integration efforts in the West African sub-region. A single currency will offer greater economic efficiency and stronger growth in the long run. The sub-region of the West African Monetary Zone (WAMZ), comprising The Gambia, Ghana, Guinea, Nigeria and Sierra Leone, with its estimated population of about 192.6 million people (World Bank, 2009), has immense natural and mineral resources, which gives it great potential for creating a viable West African market. The adoption of a single currency by these five countries would eliminate the risk of exchange rate movements and permit the integration of their capital markets. The capital markets, which are dominated by government debt instruments, would be broadened and deepened with the participation of private corporate bonds and equities. Stronger capital markets can stimulate structural reform in the banking and financial markets, and can facilitate the restructuring of the manufacturing industries and service sector.

Despite the potential benefits to be derived from a single currency, and despite the efforts of the member states to meet the benchmarks required for the commencement of the monetary union, the launch of the WAMZ monetary union has been postponed on three occasions. The target date was initially set for 1 January 2003, but was subsequently extended to 1 July 2005. The Banjul Declaration of 6 May 2005 further postponed the commencement date to 1 December 2009. The major reason for these postponements was the slow pace of macroeconomic and policy convergence in the WAMZ. The international financial crisis, on the heels of global fuel and food crises, adversely affected macroeconomic developments in the WAMZ (WAMI, 2008) and these external shocks hampered the progress of convergence in the Zone. The financial crisis also highlighted the need for a single currency to insulate the Zone member countries from external shocks. An acceleration of the integration process could enhance the region's resilience to future shocks.

This book assesses the history, progress, challenges and potential for monetary and financial integration in the WAMZ. The book has 12 chapters, which are divided among four main parts. Economic integration is the subject of Part I, in which Chapter 2 highlights the history of monetary and economic integration and the emergence of regional economic communities in Africa, and discusses the political context of Africa-wide monetary programmes, including those of the Economic Community of West African States (ECOWAS) and the WAMZ. The Banjul Action Plan (BAP), a work programme that provided a strong focus on actions and targets essential for the objectives of the WAMZ programme, is also discussed.

Chapter 3 presents an overview of the theoretical and practical underpinnings covering the Optimum Currency Area (OCA) theory (Mundell, 1961; Kenen, 1969), stages of economic integration (Holden, 2003), the experiences of the European Monetary Union (EMU) and the potential benefits and costs of a monetary union, preceding a discussion of economic integration in the WAMZ. The theoretical framework based on the OCA conditions for the establishment of a currency union is reviewed and evaluated in the context of the WAMZ countries. The stages of monetary integration, benefits and the disadvantages associated with monetary union are also assessed. The literature shows that there are potential costs and benefits inherent in the formation of a monetary union and that while those costs, including loss of independent monetary policy and asymmetric shocks, are more immediate, the benefits are long term in nature.

Chapter 4 provides a review of the economies of the WAMZ countries, their structural features, including indebtedness and patterns of trade, the risk of asymmetric shocks, business cycle synchronization, exchange rate movements, monetary policy framework and inflationary trends. It also analyses issues relating to economic distance (Alesina and Grilli, 1992). The WAMZ economies have been found to be heterogeneous in terms of both GDP and population, with only Guinea and Sierra Leone sharing common national borders, while the other countries are not geographically contiguous. Nigeria is the dominant economy within the WAMZ, constituting over 78 per cent and 86 per cent of the Zone's population and GDP, respectively. Chapter 5 provides an evaluation of the state of nominal macroeconomic convergence in the WAMZ based on a predetermined set of WAMZ criteria. The chapter underscores the economic heterogeneity as well as the asymmetric response to shocks among the member countries.

An evaluation based on the BAP shows that two of the four primary criteria, namely those of inflation rates and the fiscal deficit/GDP (excluding grants) ratio, have been the most difficult to achieve by the member countries since the launch of the WAMZ programme in 2001. The mixed performance of member countries with respect to macroeconomic convergence criteria brought to the fore the issue of whether convergence needs to be achieved *ex ante* or *ex post* (in the latter case the introduction of the common currency will force governments to speed up reforms and thus ensure convergence). The study on economic distance reveals that the cost of monetary union is relatively low for Ghana and The Gambia, but relatively high for Guinea, with Sierra Leone making progress towards reducing the cost of monetary union.

Chapter 6 explores the sustainability of fiscal policy in the WAMZ member countries, using both the accounting and present value budget constraint (PVBC) approaches (Hamilton and Flavin, 1986; Hakkio and Rush, 1991). In addition, the analysis on fiscal sustainability reveals that fiscal policies in Ghana, The Gambia, Guinea and Nigeria have been imperceptibly sustainable, while that of Sierra Leone has been unsustainable. Achieving fiscal sustainability is germane to the formation of a monetary union.

In Part II, the issue of market integration is addressed. Chapter 7 examines progress made towards a common market by the member countries of the WAMZ. It assesses the extent of trade integration of the member countries in the creation of a WAMZ common market and the institutional arrangements. In addition, labour mobility, infrastructure development and provision of logistics to support trade facilitation are also discussed. Chapter 8 discusses the evolution, structure and developments in the WAMZ financial sector. In addition, it presents an analysis of core issues relating to the extent of financial integration using both the benchmarks of the BAP and quantitative measures of financial integration based on the assumption of one price. The chapter also discusses the relevance of coordinated cross-border supervision in the aftermath of crisis and liquidity pressures and identifies barriers to financial integration. Chapter 9 articulates the role of payments system in a monetary union and the status of payments-system development in the Zone.

Part III focuses on the operational and institutional framework for monetary and financial integration in the WAMZ. Chapter 10 gives an assessment of the monetary policy transmission mechanism in the WAMZ countries and the need for improvement in data quality as well as further harmonization, especially in respect of the required standards for the common monetary policy of the WAMZ. Chapter 11 underscores the fact that legal and institutional issues are a sine qua non to the sustainability of a monetary union. The chapter adumbrates the fundamental building blocks and instruments that catalyse the efficient operation of systems and good governance for the actualization of economic and social welfare in the WAMZ. Various other legal and institutional instruments such as a Fiscal Responsibility Act, Cross-border Banking Supervision Agreement, credit information sharing, Banking Acts and acts establishing the central banks feature among the issues discussed.

Part IV highlights the way forward towards achieving lasting monetary and financial integration in the WAMZ. Chapter 12 provides a comparative analysis between the WAMZ and other monetary unions with specific reference to the Gulf Cooperation Council (GCC) and the West African Economic and Monetary Union (WAEMU). The lessons of experience suggest that the establishment of any properly functioning monetary union is a feat requiring, above all, adequate time for full preparation. The experience of other monetary unions, especially the EMU and the GCC, vividly highlights the fact that formation and sustainability of a monetary union is a long-term process, requiring political will and a culture of regionalism. The attainment of the convergence criteria would minimize the effect of asymmetric shocks in member countries. The European Union experience indicates that it took half a century to introduce the euro in 1999, with the project encountering postponements and shifts in dates along the way.

The GCC's experience is another useful example. The Gulf countries decided in 2001 to establish a monetary union by 2010 (Sturm and Siegfried, 2005; Rutledge, 2009), about the same time the WAMZ authorities decided to have their own monetary union. However, unlike the WAMZ that envisaged its monetary union in just 18 months, the GCC set a nine-year target date, despite the fact that the member countries are more homogeneous than those in the WAMZ, thus on face value being less likely to suffer heavily from asymmetric shocks. They are also culturally and historically similar, with the same language and geographical proximity. The indications are that the GCC, in spite of the gains made in real and nominal convergence over the past years, still views the common currency as a long-term project. This brings to the fore the need to build a durable and credible union.

Overall, the assessment reveals that the WAMZ does not satisfy all the OCA conditions. Nevertheless, this shortcoming does not imply that the goal of monetary integration is unattainable. The analyses demonstrate that the costs of monetary union in the WAMZ would be minimized in the long term as structural convergence takes hold. Going forward, the cost of adoption of a single currency in the WAMZ could become insignificant, especially if the establishment of a common market, financial sector integration and appropriate institutional and legal frameworks are put in place. Preparing for monetary union, therefore, involves a range of prerequisite policy reforms and institutional changes. Regardless of political considerations, the sustainability of the WAMZ monetary union depends on economic factors including the degree of nominal and real convergence, trade and financial integration, as well as institutional preparedness.

References

Alesina, A. and Grilli, V. (1992). "The European Central Bank: Reshaping Monetary Politics in Europe", in E.H. Hochreiter and P.L. Siklos (eds), *From Floating to Monetary Union: The Economic Distance between Exchange rate regimes*, SUERF – The European Money and Finance Forum, Vienna.

Hakkio, C.S. and Rush, M. (1991). "Is the Budget Deficit 'Too Large'?", *Economic Inquiry*, 29, 429–45.

Hamilton, J.D. and Flavin, M.A. (1986). "On the Limitations of Government Borrowing: A Framework for Empirical Testing", *American Economic Review*, 76(2), 353–73.

Holden, M. (2003). "Stages of Economic Integration: From Autarky to Economic Union", PRB 02–49E, February. Online: http://dsp-psd.pwgsc.gc.ca/Collection-R/LoPBdP/EB-e/prb0249-e.pdf.

Kawonishe, D. (2002). "Metamorphosis of OAU into AU: Problems and Prospects", *African Journal of International Affairs and Development*, 7(1), 84–111.

Kenen, P. (1969). "Theory of Optimum Currency Areas: An Eclectic View", in R. Mundell and A. Swoboda (eds), *Monetary Problems in the International Economy*, University of Chicago Press, Chicago.

Muchie, M. (2001). "African Union – Forward Ever, Backward Never", *New African*, September, 30.

Mundell, R.A. (1961). "A Theory of Optimum Currency Areas". *American Economic Review*, 51, 657–65.

Rutledge, E.J. (2009). *Monetary Union in the Gulf: Prospects for a Single Currency in the Arabian Peninsula*, Routledge Publishing, London and New York.

Sturm, M. and Siegfried, N. (2005). "Regional Monetary Integration in the Member States of the Gulf Cooperation Council", *ECB Occasional Paper series* 31, June.

UNCTAD (2009). *Economic Development in Africa Report: Strengthening Regional Economic Integration for Africa's Development*. United Nations, New York and Geneva.

WAMI (2008). *Convergence Report*. Online: www.wami-imao.org.

World Bank (2009). *Africa Development Indicators*. World Bank, Washington, DC.

Part I
Economic integration

2 The political context

Temitope W. Oshikoya, John H. Tei Kitcher
and Emmanuel Ukeje

Africa-wide economic integration programmes

Since the beginning of the decolonization process in the 1960s, regional integration has been part and parcel of the strategy of Africa's development. Regionalism in Africa began immediately after independence, championed mainly by the Organization of African Unity (OAU) and the United Nations' Economic Commission for Africa (ECA) (Qobo, 2007). This was in part a strategy to confront the last vestiges of colonialism on the continent while spurring political and economic progress. It was also seen as a political apparatus to address the power imbalances in the international economic cum political system.

After independence, regional integration became the fulcrum of Africa's development strategy. The ideology of Pan-Africanism,[1] which emphasizes continental unity and strong identification with ongoing anti-colonial struggles, was the linchpin of Africa's developmental framework. The fragmentation of Africa into tiny, unviable nation states led African leaders to embrace regional integration as a central element of their development strategy immediately after independence. The diminutive size and almost universally primary production structure of a typical African economy provided the rationale for pursuing mutually beneficial economic cooperation and regional integration, particularly among adjacent states.

Regional integration was viewed as a vehicle for achieving efficient industrialization with dynamic neighbourhood effects and regional spill-overs. In order to realize these benefits from integration, African countries, from the 1960s to the mid-1980s, enthusiastically established a legion of regional and sub-regional organizations. Besides economic motivations, Pan-African political aspiration for continental identity, unity and lucidity influenced the early drives for regional integration in Africa. The pursuit of these ideals derives mainly from the desire to overcome the vestiges of Africa's colonial past. Over time, the political aspiration of African unity reinforced the desire for regional and inter-regional economic cooperation as integral building blocks for continental cooperation and economic development.

In concrete terms, in the post-independence era, the ECA was the earliest advocate of regional cooperation in Africa. Right from its inception, the ECA considered the fragmented political geography of Africa as a serious impediment to the realization of its development goals. However, the idea of an immediate regional market, embracing all African countries, was considered impractical. Thus, promoting economic cooperation on sub-continental scale became an essential element of the ECA's approach. The ECA's efforts cut across the colonial francophone–anglophone divide. To this end, it sponsored several inter-governmental meetings of all the then 14 independent West African countries in 1966. Meetings were held successively in Niamey, Accra, Dakar and Monrovia to consider the draft Articles of Association for West African Economic Cooperation prepared by the ECA Secretariat. However, in spite of these efforts, the West African region remained divided between francophone and anglophone enclaves (Adedeji, 2002). The limited attempts to overcome the barrier were concentrated at the bilateral or trilateral levels, e.g. the Senegal–Gambia, Nigeria–Niger and Ghana–Guinea–Mali experiments, but these were not successful.

The idea of African integration came into its own in 1963 with the establishment of the OAU. Although the purposes of the OAU were primarily political, the organization eventually entered the realm of economic integration in 1991 with the signing of the treaty establishing the African Economic Community (AEC) by the heads of state and government (Kimunguyi, 2006). The way for this treaty had been prepared by the Lagos Plan of Action (LPA) and the Final Act of Lagos (FAL), both in 1980. The LPA had envisaged the formation of an African common market by the year 2000 which was to be achieved in stages: first the formation of free trade areas, and then later a common market and an economic union. The same process was to be followed in the three sub-regions identified by the Plan: Eastern and Southern Africa, Central Africa and West Africa.

The aim of the AEC specified in the 1991 Treaty is to promote economic, social and cultural development as well as African economic integration in order to increase self-sufficiency and endogenous development and to create a framework for development, mobilization of human resources and material. The AEC further aims to promote cooperation and development in all aspects of human activity with a view to raising the standard of life of Africa's people, maintaining economic stability and establishing a close and peaceful relationship between member states. The Treaty provides for the AEC to be set up through a gradual process, which would be achieved by coordination, harmonization and progressive integration of the activities of existing and future sub-regional economic communities (RECs) in Africa. The RECs are regarded as the building blocks of the AEC. The existing RECs are: the Arab Maghreb Union (AMU), the Economic Community of Central African States (ECCAS), the Common Market of Eastern and Southern Africa (COMESA), the Southern African Development Community (SADC) and the Economic Community of West African States (ECOWAS).

The implementation of the AEC Treaty and the establishment of the AEC have been envisaged as a six-stage process lasting 34 years (UNECA, 2008).

This starts with the strengthening of existing RECs and creating new ones where needed (five years) moving on to: stabilization of tariff and other barriers to regional trade and the strengthening of sectoral integration (eight years); establishment of free trade area and a customs union at the level of each REC (ten years); coordination and harmonization of tariffs systems among RECs, with a view to establishing an African common market and the adoption of common policies (four years); and integration of all sectors, establishment of an African Central Bank and a single African currency, setting up of an African Economic and Monetary Union and creating and electing the first Pan-African Parliament (five years). The operational provisions of the AEC Treaty accord much importance to the building up of sub-regional integration, though, as a necessary precondition for continental integration.

The Extraordinary Summit of the OAU held in Sirte, Libya on 9 September 1999 called for the establishment of an African Union in conformity with the ultimate objectives of the OAU Charter and the provisions of the AEC Treaty. Following this, at the fifth Extraordinary OAU/AEC Summit held in Sirte, Libya in March 2001, a decision declaring the establishment of the African Union (AU), based on the unanimous will of member states, was adopted. The AU is intended to, among other things: accelerate political and socio-economic integration; promote common Africa positions; promote democratic institutions, popular participation and good governance; protect human rights; promote sustainable development and the integration of African economies; and work to eradicate preventable diseases and promote good health. In 2001, the heads of state and government of all the African countries also established the New Partnership for Africa's Development (NEPAD). Regional and sub-regional approaches to development are the key element through which many of the expected results are to be accomplished.

However, in spite of the enthusiasm for and creation of a large number of regional integration organizations, African economies have continued to be constrained by political boundaries, are marginalized and remain unintegrated into the rapidly globalizing world economy. Responding to the poor outcome of their initial integration efforts, African countries are once again seeking to realize the benefits of enlarged markets with the attendant opportunities for economic transformation, growth and sustainable development. The African continent still suffers from poor infrastructure, limited trade and foreign direct investment, huge external debts and significant corruption and mismanagement. Nearly 70 per cent of sub-Saharan Africa's population lives on less than US$2 a day (World Bank, 2008). Despite these challenges, there have been positive developments. Since 1995, Africa has averaged between 2.7 and 6.5 per cent annual economic growth, including a continent-wide average growth rate of 6.0 per cent between 2005 and 2008.

The new momentum to invigorate the process of integration of African economies is reflected in the resurgence of political will expressed in the Abuja Treaty of 1991. First, the formation and strengthening of various regional blocks outside Africa (in Europe, Asia and the Americas) seems to have persuaded

African countries to reconsider the issue more seriously if they are to avoid further marginalization. Second, there has been a realization by African countries (particularly the small ones) that their respective national markets are too small to provide the benefits of economies of scale and specialization. Third, the liberalization initiatives undertaken by almost all countries in Africa has also created a conducive environment to pursue an outward-looking economic policy, which encompasses economic cooperation in general and trade liberalization policy in particular. Whether or not these factors, among others, are sufficient to take the integration initiative to a higher level remains to be seen, but they have clearly generated some movement.

ECOWAS economic and monetary integration programmes

In the West African sub-region, monetary integration pre-dated the Africa-wide efforts. As a result of different historical colonial experiences, the sub-region is largely divided into two zones, the francophone and the anglophone. The francophone West African countries were the former colonies of France and the anglophone countries, with the exception of Liberia, were former colonies of Britain. Two other countries, Guinea-Bissau and Cape Verde, were former colonies of Portugal. During the colonial period, those countries colonized by France shared the same economic programmes and institutions, likewise those colonized by Britain and Portugal.

To control the monetary matters of its colonies from a central point, the British government in 1912 established the West African Currency Board, head-quartered in London, to administer a common currency for its West African colonies, namely, The Gambia, Ghana (formerly Gold Coast), Nigeria and Sierra Leone. The currency board was characterized by a fixed parity with the pound sterling, an automatic system of issue and 100 per cent sterling cover for the local currency. However, as these countries gained independence, they created their own central banks and their own currencies, and the West African Currency Board was eventually wound up by 1964.

The franc zone, originally composed of nine French West African colonies,[2] was formed in the 1930s, when France undertook to issue currencies in these colonies that were linked to the French franc. These currencies were subsequently consolidated into the "franc de la Communauté Financière de l'Afrique" (CFA franc), which was fully convertible with the French franc at a fixed exchange rate. The French treasury guaranteed the exchange rate and ensured transferability to and from France and other territories. However, unlike the sterling zone which was abandoned after independence, the CFA franc zone was further strengthened with the establishment of a common central bank (the Central Bank of West African States, BCEAO), which has the sole responsibility of currency issue and monetary policy management throughout the francophone West African member states. In 1994, the bloc formed the West African Economic and Monetary Union (WAEMU, or UEMOA from its name in French, Union Economique et Monetaire Ouest-Africaine). Thus, while the former British West African colonies all have independent monetary policies and separate currencies, the majority of the former French colonies have maintained their union to date.

ECOWAS, comprising both the anglophone and francophone countries in West Africa, was established in 1975 (see Olukoshi, 2001), with the goal of greater economic integration. ECOWAS thus includes the distinct group of the eight countries of the WAEMU, while the others have maintained their own national currency. This second group – now consisting of Cape Verde, The Gambia, Ghana, Guinea, Nigeria, Liberia and Sierra Leone – accounts for 73 per cent of the GDP of the region and 66 per cent of the total population. Within the ECOWAS context, Nigeria accounts for 45 per cent of regional GDP, 66 per cent of total exports and more than half of the population of the region.

Economic and monetary union has been a longstanding ambition of ECOWAS, of which the revised Treaty calls for:

> co-operation and integration, leading to the establishment of an economic union in West Africa in order to raise the living standards of its peoples, and to maintain and enhance economic stability, foster relations among member states and contribute to the progress and development of the African continent.[3]

The ECOWAS Programme for West African integration includes: the ECOWAS Trade Liberalization Scheme (ETLS); the ECOWAS Monetary Cooperation Programme (EMCP); free movement of persons; development of regional transport and communications networks; strengthening the production base; and the harmonization of macroeconomic policies of member states. The Treaty, as revised in 1993, aims to accelerate the process of economic integration and strengthening political cooperation. Its long-term objectives are to establish an economic and monetary union between all member states. In the process towards economic union, the revised Treaty envisages the traditional sequencing, the intermediate stages being a free trade area, a customs union and a common market. The Heads of State first adopted the EMCP in 1987 to accelerate the process of integration within the sub-region. This programme entails the adoption of collective policy measures designed to achieve a harmonized monetary system. The end point of the EMCP is supposed to be the total monetary integration of the region. However, the programme fell short of its goal for many reasons, including the difficult economic and political experiences of some member states. According to the initial timetable, the EMCP was scheduled to take off in 1992, but this target date was not met. It was rescheduled by the Authority of Heads of State and Government of ECOWAS to the year 2000. By 1999 it was apparent that the pace of implementation of EMCP, especially the establishment of the single monetary zone, had not matched expectations. One of the major obstacles to the implementation of the EMCP was the lack of political will and leadership to implement the policies and actions aimed at the creation of a common currency. As it became clear that the 2000 target date was also too ambitious, the Authority decided at its meeting in Lomé, Togo, in December 1999, that a two-track approach to ECOWAS integration programmes be implemented.

Establishment of the West African Monetary Zone

The recognition of this problem necessitated the Authority of Heads of State and Government of ECOWAS, in December 1999 at its twenty-second Summit in Lomé, Togo, to adopt a strategy of a two-track ("Fast-Track") approach (to economic and monetary integration) initiated by Nigeria and Ghana to implementation of the EMCP. The governments of The Gambia, Ghana, Guinea, Liberia and Sierra Leone undertook consultations, while the Heads of State and Government, at their summit in Bamako, Mali in December 2000, agreed to: the establishment of a (second) West African monetary zone; the setting up of a common central bank; and the introduction of a single common currency in the zone in 2003, for eventual merger with the WAEMU zone in 2004 under the ECOWAS integration programme. The second monetary zone[4] in West Africa, known as the West African Monetary Zone (WAMZ)[5] is intended to achieve economic integration and monetary union among five non-WAEMU countries. This strategy gave renewed impetus towards the realization of the EMCP, with the ultimate aim of forming a unified monetary union for the whole of Africa. It was envisaged that the WAMZ single currency would run concurrently with the CFA franc of the WAEMU for an interim period before the creation of a single currency for the whole ECOWAS region. In April 2000, The Gambia, Ghana, Guinea, Nigeria and Sierra Leone launched the WAMZ in a bid to form a monetary union by January 2003 before merging with countries of the CFA zone by 2004 to achieve the EMCP. The action plan for the establishment of the WAMZ was to be implemented in stages, beginning January 2000, with the harmonization of macroeconomic policies through compliance with certain convergence indicators, to the operationalization of an exchange rate mechanism, culminating in the final phase, when a common currency (the eco) would be introduced.

The West African Monetary Institute (WAMI) was established by the Authority of Heads of State and Government of the five member countries in December 2000 to prepare the framework for the envisaged monetary union (WAMI, 2000). WAMI commenced operations in Accra, Ghana in March 2001. Among its tasks, the Institute was mandated to monitor the macroeconomic performance of member countries of the Zone. It was agreed that countries must satisfy all criteria before entering the monetary union if the West African Central Bank (WACB) was to start on credible and sound macroeconomic fundamentals. Thus, the WAMI was aimed at laying the foundations for the establishment of an independent WACB, as well as assisting member countries in achieving the "convergence criteria". The convergence criteria are a set of requirements which countries have to meet before being allowed to participate in the union.

The monetary union was scheduled to commence in January 2003, after a convergence process. However, due to difficulties experienced by the member countries in meeting the prescribed convergence criteria by the 2002 deadline, the programme was extended for another two-and-a-half years (July 2005) to allow more time for countries to implement more robust corrective economic measures to try to meet the targets. None of the countries attained the four

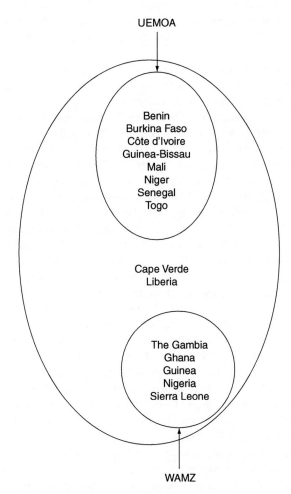

Figure 2.1 ECOWAS membership (source: www.ecowas.int).

primary and six secondary convergence criteria. Furthermore, the prior technical issues relating to statistical harmonization and payments-system developments had not been fully addressed.

The review of the first half of the convergence report prepared by WAMI in August 2004 showed that macroeconomic convergence was in its worst state since the convergence process commenced. The Authorities of WAMZ therefore concluded that 1 July 2005 was not feasible for launching the monetary union. They urged member countries to redouble efforts towards attaining the convergence criteria and directed WAMI to undertake a study on the prepared-ness of member countries for monetary union on 1 July 2005 and define a credi-ble timeframe for an enduring monetary union. Based on the results of the study, the Authorities decided on 1 December 2009 as a new target date for monetary union, and proposed an expanded work programme and an Action Plan for its delivery. The focus of the WAMZ programme was now broader, spanning not only macroeconomic convergence but also issues relating to the actualization of a single economic space.

In January 2009, WAMI prepared a status report on the WAMZ programme for consideration by the Authorities. It was clear that given the effect of the global recession, member states would be unlikely to achieve the benchmarks for macroeconomic convergence by December 2009. The Authorities once again postponed the launch of the second monetary union, until no later than January 2015.

The endorsement of a revised roadmap for the realization of a single currency for West Africa sub-region by member states of the ECOWAS ten years after the idea was first conceived should be viewed as a welcome development. The revised roadmap which targets the year 2020 for the full realization of the dream of a single currency for West Africa stipulates that between 2009 and the first quarter of 2013, ECOWAS would have achieved the harmonization of the regulatory and supervisory framework for banking and other financial institutions, the establishment of a payments-system infrastructure for cross-border transactions, the completion of the payments-system infrastructure in Guinea, The Gambia and Sierra Leone (countries lagging behind in e-payments) and the completion of the ongoing integration of the financial markets of the region. The legal instruments for the creation of the WAMZ would have been ratified. The central bank for the WAMZ, the WAMZ Secretariat as well as the West African Financial Supervisory Authority (WAFSA) would be in place by the same year. Again, a monetary union for the countries of the Zone is scheduled to be realized on or before 2015. Also contained in the roadmap are actions to be taken ahead of the new date which includes the review and harmonization of the convergence criteria, the harmonization of statistics, domestic policies and the legal, accounting and statistical framework of public finance.

The Institute's mandate was extended accordingly and WAMI continues to monitor the performance on macroeconomic convergence criteria through surveillance, policy advocacy and policy prescriptions. Furthermore, in the extended programme of the WAMZ, emphasis is placed on multilateral surveillance to ensure close coordination of member states' economic policies and sustained convergence of economic indicators. Accordingly, WAMZ member countries are enjoined to adopt regional economic policy for the Zone through effective coordination of macroeconomic policies, conduct regional economic policy in the context of an open market economy and specifically design and implement a common monetary and exchange rate policy in the Zone.

Conclusions

Despite considerable efforts to strengthen formal cooperation, the process of regional integration in West Africa has been slow. Nigeria (within WAMZ) and Côte d'Ivoire (within WAEMU/UEMOA), given their sheer economic potential, serve as core economies in these respective sub-groupings. Consequently acceleration of regional integration importantly depends on the policies and economic development in these two countries. One of the major obstacles to the implementation of the EMCP has been the lack of political will and leadership to implement the policies and actions aimed at the creation of a common currency. This lack of commitment resulted in several extensions to the dates for implementation of major aspects of the programme. In addition, the creation of the WAEMU by the countries in the CFA zone in 1994 has also hindered the advancement of the cause of ECOWAS. When the CFA zone countries decided to form the WAEMU to strengthen their political, economic and monetary solidarity, the position of the non-CFA zone members of ECOWAS was put into question.

Distrust and suspicion between member states has held back progress. Smaller countries often fear domination by the large ones. Such fears might be underpinned by socio-cultural, historical and language differences. In ECOWAS – with English, French and Portuguese being the lingua francas of the countries according to who their former colonizers were – the 'language divide' and associated political differences have militated against closer interaction among the countries (Adetula, 2004). Effective sensitization, getting all stakeholders on board and identifying with the objectives of integration have also been difficult. Awareness of the issue of economic integration has not been promoted at the grassroots level while the private sector, which is the engine of economic growth, has not been actively involved in the effort to advance integration by the various countries.

The ultimate phase of sub-regional monetary integration efforts in ECOWAS would be a merger of the WAMZ arrangement with the WAEMU, which already has a common central bank, the BCEAO. In addition to efforts at monetary integration in West Africa, the African Union is supportive of other similar efforts elsewhere in the continent to evolve a single currency and an African Central Bank. The Association of African Central Bank (AACB) Governors has recognized that achievement of the objectives of harmonization of monetary, financial and payments-systems policies and boosting intra-community trade would be predicated on, among other things, the strengthening of the sub-regional integration efforts and enhancing monetary cooperation among member states for the eventual evolvement of a monetary union in Africa. In fact, the AACB envisages that monetary cooperation, which would bring about macroeconomic convergence at sub-regional levels, would serve as building blocks for the future African Central Bank. Towards realization of this goal, the AACB has developed an African Monetary Cooperation Programme (AMCP) with stipulated convergence criteria, for implementation in the continent.

Notes

1 Regional integration and Pan-Africanism are not necessarily synonymous, but Pan-Africanism symbolizes the call for African unity which regional integration in Africa is evidently an important amplifier.

2 Before independence, the franc zone countries of West Africa comprised: Benin, Burkina Faso, Côte d'Ivoire, Guinea, Mali, Mauritania, Niger, Senegal and Togo. After independence, both Guinea and Mauritania soon withdrew from the zone, while Guinea-Bissau was admitted as a new member in 1997.
3 Article 3, Revised Treaty of ECOWAS, 24 July 1993.
4 The first monetary zone in West Africa comprises the eight francophone countries using the West African CFA franc issued by the BCEAO (known as the West African Economic and Monetary Union).
5 Countries of the WAMZ include The Gambia, Ghana, Guinea, Nigeria and Sierra Leone.

References

Adedeji, A. (2002). "History and Prospects for Regional Integration in Africa", paper presented at the Third Meeting of the African Development Forum, Addis Ababa, 5 March.

Adetula, V.A.O. (2004). "Regional Integration in Africa: Prospect for Closer Cooperation between West, East and Southern Africa", paper presented at the meeting of IDASA/ FREDSKORPSET Research Exchange Programme – Governance and Democracy, Johannesburg, South Africa, 2–4 May.

Kawonishe, D. (2002). "Metamorphosis of OAU into AU: Problems and Prospects", *African Journal of International Affairs and Development*, 7(1), 84–111.

Kimunguyi, P. (2006). "Regional Integration in Africa: Prospects and Challenges for the European Union", paper presented to the Australasian Political Studies Association Conference, University of Newcastle, Australia, 25–27 September. Online: http://www. newcastle.edu.au/Resources/Schools/Newcastle%20Business%20School/APSA/ INTLREL/Kimunguyi-Patrick.pdf.

Laporte, G. (1995). "Regional Cooperation and Integration in Africa: An Agenda for Action at the National Level", in *Regional Cooperation and Integration in the World Today: Papers from the First Open Forum*, Maastricht, 20 April, pp. 67–75.

Muchie, M. (2001). "African Union: Forward Ever, Backward Never", *New African*, September, p. 30.

Masson, P. and Pattilo, C. (2003). "The Monetary Geography of Africa", *Journal of International Economics*, 67(1), 515–20.

Olukoshi, A. (2001). "West Africa's Political Economy in the Next Mellinnium: Retrospect and Prospect", *Codesria Monograph Series*, 2.

Qobo, M. (2007). "The Challenges of Regional Integration in Africa: In the Context of Globalization and the Prospects for a United States of Africa", *ISS* paper, 145, June.

Shams, R. (2005). "The Drive to Economic Integration in Africa", Hamburg Institute of International Economics (HWWA), Discussion Paper 316.

Uche, C.U. (2002). "The Idea of a Regional Currency for Anglophone West Africa", paper presented at the tenth CODESRIA General Assembly, Kampala, Uganda, 8–12 December.

UNECA (2008). *Towards Monetary and Financial Integration in Africa: Assessing Regional Integration in Africa 111*. Online: www.uneca.org.

WAMI (2000). *Agreement, Statutes and other Provisions of the West African Monetary Zone*, ECW/AGR/WAMZ/1, December.

World Bank (2008). *World Development Indicators*, World Bank, Washington, DC.

3 Analytical framework

Temitope W. Oshikoya, John H. Tei Kitcher and Abu Bakarr Tarawalie

Introduction

This chapter examines the rationale for a monetary union drawing from both theoretical and empirical literature on stages of economic integration, optimal currency areas and lessons of experience of existing and potential monetary unions. It also outlines the potential benefits and costs of monetary integration. It concludes with some useful lessons for the WAMZ drawn from both the theory and the experience of the European Monetary Union (EMU).

Stages of economic integration

There are numerous reasons for nations to choose to harmonize their economic policies. Synchronization can produce benefits that are not probable otherwise. Every type of arrangement within which countries consent to harmonize their trade, fiscal and monetary policies could broadly be considered as economic integration. Thus the concept of economic integration basically involves the dismantling of all economic and non-economic barriers among countries participating in one form of monetary union or the other. Although it is uncommon to situate the relationships between countries within a precise pattern, formal economic integration takes place in stages, beginning with the lowering and removal of barriers to trade and culminating in the creation of a monetary union. The various stages in the process of economic integration have been identified to include:[1]

Preferential trade agreements (PTAs): These are trading agreements, where member states charge lower tariffs on imports produced by fellow member countries than they do for non-members. Thus, members of a PTA reduce the trade restrictions between themselves, while maintaining higher restrictions on goods imported from nations outside the agreement. One example has been the trading relations between Europe and the nations of Africa, the Caribbean and Pacific under the Yaoundé/Lomé Conventions.

Free trade areas (FTAs): These are PTAs without any tariffs on fellow members' goods. In other words, in an FTA, member countries eliminate internal tariffs and non-tariff barriers among themselves but have different external tariffs for non-members. Thus, it involves the elimination of all forms of barriers and restrictions on mutual trade between the signatory states, as for example in the Latin American Free Trade Association (LAFTA) and the European Free Trade Association (EFTA). An FTA is a complicated process where procedures have to be established to deal with intermediate goods, as well as preventing the re-exportation of goods from the country with the lowest tariff, and enforcement of the rules of origin.

Customs unions: In these arrangements, all the conditions of an FTA hold, with the addition of a common external tariff (CET) on imports from non-members of the union. In other words, a customs union builds on an FTA by, in addition to removing internal barriers, also requiring participating countries to harmonize their external trade policies. In addition to the CET, import quotas are imposed on products entering the region from third-party countries, and there may be common trade remedy policies such as anti-dumping and countervailing measures, but without free movement of capital and labour across member countries (e.g. the Central African Customs Union). The rules of origin are not relevant in a customs union, since any product entering the customs union area would be subject to the same tariff rates and/or import quotas regardless of the points of entry.

Common markets: These apply the same conditions as a customs union, plus the free movement of capital and labour within the economic group. Thus, in addition to containing the provisions of a customs union, a common market removes all barriers to the mobility of people, capital and other resources within the area in question, as well as eliminating non-tariff barriers to trade, such as the regulatory treatment of product standards. A common market is also associated with a broad convergence of fiscal and monetary policies due to the increased economic interdependence within the region and the effect that one member country's policies can have on other members.

Monetary unions: These involve all the conditions of a common market, as well as the harmonization of financial, economic and legal policies. Specifically, member countries accept a common currency administered by a supranational authority in addition to all of the characteristics of common market. The closest arrangement that mimics this today is the EMU.

The identified stages of integration (Box 3.1) represent the processes through which efforts at integrating different national economies should be pursued. For example, to reach the *customs union* stage, the conditions of a *free trade area* must exist among the countries. Similarly, to reach the *common market* stage, conditions for a *customs union* are a precondition. The achievement of *monetary union* is designed to be the last stage in the process of economic integration. While this arrangement seems to suggest that attempts to by-pass any one stage, or failure to follow this process in sequential order, could result in problems for the integration effort, it is also pertinent to note that the fact that certain integration processes have evolved in stages does not mean that a specified time-frame is necessarily attached to any particular stage. This may suggest that the time needed to transit from one stage to the other is critically dependent on the level of commitment of each of the integrating countries in the implementation of the required policies and programmes relevant to each of the different stages of integration.

Box 3.1 Stages of economic integration

Preferential trade agreements

In the establishment of preferential trading relations, member states charge lower tariffs to imports produced by fellow member countries than they do for non-members (e.g. ACP–EEC trading relations based on the Yaoundé/Lomé Conventions).

Free trade area

This involves the elimination of all forms of barriers and restrictions on mutual trade between signatory states (e.g. Latin American Free Trade Association (LAFTA), European Free Trade Association (EFTA)).

Customs union

In this arrangement all the conditions of a free trade area hold, in addition to the establishment of a common external tariff (CET) against imports from non-members of the union (e.g. the Central Africa Customs Union).

Common market

All conditions of a customs union hold, plus the free movement of capital and labour within the economic group (e.g. the European Economic Community).

Monetary union

This involves all the conditions of a common market, as well as the harmonization of financial, economic and legal policies. The closest arrangement to mimic this today is the EMU.

Source: Holden (2003)

Theory of monetary integration: optimum currency area

The relevant theory that permeates the discussion on monetary integration is that of the Optimum Currency Area (OCA), which addresses the central question of under what conditions a monetary union is ideal. While several studies have examined this issue (Box 3.2), the main OCA conditions are summarized below.

Mundell (1961) defines the optimum currency area as a region in which factors of production are internally mobile but internationally immobile, so as to facilitate the intra-regional redistribution of resources in response to demand shifts. In this regard, an OCA is considered to be the optimal geographic area of a common currency, or of several currencies, whose exchange rates are irrevocably pegged and might be unified. The common currency, or the pegged currencies, can fluctuate only in unison against the rest of the world. The domain of an OCA is defined by the sovereign countries choosing to adopt a single currency or to irrevocably peg their exchange rates. Optimality is defined in terms of several OCA criteria, including the mobility of labour and other factors of production, economic openness, diversification in production and consumption, price and wage flexibility, similarity of supply and demand shocks and business cycles, fiscal integration and similarity of inflation rates (Mongelli, 2002). Sharing the above properties reduces the usefulness of nominal exchange rate adjustments within the currency area by fostering an internal and external balance, reducing the impact of some types of shocks or facilitating the adjustment thereafter. Countries would thus form a currency area in expectation that current and future benefits would exceed the costs.

The OCA theory emerged from the debate on the advantages and disadvantages of fixed versus flexible exchange rate regimes. The OCA theory began with Mundell (1961), McKinnon (1963) and Kenen (1969). Three main OCA criteria for monetary integration arose from a debate that centred on factor mobility, the degree of economic openness and diversification in production and consumption.[2]

The first criterion, according to Mundell (1961), relates to the mobility of factors of production, including labour. High-factor market integration and sufficient factor mobility within a group of partner countries could reduce the need to alter real factor prices and the nominal exchange rate between countries in response to disturbances. If one country suffers from depression due to a negative shock, factors of production may move from this country to another which is hit by a positive shock. Hence, prices of these factors do not need to fall so sharply in the depressed economy and rise in the booming economy. Factor mobility is then able to compensate for the exchange rate changes.

Mundell (1961) presumed that people had their expectations stationary, in other words they did not anticipate future movements in the price level, interest rates, the exchange rate or in government policy itself. However, in a related study, Mundell (1973) admitted the existence of private agents' expectations and identified a central fact that better reserve pooling and portfolio diversification can mitigate asymmetric shocks within countries using a common currency. A country hit by an adverse shock can better share the loss with a trading partner because both countries hold claims on each other's output in a common currency. And the larger the portion of currencies that is backed up by internationally acceptable money, the greater the reserve needed for unexpected events. Therefore, if some countries decide to form a currency area, the domain of risk-sharing is extended. A common currency area thus provides benefits for its members by offering insurance against region-specific shocks.

The second criterion, designated by McKinnon (1963), is the degree of economic openness. The higher the degree of openness, the more changes in international prices of tradables are likely to be transmitted to the domestic cost of living. Also devaluation would be more rapidly transmitted to the price of tradables and the cost of living, negating its intended effects. Hence, the nominal exchange rate would be less useful as an adjustment instrument for small and open economies.

Kenen (1969) outlined the third criterion: diversification in production and consumption.[3] A high diversification in production and consumption diminishes the possible impact of shocks specific to any particular sector. Therefore diversification reduces the need for changes in the terms of trade via the nominal exchange rate and provides a hedge against an array of disturbances. More diversified partner countries are more likely to endure small costs from forsaking nominal exchange rate changes among them and find a common currency beneficial.

Other criteria include: price and wage flexibility; similarity of supply and demand shocks and business cycles; fiscal transfers; financial market integration; and similarities of inflation rates. When nominal prices and wages are flexible between and within countries contemplating a common currency, the transition towards adjustment following a shock is less likely to be associated with sustained unemployment in one country and/or inflation in another. This will lessen the need for nominal exchange rate adjustment. In this case, the loss of direct control over the nominal exchange rate instrument need not represent a cost. Price and wage flexibility are particularly important in the very short run, when the factor mobility is partly restricted, to facilitate the adjustment process following a shock. Permanent shocks will entail permanent changes in real prices and wages.

Another essential criterion is the similarity of supply and demand shocks and business cycles in countries using a common currency. Monetary and exchange rate policy cannot be used as a stabilization tool if a member country is, for example, hit by an asymmetric shock. Hence, business cycles of countries considering establishing a currency area must be correlated to a maximum extent.

Fiscal transfers are essentially a non-market-based adjustment process. The intention is the redistribution of financial resources from relatively richer to relatively poorer countries or from countries hit by a positive shock to countries hit by a negative shock. Admittedly, these two objectives could be incompatible: a country hit by a positive shock could be at the same time a relatively poorer country. Besides, the system of fiscal transfers requires a certain degree of political integration.

Financial market integration is an essential criterion that can reduce the need for exchange rate adjustment (Ingram, 1962). It helps to moderate temporary adverse disturbances through capital inflows (by borrowing from surplus areas or de-cumulating net foreign assets that can be reverted when the shock is over). Under a high degree of financial integration, even modest changes in interest rates would elicit equilibrating capital movements across partner countries. This would reduce differences in long-term interest rates, easing the financing of external imbalances but also fostering an efficient allocation of resources.

Similarities of inflation rates are also needed to create an OCA. External imbalances can arise from persistent differences in national inflation rates resulting, *inter alia*, from: disparities in structural developments; diversities in labour market institutions; differences in economic policies; and diverse social preferences. When inflation rates between countries are similar over time, terms of trade will also remain fairly stable. This will foster more equilibrated current account transactions and trade, and reduce the need for nominal exchange rate adjustment.

In real life there would almost certainly be no monetary union, even within the same country, if each and every one of the conditions of the OCA had to be satisfied concurrently and in full. Consequently, the creation of a monetary union and the introduction of a common currency generally deviate from the theory of the OCA in some areas. Furthermore, as observed by Kim (2007), it has to be taken into account that the establishment of a monetary union with a single currency is likely to stimulate trade integration and thus improve *ex post* the conditions for a monetary union. In reality, countries that are decidedly integrated with each other in terms of trade and other economic relationships are likely to constitute a monetary union.

Overall, there are basically two approaches to monetary union. It is either the case that one market generates the need and conditions for one money or else it can be the case that one money creates the need for one market. While the European experience followed the earlier model, the CFA zone in West and Central Africa essentially follows the 'one money seeking to create one market' paradigm. In this context it is useful to examine the relevance of the experience of the EMU and other monetary unions for the WAMZ.

Potential benefits and costs of monetary integration

The ultimate goal of regional integration is to create a common economic space among the participating countries. Monetary and economic integration may evolve from trade links as well as from historical and cultural ties. The process entails the harmonization of macroeconomic policies, legal frameworks and institutional architecture towards nominal and real convergence. There are benefits as well as costs associated in the pursuit of monetary integration.

Benefits

The potential advantages of a monetary union include a reduction in transaction costs, consolidation of the single market, price convergence and price stability. The amounts spent on foreign exchange transactions and exchange rate hedging will be eliminated. The eradication of these costs will boost trade within the member countries of the union. It will also be especially helpful to small and medium-sized enterprises, which may not be able to reap sizeable economies of scale. Furthermore, the consolidation of the single market is important in itself, potentially increasing efficiency in production because of increased specialization and economies of scale. The principal gains from monetary integration are as follows:

1   Monetary and financial integration may attract foreign direct investment (FDI) both from within and outside the monetary integration arrangement as a result of (i) market enlargement (particularly for "lumpy" investment that might only be viable above a certain size), and (ii) production rationalization (reduced distortion and lower marginal cost in production), which may result in economies of large-scale production (see Kritzinger-Van Niekerk, 2005).

2   The low capacity of many countries usually makes cooperation in international negotiations an attractive option, as cooperation can increase the countries' bargaining power and visibility, which would create an improvement in integration of markets for goods, services and factors.

3   Monetary integration would result in the elimination of exchange rate risk and uncertainty among member states. Coupled with stable prices and interest rates, intra-regional trade and investment flows would be less volatile.

4   Conducting economic activities in the same currency also reduces transaction costs by eliminating the costs of using different currencies.

5   A monetary union can act as an external "agent of restraint", providing more policy discipline than would otherwise be the case (Collier, 1991). In particular, a supranational agency of restraint would be more insulated from political pressures from one national government than a national institution, and therefore better able to focus on a given economic objective.

6   Developmental and environmental efficiency gains may thus arise from adopting a regionally integrated approach towards the provision or protection of regional public goods[4] (such as environmental and water management, migration and HIV prevention), which cannot be effectively addressed individually but are best tackled in a cooperative framework. In this regard, monetary integration can also be an effective approach towards conflict prevention by establishing ties with economic partners in a region.

7   Monetary integration would enhance the pooling of national reserves of foreign currencies. By internalizing their foreign trade, countries in a monetary integration reduce their demand for foreign currency reserves, which can easily be spent on or invested in alternative and more productive uses.

8   By unifying monetary and coordinating fiscal policies, participating countries are led to fewer distortions while combating macroeconomic disequilibria. This would result in a greater internal monetary stability and an increase in influence in international monetary affairs, resulting in economic growths and stable macroeconomic performance.

9   Price comparability and transparency may arise from monetary integration. This will boost competition and specialization in tradable goods[5] and services, with the result of increasing export earnings.

Costs

1   The loss of a country's sovereignty to use the exchange rate and monetary policy for stabilization is considered the most important cost of monetary integration.
2   Another cost of monetary integration is the loss of seignorage (inflation tax), as well as loss of revenue from tariff, customs duties, etc. Seignorage is the revenue the government obtains by financing its budget deficit through printing money rather than selling debt. The reduction in seignorage and tariff revenue may impact negatively on a government's ability to finance social, health and education programmes, among others.
3   Monetary integration may discourage infant industries because of external competition; some sectors in each country will suffer from competition with more efficient producers in the partner markets.

An examination of the benefits and costs brings to the fore the importance of sequencing and achieving a sufficient measure of compliance with key conditions to ensure net economic benefits. As noted earlier, even successful monetary unions did not fully comply with all the theoretical optimal currency conditions. The key to a smooth, and politically sustainable, transition to a monetary union is policy convergence, particularly in inflation, exchange rate, public debt levels and fiscal stances. The risk of costly adjustment is reduced by flexibility within and between the economies, including mobile capital and labour and diversification. Thus, the immediate and essential priority before the formation of a monetary union should be to achieve policy convergence, accompanied by efforts to increase flexibility and integration.

Convergence criteria are usually drawn up in an effort to bring convergence to the participating economies within the monetary union. However, this is an optimistic objective and did not really account for the costs that the loss in sovereign monetary policy entails. Economic policy would become very rigid within the participating countries as governments lose the option of devaluation, and monetary policy would be set by a supranational central bank. In the event of a detrimental asymmetric shock that puts the economies in recession, the governments would be very limited in their policy response options. They cannot devalue to restore competitiveness or decrease interest rates, and fiscal policy would also likely be restricted especially in the light of prior agreements which limit yearly budget deficits of the countries. Basically, governments would only be left with microeconomic options to boost the economy which may help to increase employment and output in the long run but would do little in the short run during a recession. However, overall monetary integration can be expected to facilitate economic convergence and therefore make asymmetric shocks less likely to occur.

Box 3.2 discusses the empirical evidence of the benefits and costs of existing monetary unions in Africa. Much of the literature on economic and monetary integration in Africa investigates the critical challenges of sustaining a monetary union and financing a fixed exchange rate regime given that most of the unions in Africa suffered setbacks after the initial enthusiasm of the early 1960s. Furthermore, economic problems as well as political instability can cause member states to stray from regional monetary arrangements: for instance, the East African Currency Board collapsed in 1966, soon after member states secured independence, while both the CFA zone and the original rand monetary area lost some members over time and faced financial problems. Botswana left the rand monetary area in 1976; Mauritania left the West African CFA monetary union in 1973 followed by Mali (although the latter re-entered in 1984).

Box 3.2 Benefits and costs of monetary union: empirical evidence from Africa

Substantial literature has been dedicated, albeit with data constraints, to measuring the benefits and costs of monetary integration in Africa.

Enhanced trade: A major strand of empirical research on the benefits of monetary union is rooted in the standard international trade theory. Alesina *et al.* (2002), Frankel and Rose (2002), Glick and Rose (2001), Rose (2000) and Tenreyro and Barro (2003) all find evidence that currency unions lead to increased trade linkages between member states.

Economic Growth: Looking more specifically at the relationship between growth and common currencies, Edwards and Magendzo (2003) find that there is no significant difference between the growth performance of dollarized countries and countries with a domestic currency. Devrajan and de Melo (1987) demonstrate how participation in the CFA zone shielded member states from the negative impact of global economic shocks in the 1970s. The authors noted that individual and aggregate measures of the zone's GDP growth are higher than those of other countries in sub-Saharan Africa.

Business Cycles: Most evaluations have focused on the CFA zone and criticize the striking lack of business cycle synchrony. Bayoumi and Ostry (1997) opined that one of the major shortcomings of the CFA zone lies in its insufficient homogeneity. Although the authors find high inflation correlations for CFA countries, the coherence of economic growth across countries could not be established, indeed negative correlations were reported in some cases. The authors explained the growth asymmetry in terms of the high specialization of member countries in the production of primary products, which makes them susceptible to external shocks. Their findings indicated that endogeneity may not apply to West African countries.

Asymmetry Shocks: Fielding and Shields (2001) applied the OCA theory to the two francophone monetary unions. The paper focused on shocks to aggregate output growth and to aggregate price inflation applying a structural representation of the macroeconomy of each member of the CFA and Kenya. The cost of CFA membership in terms of lost monetary autonomy would be larger than in a world where a monetary response to a shock is immediate. The study concluded that the cost of monetary union membership will depend on the extent to which price and output shocks are correlated across countries and the degree of similarity in the long-run effect of the shocks on the macroeconomy.

Anyanwu (2003) used panel economic indicators for individual members of WAEMU as well as non-WAEMU ECOWAS counterparts to determine whether the monetary union has brought price and output, fiscal and trade stabilization during the period 1990–2001. The result revealed that with respect to the macroeconomic effect of monetary unions on trade and output, a monetary union is beneficial to bilateral trade and economic growth. The results suggested that economic growth stability was greater in the WAEMU countries than in non-WAEMU countries during the study period, but the reverse was the case for inflation. Inflation in the WAEMU region was higher than in the non-WAEMU region.

Studies that apply the gravity model of trade appear to have presented a robust support for monetary integration. Rose (2000), Engel and Rose (2002) as well as Frankel and Rose (2002) have generated a substantial literature on the relationship between currency integration and intra-regional trade. The conclusion of these studies is that the use of a common currency increases trade three-fold. Anyanwu (2003) supplements the basic gravity model to control for the CFA's devaluation period and the volatility of nominal exchange rates, while Carrère (2004) compares the effects of currency unions versus trade agreements. Their findings further emphasized the view that participation in a monetary zone increases trade for CFA countries.

Lessons from the experience of the European Monetary Union

The European Monetary Union (EMU)[6] came into being on 1 January 1999, when the third stage of the process set forth in the Maastricht Treaty was launched. Countries adjudged to have satisfied the Maastricht criteria entered the single currency zone, giving up their monetary policy to the European Central Bank (ECB) and committing to keeping their fiscal policy in line with the limits described by the Stability and Growth Pact. European convergence started in 1952 with the establishment of the European Coal and Steel Community (ECSC) by six European countries. A key milestone was the signing of the Treaty of Rome which established the European Economic Community (EEC) in 1958. The Werner Report of 1970 advocated monetary union by 1980. However, because of the world oil crisis, during which the price of oil quadrupled and inflation and unemployment rose sharply, the focus shifted away from monetary union, and the plans were dropped.

In 1979, the European Monetary System (EMS) was established to link European currencies and to avoid large fluctuations between their respective values. It created the European Exchange Rate Mechanism (ERM) under which the exchange rates of each member state's currency was to be restricted to narrow fluctuations (+/–2.25 per cent) on either side of a reference value. This reference value was established in an aggregated basket of all the participating currencies called the European Currency Unit (ECU), which was weighted according to the size of the member state's economies.

The European Commission (EC) passed the Single European Act in February 1986, which aimed to remove institutional and economic barriers between EC member states and established the goal of a common European market. It took some time for the member states to remove all the barriers to trade between them and to turn their "common market" into a genuine single market in which goods, services, people and capital could move around freely. The Single Market was formally completed at the end of 1992. By the close of the 1990s, it had become increasingly easy for people to move around in Europe, as passport and customs checks were abolished at most of the European Union's internal borders.

In 1989, the Delors Report proposed a realization of the EMU in three stages. The first stage officially began in 1990, when exchange rate controls were abolished, thus freeing capital movements within the EEC. In 1992, the three stages envisioned by the Delors Commission were formalized in the Maastricht Treaty, including economic convergence criteria for adoption of the common currency. In effect, this transformed the EEC into the European Union (EU).

In the second stage of the EMU, the European Monetary Institute (EMI) was established as a forerunner of the European Central Bank (ECB). In June 1997, the European Council in Amsterdam agreed to the Stability and Growth Pact and set up the ERM II, which would succeed the EMS and the ERM after the launch of the euro. The following year the European Council in Brussels selected 11 countries to adopt the euro in 1999 and the ECB came into being, tasked with establishing monetary policy for the EU and with overseeing the activities of the European System of Central Banks.

To join the EU, a country must meet the Copenhagen criteria, defined at the 1993 Copenhagen European Council. These require a stable democracy which respects human rights and the rule of law; a functioning market economy capable of competition within the EU; and the acceptance of the obligations of membership, including EU law. In addition, member states are expected to satisfy certain primary convergence criteria, which includes: inflation (should not exceed by more than 1.5 percentage points the three best-performing member states); budget deficit (should not exceed 3 per cent of GDP); gross public debt (should not exceed 60 per cent of GDP); and interest rates (average of the lowest six countries plus 2 percentage points). Evaluation of a country's fulfilment of the criteria is the responsibility of the European Council.

The EU has developed a single market through a standardized system of laws which apply in all member states, ensuring the freedom of movement of people, goods, services and capital. It maintains common policies on trade, agriculture, fisheries and regional development. A common currency, the euro, has been adopted by 16 member states that are thus known as the Eurozone. The EU has developed a limited role in foreign policy, having representation at the World Trade Organization, G8 summits and at the United Nations. It enacts legislation in justice and home affairs, including the abolition of passport controls between many member states which form part of the Schengen Area. Twenty-one EU countries are also members of NATO.

The experience of the EMU in creating a monetary union highlights a number of steps that were taken well before the euro was launched. The EMU followed a lengthy and high degree of policy and institutional preparedness and the introduction of the euro was the product of over 40 years of remarkable cooperation among sovereign states with great diversity of economic, social and political interests. Indeed, in spite of their higher level of development, the long transition period enabled the countries to prepare and show that they have converged to low fiscal deficits, low rates of inflation and stable exchange rates before the union was started. The Maastricht criteria assisted the countries to move forward by specifying quantitative benchmarks for progress, establishing mileposts and creating transparency and oversight mechanisms to monitor progress achieved.

The EMU's Maastricht approach also showed that transition may need to be gradual if there is wide asymmetry among member states at the beginning, while fast-tracking stands a chance of succeeding where stability and prudence has already taken root among the members. Thus, it would be appropriate for flexibility in progression to integration through allowing room for variable speed, variable geometry and variable depth.

Another important lesson from the experience of the EMU is that for macroeconomic convergence to work, there must be key determinants in place, such as: building consensus in developing the convergence criteria and its implementation modalities, as well as commitment to agreed obligations; prioritization in the design of policy objectives and strategies, as well as the setting up of relevant institutions and assigning mandates at the national and regional levels; equitable, objective and transparent mechanisms for determining and allocating the costs, benefits and corrective measures that integration entails; an appropriate, independent supranational authority and requisite regional institutions (e.g. a single central bank), with a clear focus and realistic transition framework towards integration – such a supranational authority should be adequately empowered with rules for enforcing and penalizing any errant behaviour by non-compliant members.

Establishment of supranational institutions also contributed immensely to the European integration process. Institutional support was provided by the common market, Single European Act, the European Commission and extensive policy harmonization in many areas. The achievement of the single market in Europe paved the way for the introduction of the single currency. In the words of the European Commission:

> a single currency is the natural complement of a single market. The full potential of the latter is not achieved without the former ... there is a need for economic and monetary union in part to consolidate the potential gains from completing the internal market, without which there would be risks of weakening the present momentum of the 1992 progress.

Also, the European Commission was invested with the power to propose directives and regulations, which, if approved by the European Council and

European Parliament, had direct effect, in that they superseded national legislation in the area concerned. The provision of defined extensive legal framework to back up the activities of the institutions and organs of the Community and upholding of or respect for these provisions by both the direct operators and member states was also crucial.

The European experience also shows that the EMU is essentially a political agreement, of which economic integration and monetary union are components. The member states of the EU demonstrated a growing willingness to sacrifice national sovereignty – in macroeconomic management, structural policies and, eventually, politics.

The EMU certainly offers important lessons for the WAMZ in order to appreciate the risks and the opportunities, and the way they were resolved. The EMU project also suffered shifts in target dates along the way. The postponements of the launch date of the WAMZ monetary union are therefore not unique. Monetary union in the WAMZ should be premised on strong political will and the commitments by member states to undertake policies and programmes that are needed to strengthen the overall economic integration efforts in the sub-region. Without political will and a great deal of groundwork a monetary union cannot be made to work even in an homogeneous and historically connected region such as western Europe. These measures showed that the EU did witness a very significant deepening of reciprocal trade among its member countries over 50 years. It required not only the removal of tariff and non-tariff barriers but also very substantial institution-building over a long period.

Box 3.3 Chronology of European integration

1962 The European Commission makes its first proposal (Marjolin Memorandum) for economic and monetary union.

May 1964 A Committee of Governors of the central banks of the member states of the EEC is formed to institutionalize the cooperation among EEC central banks.

1971 The Werner Report sets out a plan to realize an economic and monetary union in the Community by 1980.

April 1972 A system (the "snake") for the progressive narrowing of the margins of fluctuation between the currencies of the member states of the EEC is established.

April 1973 The European Monetary Cooperation Fund (EMCF) is set up to ensure the proper operation of the snake.

March 1979 The European Monetary System (EMS) is created.

February 1986 The Single European Act (SEA) is signed.

June 1988 The European Council mandates a committee of experts under the chairmanship of Jacques Delors (the Delors Committee) to make proposals for the realization of EMU.

May 1989 The Delors Report is submitted to the European Council.

June 1989 The European Council agrees on the realization of EMU in three stages.

July 1990 Stage One of EMU begins.

December 1990 An Intergovernmental Conference to prepare for Stages Two and Three of EMU is launched.

February 1992 The Treaty on European Union (the Maastricht Treaty) is signed.
October 1993 Frankfurt am Main is chosen as the seat of the EMI and of the ECB and a President of the EMI is nominated.
November 1993 The Treaty on European Union enters into force.
December 1993 Alexandre Lamfalussy is appointed as President of the EMI, to be established on 1 January 1994.
January 1994 Stage Two of EMU begins and the EMI is established.
December 1995 The Madrid European Council decides on the name of the single currency and sets out the scenario for its adoption and the cash changeover.
December 1996 The EMI presents specimen euro banknotes to the European Council.
June 1997 The European Council agrees on the Stability and Growth Pact.
May 1998 Belgium, Germany, Spain, France, Ireland, Italy, Luxembourg, the Netherlands, Austria, Portugal and Finland are considered to fulfil the necessary conditions for the adoption of the euro as their single currency; the Members of the Executive Board of the ECB are appointed.
June 1998 The ECB and the ESCB are established.
October 1998 The ECB announces the strategy and the operational framework for the single monetary policy it will conduct from 1 January 1999.
January 1999 Stage Three of EMU begins; the euro becomes the single currency of the euro area; conversion rates are fixed irrevocably for the former national currencies of the participating member states; a single monetary policy is conducted for the euro area.
January 2001 Greece becomes the twelfth EU member state to join the euro area.
January 2002 The euro cash changeover: euro banknotes and coins are introduced and become sole legal tender in the euro area by the end of February 2000.
May 2004 The national central banks of the ten new EU member states join the ESCB.

Source: Scheller (2004)

Conclusions

Several lessons for the WAMZ can be gleaned from the theory and relevant experiences relating to economic and monetary integration.

Successful integration requires the widest possible intra-regional economic integration agenda – including trade and financial integration as well as labour and product market integration. In other words, although the attainment of a common market status is essential, it is not necessarily a sufficient condition of monetary integration. OCA theory points to seemingly ideal conditions for countries' participation in a monetary union based purely on theoretical conjecture.

Even though a common currency should be beneficial if it is executed properly, several transitional steps must be accomplished first. The adoption of convergence criteria as a precondition for the commencement of the monetary union in WAMZ, as was the case in the EU, signifies adequate safeguards to help the region attain OCA status *ex post*. It is desirable that monetary and fiscal policies of the countries that are going to join the common currency are harmonized before creating a common currency.

The linkage between national economic development policies and regional policies needs to be strengthened. One way to realize this is by incorporating regional integration objectives into national development plans of member countries. This will reduce the conflict of objectives, harmonize development policies aimed at fostering greater compatibility and achieve convergence between national and regional plans and policies.

Overall, it is recognized that there are adjustment costs as barriers to trade are removed. Some firms will not be able to meet the foreign competition, and will die or contract. Consequently, a burden-sharing mechanism to equitably share the short-run costs of adjustment is important to reap the medium- and longer-run benefits of economic integration and monetary union. On monetary integration, Dodge (2003) is of the view that it is an issue that should be considered once progress has been made towards establishing a single market for goods and services, capital and labour. Without a single well-functioning market for labour, a single currency could impose great adjustment costs on workers. Furthermore, fiscal transfers are essentially a non-market-based adjustment process. However, though the system of fiscal transfers requires a certain degree of political integration it is doubtful if this could be applicable in the WAMZ given that even in the European experience it was stepped down.

Monetary integration can provide the vehicle for low inflation as the monetary policy is delegated to an independent supranational monetary authority. A monetary union with an independent supranational central bank can therefore be expected to deliver low inflation. Various studies, including Kydland and Prescott (1997), Barro and Gordon (1983), Persson and Tabellini (1993), Rogoff (1985) and Walsh (1995) have shown how difficult it is for government to commit their monetary policies to the pursuit of low inflation. Alesina and Summers (1993), Cukierman (1992) and Grilli *et al.* (1991) found that central bank independence is associated with low inflation.

The institutional and structural architecture – such as the payments system, statistical, banking system regulations and commercial law harmonization – are anchors that are expected to ensure some degree of OCA compliance.

As shown by the case of the euro area, monetary union has been largely driven by political and economic considerations. Monetary union in the WAMZ should similarly be premised upon the strong political will and commitment of member states to undertake policies and programmes that are needed to strengthen the overall economic integration efforts in the sub-region.

Notes

1   See Holden (2003) for detailed analysis on the stages of economic integration.
2   See Horvath and Komarek for detailed analysis.
3   See Max Milbredt (2008) for detailed analysis.
4   Public goods are goods whose use by one country does not reduce (or hardly reduces) the use by others. They are non-excludable and exhibit non-rivalry of consumption.

5   Tradable goods are goods meant for international trade, i.e. they have imports and exports potential.
6   See www.unc.edu/depts/europe/conferences/eu/pages/emu4.htm and www.clas.ufl. edu/users/kreppel/euro.pdf.

References

Alesina, A. and Summers, L. (1993). "Central Bank Independence and Macroeconomic Performance: Some Comparative Evidence", *Journal of Money, Credit, and Banking*, 25(2) (May), 151–62.

Alesina, A. and Barro, R.J. (2002). "Currency Unions", *Quarterly Journal of Economics*, 117(2) (May), 409–36.

Anyanwu, J.C. (2003). "Estimating the Macroeconomic Effects of Monetary Unions: The Case of Trade and Output", *African Development Review–Revue*, 15(2–3) (December).

Barro, R.J. and Gordon, D.B. (1983). "A Positive Theory of Monetary Policy in a Natural Rate Model", *The Journal of Political Economy*, 91(4).

Bayoumi, T. and Ostry, J.D. (1997). "Macroeconomic Shocks and Trade Flows within Sub-Saharan Africa: Implications for Optimum Currency Arrangements", *Journal of African Economies*, 6(3), 412–44.

Carrère, C. (2004). "African Regional Agreements: Impact on Trade with or without Currency Unions", *Journal of African Economies*, 13(2), 199–239.

CePova, F. (2008). "Chronology of European Integration", EPP-ED Group, European Parliament. Online: www.epp-ed.eu.

Collier, P. (1991). "Africa's External Economic Relations, 1960–90", *African Affairs*, 90, 339–56.

Collier, P. (1998). "Globalization: Implications for Africa", in Z. Igbal and M.S. Khan (eds), *Trade Reform and Regional Integration in Africa*, Washington, DC: IMF.

Cukierman, A. (1992). *Central Bank Strategy, Credibility, and Independence: Theory and Evidence*, Cambridge, MA: MIT Press.

De Grauwe, P. (1997). *The Economics of Monetary Integration*, New York: Oxford University Press.

Deme, M. (1995). "The Impact of ECOWAS on Intraregional Trade-Flows: An Empirical Investigation", *Review of Black Political Economy*, 23(3) (Winter).

Devarajan, S. and Melo, J. (1987). "Evaluating Participation in African Monetary Unions: A Statistical Analysis of the CFA Zones", *World Development*, 15(4) (April).

Frankel, J.A. and Rose, A.K. (1997). "The Endogeneity of the Optimum Currency Area Criteria", *Economic Journal*, 108(449), 1009–25.

Frankel, J.A. and Rose, A.K. (2002). "An Estimate of the Effect of Common Currencies on Trade and Income", *Quarterly Journal of Economics*, 117(2) (May), 437–66.

Fielding, D. and Shields, K. (2000). "Is the Franc Zone an Optimal Currency Area?" *University of Leicester Working Paper*, 00/1.

Fielding, D. and Shields, K. (2002). "Currency Unions and International Integration: Evidence from the CFA and the ECCU", *University of Leicester Working Paper*, 02/8.

Feldstein, M. and Horioka C. (1980). "Domestic Saving and International Capital Flows", *Economic Journal*, 90(358), 314–29.

Glick, R. and Rose, A.K. (2001). "Does a Currency Union Affect Trade? The Time Series Evidence", *NBER Working Paper*, No. 8396.

Grilli, V. and Tabellini, G. (1991). "Political and Monetary Institutions and Public Financial Policies in the Industrial Countries", *Economic Policy*, 13, 341–92.

Hanink, D.M. and Owusu, J.H. (1998). "Has ECOWAS Promoted Trade among Its Members?" *Journal of African Economies*, 7(3) (October).

Holden, M. (2003). "Stages of Economic Integration: From Autarky to Economic Union", *Parliamentary Research Branch*, 02–49E.

Kenen, P. (1969). "Theory of Optimum Currency Areas: An Eclectic View", in R. Mundell and A. Swoboda (eds), *Monetary Problems in the International Economy*, Chicago: University of Chicago Press.

Kim, I. (2007). "The Evolutionary Process of East Asia's Monetary Integration", *The International Journal of Economic Policy Studies*, 2.

Kydland, F. and Prescott, E. (1997). "Rules Rather Than Discretion: The Inconsistency of Optimal Plans", *Journal of Political Economy*, 85, 473–91.

Masson, P. and Patillo, C. (2001). "Monetary Union in West Africa (ECOWAS): Is It Desirable and How Could It Be Achieved?" *IMF Occasional Paper*, 204.

McKinnon, R.I. (1963). "Optimal Currency Areas", *American Economic Review*, 53(4), 717–25.

Milbredt M. (2008). "The Theory of Optimum Currency Areas". Online: http://qed.econ. queensu.ca/pub/faculty/smithgw/econ826/exercises/Optimum%20Currency%20Areas. pdf.

Mongelli, F.S. (2002). "Economics of Monetary Union". Online: www.wiwi.uni-frankfurt.de/profs/klump/d/emu2002_lecture 1.pdf.

Mundell, R.A. (1961). "A Theory of Optimum Currency Areas", *American Economic Review*, 51, 657–65.

Mundell, R.A. (1973). "Uncommon Arguments for Common Currencies", in H. Johnson and A. Swoboda (eds), *The Economics of Common Currencies*, London: George Allen & Unwin Ltd., pp. 114–32.

Mundell, R.A. (2002). "Does Africa Need a Common Currency?" in *Third African Development Forum: Defining Priorities for Regional Integration*, Addis Ababa: Economic Commission for Africa.

Persson, T. and Tabellini, G. (1993). 'Designing Institutions for Monetary Stability", *Carnegic Rochester Conference Series*, 39, 53–84.

Persson, T. (2001). "Currency Unions and Trade: How Large is the Treatment Effect?" *Economic Policy*, October.

Ricci, L.A. (1997). "A Model of an Optimum Currency Area", *IMF Working Paper*, WP/97/76, September, LI, 657–65.

Rogoff, K. (1985). "The Optimal Degree of Commitment to an Intermediate Monetary Target", *Quarterly Journal of Economics*, 110, 1169–90.

Rose, A. (2000). "One Money, One Market: The Effect of Common Currencies on Trade", *Economic Policy*, 30 (April), 7–33.

Rose, A. and Engel, C. (2002). "Currency Unions and International Integration", *Journal of Money, Credit and Banking*, 34(4) (November), 1067–89.

Scheller, H.K. (2004). "The European Central Bank: History, Role and Function". Online: www.ecb.int/pub/pdf/other/ecbhistoryrolefunctions2004en.pdf.

Sebastian E.S. and Magendzo, I. (2003). "Strictly Dollarisation and Economic Performance: An Empirical Investigation", *NBER Working Papers*, 9820.

Skudelny, F. (2003). "Exchange Rate Uncertainty and Trade: a Survey", mimeo, Katholieke Universiteit Leuven.

Tenreyro, S. and Barro, R.J. (2003). "Economic Effects of Currency Unions", *NBER Working Paper*, 9435.

Walsh, C.E. (1995). "Optimal Contracts for Central Banks", *Anurkan Economic Review*, 85, 150–67.

4 Characteristics and structural convergence of the WAMZ economies

*Temitope W. Oshikoya, Emmanuel Onwioduokit,
Abu Bakarr Tarawalie and Rohey Khan*

Introduction

This chapter presents a brief synopsis of the economies of the WAMZ countries, including The Gambia, Ghana, Guinea, Nigeria and Sierra Leone. It discusses their structural economic features, indebtedness, patterns of trade, risk of asymmetric shocks, business cycle synchronization and exchange rate movements and analyses issues relating to economic distance in the WAMZ.

Key features of the WAMZ economies

The WAMZ is heterogeneous in terms of gross domestic product (GDP) as well as population. In addition, the economies are very open, but tend to rely on very few export goods. The Zone covers a total land area of 1.49 million square kilometres. With the exception of Guinea and Sierra Leone that share national borders, the other countries are not geographically contiguous. The WAMZ has a total combined population of 192.6 million people, representing 66 per cent and 20 per cent of the population of the Economic Community of West African States (ECOWAS) and Africa respectively (World Bank, 2008a), and a combined GDP of US$340 billion (purchasing power parity), representing 73 per cent and 19 per cent of ECOWAS and Africa, respectively.

While the Zone is relatively large geographically, it is still a small open economy in global terms, accounting for less than 1 per cent of the global economy. As a result, even after full integration of the economies, the Zone will still be considered a small open economy, with a strong possibility of imported inflation with implications for the conduct of monetary policy and the choice of targets and instruments within the monetary union.

Nigeria is the dominant economy in the WAMZ, accounting for over 78 per cent of the population and 86 per cent of the Zone's GDP (World Bank, 2008b). Nigeria's economy is oil-based, with the sector contributing about 40 per cent of GDP, 80 per cent of total revenue and 90 per cent of foreign exchange earnings (see Nigeria, 2008). The next largest economy within the Zone is Ghana with 9.2 per cent of the Zone's GDP, while The Gambia is the smallest economy constituting about 0.6 per cent of the GDP.

Table 4.1 WAMZ countries key indicators (2008)

Country	Population (millions)	Population age composition (%), ages 0–14	Land area (1,000 km²)	Gross Domestic Product		
				US$ billion (PPP)	Average annual GDP growth 2001–2008	Per capita US$
The Gambia	1.8	40	10.4	2.1	4.9	1,317
Ghana	23.9	39	235.5	31.3	5.6	1,425
Guinea	9.5	44	245.9	9.7	3.1	973
Nigeria	151.3	44	923.8	291.7	5.2	2,027
Sierra Leone	5.9	79	71.7	4.0	11.0	592

Sources: World Bank (2008) and (2007).

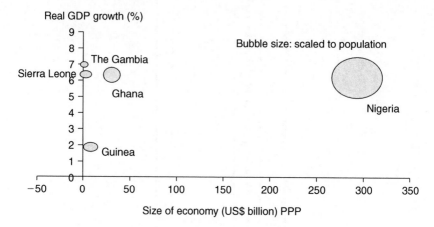

Figure 4.1 WAMZ countries: population, GDP growth and size of economies (2007) (sources: World Bank (2008) and WAMI (2007)).

A decision-making framework that allows the political weight of Nigeria to equal its economic weight may create a sense of dominance by Nigeria that would make monetary zone decisions less acceptable to the other countries. To create a sense of ownership of decisions by all countries, a delicate choice is required that permits: decentralization and a degree of local autonomy; governance by rules agreed by consensus rather than governance by discretion; and having discretionary powers given to a governing board where the members would be selected in such a way that it would be possible to have a high degree of confidence allowing member countries to think of themselves as individuals seeking the interests of the WAMZ as a whole.

Structure of production and demand in the WAMZ

Apart from Nigeria, sectoral distribution of output in the WAMZ economies shows some similarities, with services and agriculture dominating. In The Gambia, the services sector remains the dominant sector, while in Ghana, contributions from agriculture and the services sectors are quite similar. In Guinea, the services sector was the largest contributor to GDP from 2000 through 2006; however, in 2007, the industrial sector (especially mining) had the largest share of GDP. In Nigeria, the industrial sector (petroleum) remains the largest contributor to output, while in Sierra Leone the agricultural sector continues to provide the dominant share in output growth. It is important to note that although the current production structures in the WAMZ appear divergent, diversification in production, discovery and exploitation of oil in some member countries in the future may increase structural similarities.

Across WAMZ countries, household final consumption expenditure accounts for the greatest share of aggregate demand,[1] followed by gross capital formation

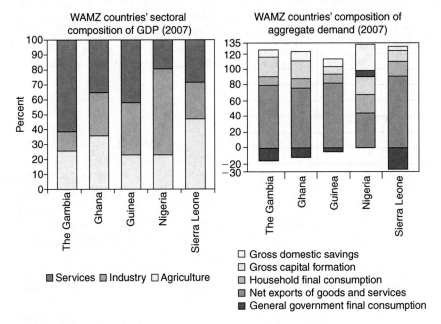

Figure 4.2 WAMZ countries' sectoral composition of GDP and aggregate demand
(sources: World Bank (2007) and WAMI (2007) database).

in the case of The Gambia, Ghana and Nigeria. In Guinea and Sierra Leone,
however, general government final expenditure follows household consumption.
Net exports[2] are generally negative, except in Nigeria where a positive 9 per cent
of GDP was recorded. Gross domestic savings were generally low in all the
countries with the exception of Nigeria.

Business cycle synchronization[3]

Optimum Currency Area theory stresses the importance of the synchronization
in cyclical economic activity for members of a monetary union. In particular, the
higher the correlation of business cycles, the lower the stabilization cost of
giving up an independent monetary policy. If a member economy's business
cycle is very highly correlated with the union-wide cyclical output, then monetary policy conducted by the common central bank will be a very close substitute
for the country's own independent monetary policy. If the economy's business
cycle is weakly correlated (or, worse, negatively correlated) with the union's
cyclical output, then the common monetary policy will be a poor substitute for
that economy's own independent monetary policy, and may end up actually
being destabilizing.

Annual data on real GDP,[4] broad money supply, nominal interest rate and real
interest rate were used to evaluate business cycle synchronization as well as

identifying the channels of risk sharing that existed in the WAMZ. Table 4.2 gives the descriptive statistics of the variables including their correlation, mean and standard deviation. Although the correlation among the five countries generally appears low, Ghana and Nigeria showed relatively high correlations in most of the variables, including real and nominal interest rates as well as real GDP growth, to some extent.

Asymmetry of shocks

The occurrence of asymmetric shocks is a potential source of conflict in a monetary union (Houssa and Leuven, 2004; Blanchard and Quah, 1989). Terms of trade shocks (see Table 4.3), natural disasters and other shocks to the real economy can affect different countries differently at any particular point in time. The dilemma for the monetary union central bank would arise when the appropriate policy response differs for the different countries. On the other hand, if the real effects of shocks tend to be symmetrical, then there is no dilemma, since a common policy would be required in addressing such a shock.

The WAMZ economies are prone to relatively large and asymmetric shocks, given the member countries' heavy reliance on exports of different primary commodities. Nigeria, Sierra Leone and Guinea each depend on a single commodity for over 50 per cent of their export earnings. The massive terms of trade shocks in the Zone's largest economy, Nigeria, stand out and are underpinned by the volatility of world oil prices.

Furthermore, these shocks have a low correlation, mainly because the prices of the different commodities exported exhibit a low correlation. Nigeria's terms of trade movements in particular had a negative correlation with the other four countries. However, Ghana is expected to join Nigeria as an oil exporter and this may improve, to some level, the degree of correlations between the two major countries of the Zone.

A dilemma for the West African Central Bank (WACB) would arise when the appropriate policy response differs for the different countries. For example, monetary and exchange rate policies can help to insulate output from terms of trade fluctuations, via flexible exchange rates and interest rate adjustment. In addition, member countries could use prudent fiscal policies to cushion the effect of such asymmetric shocks.

Deterioration in the terms of trade[5] tends to tighten money and credit markets, while improvements in the terms of trade tend to relax these markets. Deterioration in terms of trade may reduce earnings from exports, which may have dampening effect on the money supply. In addition, to avoid excessive depreciation[6] of the domestic currency arising from decline in export earnings, the monetary authorities may reduce the money supply (domestic credit). Furthermore, banks may also reduce the availability of credits to creditors. Thus, when terms of trade deteriorate, the eco is expected to depreciate in the foreign exchange markets and interest rate is also expected to decrease. The opposite should be allowed to happen when terms of trade improve: the eco should appreciate and interest rates

Table 4.2 Correlation of key economic indicators

Real GDP growth	The Gambia	Ghana	Guinea	Nigeria	Sierra Leone	Mean	Standard deviation
The Gambia	1.00					6.08	0.91
Ghana	0.99	1.00				5.65	0.98
Guinea	0.37	0.42	1.00			2.95	0.07
Nigeria	0.98	0.96	0.17	1.00		6.31	0.22
Sierra Leone	-0.99	-0.99	-0.41	-0.97	1.00	11.86	5.71
Broad money supply growth							
The Gambia	1.00					21.63	12.12
Ghana	0.50	1.00				35.00	11.77
Guinea	0.34	-0.34	1.00			28.35	17.62
Nigeria	-0.42	0.16	-0.38	1.00		31.25	16.37
Sierra Leone	0.00	0.19	-0.16	-0.41	1.00	25.34	5.31
Nominal interest rates							
The Gambia	1.00					19.00	7.44
Ghana	0.22	1.00				16.74	6.55
Guinea	-0.55	-0.86	1.00			17.44	4.19
Nigeria	0.41	0.91	-0.79	1.00		12.42	4.59
Sierra Leone	0.54	-0.25	-0.17	-0.14	1.00	19.04	4.76
Real interest rates							
The Gambia	1.00					11.51	5.16
Ghana	-0.13	1.00				0.8	5.28
Guinea	-0.79	0.25	1.00			-0.72	10.33
Nigeria	-0.06	0.80	0.16	1.00		0.06	4.42
Sierra Leone	-0.06	0.82	0.31	0.49	1.00	9.52	4.72

Source: WAMI (2008).

Table 4.3 Terms of trade shocks in the WAMZ

	Correlations of terms of trade shocks					Standard deviation of shocks
	The Gambia	Ghana	Guinea	Nigeria	Sierra Leone	
The Gambia	1.000					9.9
Ghana	0.453	1.000				14.3
Guinea	0.315	0.054	1.000			11.1
Nigeria	−0.261	−0.515	−0.042	1.000		26.0
Sierra Leone	0.156	−0.206	0.202	−0.019	1.000	14.0

Source: WAMI (2008).

increase. Such a strategy calls for appropriate intervention in foreign exchange and money markets by the WACB, or changes in the WACB interest rates or exchange rates. If the real effects of such external shocks remained uniform across the WAMZ, then there is no dilemma for the WACB. A dilemma would arise when the real effects of such shocks tend to differ across countries within the Zone.

The authorities, governments and the WACB could greatly mitigate the effects of an external shock to one country within the Zone through the creation of an enabling environment involving the implementation of certain measures, while providing compensatory developments in other parts of the Zone. The most important of these measures would be the integration of the financial markets. With such integration, banks could obtain liquidity anywhere in the WAMZ and competition would become vibrant in the financial markets, allowing investors to diversify their portfolio across the Zone, as well as encouraging cross-border borrowing by firms and households. To foster financial market integration, the payment systems and the legal and regulatory systems would, *inter alia*, need to be harmonized in fundamental ways. Such harmonization would greatly assist the conduct of monetary policy. Fostering integration of markets would also involve removing barriers to entry and forces that engender segmentation of the markets for particular assets (e.g. government securities or foreign exchange) across regions or across groups of firms of the same country.

Exchange rate movements

A low synchronization in exchange rate movements would likely hinder the cooperation between members of a monetary union. Comparing the correlation of real exchange rates (RER), there is clear evidence of strong similarity in RER movement among most of the countries, especially between The Gambia and Sierra Leone (97 per cent), Ghana and Nigeria (91 per cent) and The Gambia and Guinea (82 per cent). This is a positive trend for the formation of a monetary union. Only Guinea's RER movements appeared to diverge strongly from the rest of the countries. The Gambia's real exchange rate was the most volatile with a standard deviation of 19.5, while Guinea's currency was the most stable with a standard deviation of 2.3 during the period covered. It is envisaged that high correlation of real exchange rates among countries of the Zone prior to the formation of a monetary union would pave the way for the smooth adoption of a unified exchange rate mechanism that would be less costly. It would also enhance the effective functioning of a common monetary policy, as well as easing the effects of external shocks through the use of exchange rate policy.

Trends in structural convergence

In terms of structural convergence, apart from Nigeria, the differences in sectoral distribution of output and GDP sizes among the countries, while significant, were not impediments to the formation of a monetary union. Interestingly, Ghana and Nigeria showed high correlations in key economic variables (business cycle synchronization indicators). It is also important to emphasize that the apparent overall structural heterogeneity of the WAMZ countries is more likely to be reduced in the future. Nigeria, the largest economy and currently the only oil producing/exporting country in the Zone, is pursuing policies to diversify its economy away from the excessive dependence on oil, while Ghana may at the same time become more correlated with Nigeria as its oil production develops.

External and domestic debt in WAMZ

External debt acts as a burden on governments' fiscal operations and hence has major implications for monetary union convergence in WAMZ. Financing of huge external debt may cause governments to redirect expenditure to non-priority areas. In addition, it also serves as a burden on future generations, as well as a signal for future tax increases to finance the debt burden based on the Ricardian equivalence doctrine.[7]

In 2001, Nigeria's external debt remained extremely high, compared to other countries within the Zone (Figure 4.3). However, the external debt position improved significantly during 2007 and 2008. The Gambia, on the other hand, incurred the lowest external debt in 2001, but it slightly increased in 2007 and 2008, despite attaining the Heavily Indebted Poor Countries (HIPC) Initiative

Table 4.4 Correlation of real exchange rates (2000 = 100): 2002–2006

	The Gambia	*Ghana*	*Guinea*	*Nigeria*	*Sierra Leone*	*Mean*	*Standard deviation*
The Gambia	1.000					*61.6*	*19.5*
Ghana	0.823	1.000				*110.1*	*10.9*
Guinea	−0.972	−0.680	1.000			*106.2*	*2.3*
Nigeria	0.536	0.914	−0.358	1.000		*120.3*	*13.2*
Sierra Leone	0.967	0.750	−0.935	0.417	1.000	*78.7*	*13.5*

Source: IMF (2008).

completion point. Guinea's external debt moderated within US$5 billion during the entire period, while Sierra Leone's external debt declined significantly in 2007 and 2008 due to debt cancellation. Ghana's debt also halved between 2001 and 2007, arising from the debt cancellation under the HIPC debt relief. However, in 2008 the level increased slightly by 5 per cent.

Fiscal discipline is crucial for the success of a monetary union. Without it, large differences in member countries' fiscal stances can create tensions, leading to political disagreements and hindering other key macroeconomic convergence requirements for the smooth functioning of the union, such as price stability. It is therefore important that countries achieve fiscal convergence prior to the introduction of the common currency. Applying one of the traditional fiscal convergence indicators, namely government domestic debt, it was observed that the WAMZ countries' debt profile followed a mixed but declining trend. The trend in domestic debt as shown in Figure 4.5 reveals that The

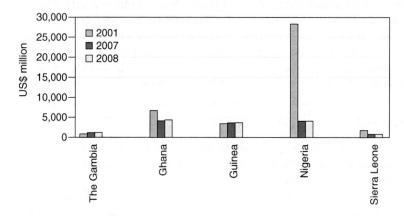

Figure 4.3 WAMZ countries' external debt ($ million) (source: WAMI (2008)).

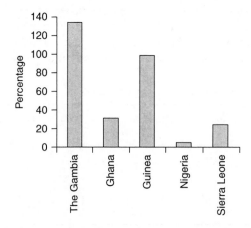

Figure 4.4 WAMZ countries' external debt (% of GDP) (source: WAMI (2008)).

Gambia incurred huge domestic debt relative to all other countries during the review period. Furthermore, Ghana's domestic debt also remained high during the period, while Nigeria's debt declined consistently between 2001 and 2007, but increased in 2008. For Sierra Leone, domestic debt was relatively stable, averaging 10 per cent of GDP during the period.

Box 4.1 The HIPC Initiative in the WAMZ

The HIPC Initiative was first launched in 1996 by the International Monetary Fund (IMF) and World Bank, with the aim of easing the debt burdens of poor countries. It entails coordinated action by the international financial community, including multilateral organizations and governments, to reduce to sustainable levels the external debt burdens of the most heavily indebted poor countries.

Once a country has met or made sufficient progress in meeting pre-set criteria, the Executive Boards of the IMF and the International Development Association (IDA, World Bank) formally decide on its eligibility for debt relief, and the international community makes commitments to reduce debt to the sustainability threshold. This is called the decision point. The country can then receive interim relief on its debt service falling due. In order to receive a full and irrevocable reduction in debt, however, the country is expected to: establish a further track record of good performance under IMF and IDA-supported programmes; implement key reforms agreed at the decision point and adopt a Poverty Reduction Strategy Paper for at least one year. After it has met these criteria, a country can reach its completion point, whereupon lenders provide full debt relief.

In the WAMZ, as at the end of November 2008, The Gambia, Ghana and Sierra Leone had reached completion point, while Guinea was between decision point and completion point. The debt relief for The Gambia was US$91 million, for Ghana US$3,700 million and for Sierra Leone US$950 million.

Source: www.worldbank.org

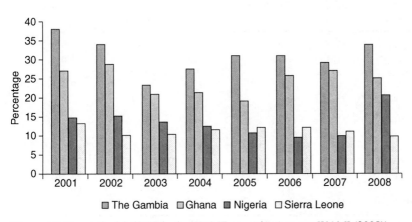

Figure 4.5 Domestic debt/GDP in the WAMZ countries (source: WAMI (2008)).

Structure of merchandise imports and exports

The pattern of merchandise imports and exports has a significant impact on the visible trade balance, hence on current account and balance of payments. The pattern of trade differs across countries and is largely based on the structure of the economy, availability of natural resources and domestic demand. However, the uneven distribution of natural resources and differences in tastes also influence trade between the member countries. There are major intra-industry trades in the WAMZ countries as is evident in the structure of their merchandise export and import shown in Table 4.5. The structure of merchandise exports shows that food products remain the major exports of The Gambia, Ghana and Sierra Leone, followed by manufactures. Fuel, agricultural raw materials, ores and metals account for a small proportion of total exports in these countries. However, crude oil accounts for over 97 per cent of Nigeria's exports, while manufactures account for the rest. In Guinea, ores and metals form the greatest share of merchandise exports, while manufactures and food represent 25.3 per cent and 2 per cent, respectively.

Conversely, manufactures form the largest share of merchandise imports for all the countries except Sierra Leone, whose major import is fuel. Food imports also contribute significantly to merchandise imports for all the countries. In addition, fuel imports are relatively high for The Gambia, Guinea and Nigeria.

Survey-based indicators

Survey-based indicators may also be used to ascertain possible structural weaknesses that could eventually undermine external stability in the WAMZ countries. The World Bank *Doing Business* indices showed the performance of the member countries in nine key indicators (Table 4.6). Overall, Ghana and Nigeria

Table 4.5 Structures of exports and imports (2006)

Exports (% of total)	Food	Agriculture raw materials	Fuel	Ores and metals	Manufactures
The Gambia	81.0	4.0	0.0	0.0	14.0
Ghana	61.0	4.0	1.0	3.0	31.0
Guinea	2.0	0.8	0.1	71.6	25.3
Nigeria	0.0	0.0	97.9	0.0	2.1
Sierra Leone	91.6	0.8	0.0	0.1	7.5
Imports (% of total)					
The Gambia	31.0	2.0	17.0	1.0	49.0
Ghana	13.0	1.0	14.0	1.0	70.0
Guinea	23.1	1.2	21.7	0.8	53.0
Nigeria	15.5	0.6	16.0	1.6	66.3
Sierra Leone	22.5	7.6	39.7	0.8	29.3

Sources: World Bank (2008) and (2007).

achieved the best performances, followed by The Gambia, Sierra Leone and Guinea. The difficulty encountered in paying taxes, registering property and getting credit are particularly high in the WAMZ.

The major strengths for the member countries indicated by the indices were in enforcing contracts, employing workers and trading across borders. The report also suggested that the WAMZ countries compared favourably with other ECOWAS countries in the ease of doing business with Ghana, Nigeria and The Gambia, which were placed in the top three in the overall ranking in the sub-region.

Monetary policy framework in the WAMZ

With the advent of economic liberalization and deregulation of the financial system, the conduct of monetary policy in the WAMZ was premised on the use of indirect instruments. In implementing monetary policy, the WAMZ central banks used their influence on money market conditions via reserve requirements, rediscount window, open market operations, foreign exchange swaps, etc. to achieve their objective of price stability. They implemented monetary policy primarily through the control of monetary aggregates at the level adjudged consistent with a programmed rate of economic growth. With this framework, monetary aggregates are the intermediate target, with reserve money being the operational target, channelled through open market operations. In The Gambia, the conduct of monetary policy by the Central Bank of The Gambia (CBG) is through monetary targeting framework, where the central bank sets an intermediate target for growth in broad money (the nominal anchor) and uses reserve money as its operational target.

In Ghana, the Bank of Ghana (BOG) adopted an inflation targeting framework in 2007 (Addison, 2001), using a core measure of the consumer price index, which excluded energy and utility prices. Prior to 2007, the strategy for monetary management was based on monetary targeting. The strategy for

Table 4.6 WAMZ: *Doing Business* indicators (2009)

	The Gambia	Ghana	Guinea	Nigeria	Sierra Leone
Starting a business	101	137	177	91	53
Employing workers	55	145	114	27	173
Registering property	111	31	157	176	163
Getting credit	131	109	163	84	145
Protecting investors	170	38	170	53	53
Paying taxes	175	65	168	120	160
Trading across borders	73	76	110	144	132
Enforcing contracts	63	50	131	90	145
Closing a business	120	104	109	91	145
Overall rank	130	87	171	118	156

Source: World Bank (2009).

monetary management in Guinea is also based on monetary targeting framework. However, the central bank sets two intermediate targets: a minimum amount of net foreign assets of the central bank and a ceiling on the net credit to government. The conduct of monetary policy in Nigeria is also based on monetary targeting.

In November 2006, the Monetary Policy Committee of the Central Bank of Nigeria (CBN) adopted a new monetary policy framework involving the introduction of a new Monetary Policy Rate (MPR) that replaced the Minimum Rediscount Rate (MRR). The MPR determines the lower and upper band of the CBN standing facility and is expected to have the capability of acting as the nominal anchor for other rates. Monetary targeting also remained the vibrant monetary policy framework for the conduct of monetary policy in Sierra Leone

Inflationary trends

The achievement of single-digit inflation on a sustainable basis proved to be challenging for WAMZ member countries over the years, with mixed performance during the period 2001–2008. While inflation rates were generally high between 2001 and 2005, there was marked improvement in 2006, in which The Gambia, Nigeria and Sierra Leone recorded single-digit inflation rates of 0.4, 8.5 and 8.3 per cent, respectively (WAMI, 2008). However, Ghana's inflation rate of 10.5 per cent in 2006 was the lowest rate it achieved during the period 2001–2008, while Guinea's inflation rate of 39.1 per cent was the highest during the reference period. There was an inflation rate rebound in 2007 and 2008, as inflation rates accelerated in all WAMZ member countries, engendered by escalation in global food and fuel prices as well as monetary expansion arising from deficit financing from government.

Fiscal deficit (excluding grants) as a ratio of GDP

Fiscal policy slippages remained a major factor that inhibits the attainment of the WAMZ fiscal deficit criterion[8] by member countries. Fiscal performance was generally unsatisfactory during 2001–2004, but improved significantly in 2006. The fiscal position of The Gambia, Guinea and Nigeria remained relatively strong as these countries satisfied the WAMZ criterion in most of the period under review. However, Sierra Leone and Ghana never satisfied this criterion, indicating a weak fiscal position in these countries.

Economic distance in the WAMZ

The notion of economic distance gives an indication of the likely costs of forming a monetary union. The typical approach when analysing and comparing the similarities in the economic structure of one partner of a monetary union to that of their largest trading partner is by measuring the correlation coefficients of output growth and inflation. In accordance with this concept, the cost of a monetary union depends on the volatility of output growth and inflation between the target and candidate countries. In other words, the greater the differences between the candidate and target countries' output variance and the smaller the correlation between the candidate and target countries' output growth, the larger are the potential costs of forming a monetary union.[9] The measure of economic distance is defined in such a way that, the higher the economic distance, the greater the costs of joining a monetary union. In this regard, economic distance gives an indication of the deviation of the candidate countries' output growth and inflation from the target country. A high positive correlation coefficient means a convergence of business cycles and similarities in the partners' economic structures, and consequently any external shock would impact the member countries in the same direction. A negative correlation implies a divergence of business cycles. The similarity of economic structure lessens the instability of output and inflation. Also, the similarities reduce the possibilities of different cycle paths in a given country relative to the other members of the monetary union. For the countries of the WAMZ, Nigeria was considered the target country due to its relative size, structure of its economy and contribution to the WAMZ programme, while Ghana, Guinea, The Gambia and Sierra Leone were jointly considered as candidate countries.

The results of the economic distance are shown in Figures 4.6 and 4.7. The data set was divided into two sub-samples, i.e. the period before the implementation of WAMZ programme (1993–2000) and the period corresponding to the WAMZ programme. The breakdown of the data into two sub-samples provided a valid judgement on the costs of joining a monetary union, by comparing the economic distance for the two periods. Figure 4.6 plots the output growth correlation coefficients and standard deviation between the candidate and target countries respectively for the two periods. It is evident from Figure 4.6 that output growth correlation rose for Ghana during the WAMZ period compared to a lower value during 1993–2000. On the other hand, output volatility as measured by the standard deviation marginally decreased between 2001 and 2008. This result showed that the cost of Ghana forming a monetary union with Nigeria declined substantially during the WAMZ period, due to the rise in output growth correlation and decline in output volatility.

The Gambia's situation showed much improvement in reducing the cost of entering a monetary union. The result revealed that output growth correlation between The Gambia and Nigeria increased during the WAMZ period relative to the *ex-ante* sub-sample period 1993–2000. In addition, output volatility also declined significantly during the period 2001–2008 compared with 1993–2000. This analysis also showed that the cost of The Gambia joining a monetary union with Nigeria was comparatively lower during the WAMZ period, relative to the period prior to the WAMZ programme. The result was mixed for Sierra Leone, with a sharp fall in output volatility being offset by a fall in output growth correlation. However, despite the cost of joining a monetary union for Sierra Leone being high, the result showed that the country made significant progress towards reducing the cost of monetary union as evidenced by the positive output growth correlation with Nigeria and the significant decline in output volatility. In the case of Guinea, the cost of joining a monetary union increased during the WAMZ period. The result showed that the output growth correlation with Nigeria became negative during the WAMZ period relative to a positive value prior to the WAMZ period. Furthermore, the output volatility which remained negative in both periods also increased during the WAMZ period.

Figure 4.7 gives a stylized presentation of inflation correlation coefficient and volatility between the candidate and target countries respectively. The results revealed that the inflation correlation coefficient between Ghana and Nigeria increased during the WAMZ period from a lower value during 1993–2000. In addition, inflation volatility, which remained negative in both periods, declined

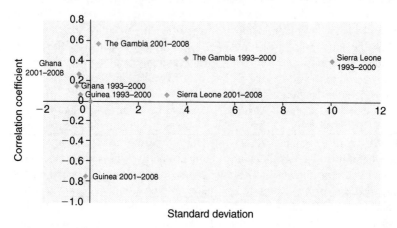

Figure 4.6 Economic distance output growth; Nigeria as target country (source: IMF (2008)).

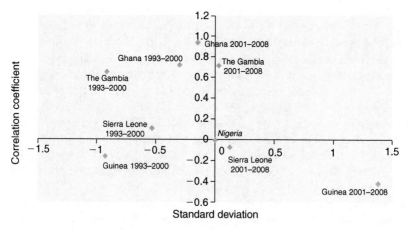

Figure 4.7 Economic distance inflation; Nigeria as target country (source: IMF (2008)).

in absolute terms during 2001–2008. These developments give an indication that the cost of monetary union was lower for Ghana. This result was not at variance with the result on output growth. For The Gambia, the result revealed that the cost of monetary union declined during the WAMZ period relative to the period before the implementation of WAMZ. This was justified on the grounds that the inflation correlation coefficient increased during the WAMZ period compared with a much lower value during 1993–2000. In addition, inflation volatility between The Gambia and Nigeria declined during the WAMZ period. The picture for Sierra Leone indicated that the cost of monetary union remained higher. The inflation correlation coefficient was negative during the WAMZ period compared with a positive relationship prior to the WAMZ period. Also, the inflation volatility, which was negative during 1993–2000, increased to a positive value during the period corresponding with the WAMZ programme. Finally, Guinea has consistently maintained a negative inflation correlation with Nigeria for both periods, with the value decreasing during the WAMZ period. In addition, the country experienced increased inflation volatility during the WAMZ period. Conclusively, the result showed that the cost of monetary union remained higher for Guinea.

The measure of economic distance shown in Table 4.7 also confirms the preceding results. The result revealed that economic distance in terms of output growth was much lower during the WAMZ period, and the inflation variance was also lower for both periods. The results suggest that Ghana is a good candidate for monetary union. The result also showed that The Gambia had made great effort in reducing the cost of joining a monetary union with the target country, as evidenced by a reduction in output growth variance by more than half during the WAMZ period, relative to the period 1993–2000. The results seem to re-echo the progress made by The Gambia towards meeting the convergence criteria. For Sierra Leone, the result showed that the costs of joining a monetary union with Nigeria are quite high in both periods as evidenced by the

Table 4.7 Economic distance; Nigeria as target country

Candidate country	2001–2008	
	Output growth	Inflation
Ghana	0.90	0.85
Guinea	1.94	2.76
The Gambia	1.39	1.07
Sierra Leone	4.29	1.55
	1993–2000	
Ghana	0.97	0.74
Guinea	1.12	1.16
The Gambia	3.03	0.35
Sierra Leone	6.67	1.01

Source: IMF (2008).

large economic distance for output growth and inflation. However, Sierra Leone appeared to have made efforts in reducing the costs as measured by both the fall in output and inflation variances from 6.67 and 2.44 during 1993–2000 to 4.29 and 1.55 during 2001–2008, respectively. In the case of Guinea, the cost of joining a monetary union with Nigeria has actually increased during the WAMZ period. Comparatively, prior to the implementation of the WAMZ programme, the cost of monetary union based on output growth tends to be lower for Guinea as evidenced by the low economic distance values of 1.12 and 0.97 of output and inflation variances, respectively. However, during the WAMZ programme, there were marked increases of 1.94 for output variance and the value almost tripled in the inflation variance.

Overall, while the costs of joining a monetary union remained high for countries such as Sierra Leone and Guinea, comparison of the two sets of data showed that the costs of monetary union corresponding with the WAMZ programme tends to be lower relative to the *ex ante* WAMZ period. In essence, the WAMZ programme helped to lower economic distance measured by output and inflation variances between the target country and the candidate countries. The long-term costs of forming a monetary union between Nigeria and the candidate countries are likely to continue to decline with the consistent implementation of the WAMZ programme.

Conclusions

The countries of the WAMZ are heterogeneous in terms of GDP and population and do not share common borders except Guinea and Sierra Leone. The Zone's economies are prone to relatively large and asymmetric shocks, given the member countries' heavy reliance on exports of different primary commodities. These asymmetric shocks pose potential risks to the WAMZ economies towards the formation of a monetary union. However, despite the heterogeneity in the economic structure of the WAMZ countries, there are clear indications that the cost of joining a monetary union is relatively low, according to the evidence on the volatility and variation of output growth and inflation. Nevertheless, asymmetric shocks would require close harmonization of financial markets and carefully coordinated application of policy, as well as fiscal discipline across the Zone.

Notes

1 Aggregate demand is defined as the total demand for goods and services (at any time by all groups within a national economy) that makes up the GDP. Component-wise, aggregate demand comprises consumption expenditure, investment expenditure, government expenditure and net exports.
2 Net export is the difference between exports and imports. A negative value implies export is less than import, while a positive value indicates export is greater than imports.
3 See Ambler *et al.* (2004), Backus *et al.* (1992) and Canova (1998).

4 Real GDP was de-trended using the Hodrick–Prescott filter, which separated the data into temporary and permanent components. The de-trended value (permanent component) of real GDP was used in the correlation analysis.
5 Deterioration in terms of trade implies export prices are lower than import prices.
6 Depreciation is a reduction in the value of the domestic currency in relation to other currencies.
7 Ricardian equivalence is an economic theory that suggests consumers internalize the government's budget constraint and thus the timing of any tax change does not affect their change in spending. Consequently, Ricardian equivalence suggests that it does not matter whether a government finances its spending with debt or a tax increase, the effect on total level of demand in an economy being the same.
8 Members countries' fiscal deficit (excluding grant) should not exceed 4 per cent of GDP.
9 These two factors define the notion of economic distance (Alesina and Grilli, 1992). To better understand the notion of economic distance, a simple model which assumes a standard loss function for the central bank, wherein inflation variability and output variability as determinants is used. $ED = \left\{ \left(\frac{\sigma_C}{\sigma_T} \right)^2 + (1 - \rho_i)^2 \right\}^{\frac{1}{2}}$. Where: ED is economic distance, σ_C is the standard deviation of output or inflation in the candidate country; σ_T is the standard deviation of output or inflation in the target country and ρ_i represents the correlation coefficient of output or inflation between the candidate and target countries. Based on the equation above, the larger the economic distance, the greater the costs of monetary union, and the smaller the economic distance, the lower the cost of monetary union.

References

Addison, E.K.Y. (2001). "Monetary Management in Ghana", paper presented at the Conference on Monetary Policy Frameworks in Africa, Pretoria, South Africa, 17–19 September. Online: www.reservebank.co.za/internet/publication.nsf/LADV/ghana.

Alesina, A. and Grilli, V. (1992). "The European Central Bank: Reshaping Monetary Politics in Europe", in E.H. Hochreiter and P.L. Siklos (eds), *From Floating to Monetary Union: The Economic Distance between Exchange Rate Regimes*, Vienna: SUERF – The European Money and Finance Forum.

Ambler, S., Cardia, E. and Zimmermann, C. (2004). "International Business Cycles: What Are the Facts?" *Journal of Monetary Economics*, 51(2), 257–76.

Backus, D.K., Kehoe, P.J. and Kydland, F.E. (1992). "International Real Business Cycles", *Journal of Political Economy*, 745–75.

Blanchard, O.J. and Quah, D. (1989). "The Dynamic Effects of Aggregate Demand and Supply Disturbances", *American Economic Review*, 79, 4655–73.

Canova, F. (1998). "Detrending and Business Cycle Facts", *Journal of Monetary Economics*, 41, 475–512.

Houssa, R. and Leuven, K.U. (2004). "Monetary Union in West Africa and Asymmetric Shocks: A Dynamic Structural Factor Model Approach", *Centre for Economic Studies Discussion Paper Series*, 04.11, November.

IMF (2008). *International Financial Statistics Year Book*, Washington, DC: IMF.

Kalemli-Ozcan, S., Sorensen, B.E. and Yosha, O. (2001). "Economic Integration, Industrial Specialization, and the Asymmetry of Macroeconomic Fluctuations", *Journal of International Economics*, 55(1) (October), 107–37.

Nigeria (2008). *Report of the Annual National Debt Sustainability Analysis (DSA)*, Debt Management Office, Nigeria.

WAMI (2008). *Convergence Report*. Online: www.wami-imao.org.

World Bank (2008a). *Africa Development Indicators*, Washington, DC: World Bank.

World Bank (2008b). *World Development Indicators*, Washington, DC: World Bank.

World Bank (2009). *Doing Business World Bank Report*. Online: www.doingbusiness.org/EconomyRanking.

5 Nominal macroeconomic convergence

Emmanuel Onwioduokit, Lamin Jarju, Tidiane Syllah, Jibrin Yakubu and Hilton Jarrett

Introduction

It is generally agreed that monetary integration has a higher degree of success if the economies in question are converging, i.e. their macroeconomic fundamentals and policies approach each other. Convergence does not mean equality, since short-run departures are expected. However, when there are significant differences in performance, countries will react differently to shocks, thus necessitating country-specific responses which may be injurious to the entire group. In order for convergence to be meaningful, it should take place with respect to some targets.

In the WAMZ, the disparities in economic performance have necessitated the adoption of convergence criteria. In 2001 the WAMZ countries agreed on four primary convergence criteria: single-digit inflation; fiscal deficit GDP ratio of 4 per cent; central bank financing of government fiscal operations to be limited to 10 per cent of the previous year's tax revenue; and gross foreign reserves to be equivalent to three months of normal imports. In addition, a set of six secondary convergence criteria was agreed on: non-accumulation of payment arrears; tax revenue/GDP ratio of at least 20 per cent; salary mass/total tax revenue of not more than 35 per cent; public sector investment from domestic receipts to be greater than or equal to 20 per cent; positive real interest rates; and exchange rates to fluctuate within ±15 per cent in the WAMZ exchange rate mechanism (ERM).

Taken together, these criteria reflect the link between fiscal outcomes and balance of payments viability as well as recognition of the fact that rapid price increases could have a destabilizing impact on the economy. The key concern in the articulation of the convergence criteria is that fiscal dominance should not adversely impede the objective of price stability in a monetary union.

In WAMZ, inflation convergence is used to ensure domestic price stability; foreign exchange reserve to ensure the price level stability of domestic currency in relation to foreign currencies; fiscal deficit cap to ensure limiting the adverse impact of excessive fiscal expenditures on price level stability; while the central banking financing government expenditure cap is also directed at attaining and ensuring funding price stability.

Admittedly, regional integration stages can have a great impact on price stability, especially in developing regions. It is relatively difficult for developing regions to maintain price stability in free trade areas and customs unions. But in common markets, price level stability can be relatively easier to achieve because commodity price levels, funding price levels (long-run interest rates) and foreign exchange rate stability tend to be stabilized; fiscal deficits can also be more easily managed with better policy coordination, as was the case in the Eurozone experience.

Conceptual issues

Fundamental to appreciating the rationale for convergence criteria in a monetary union is the understanding of what monetary union means and the kind of environment it requires to thrive. Monetary union possesses three essential characteristics. First, membership of a monetary union implies relinquishing monetary sovereignty, including central monetary policy and centralized determination of interest rates. Second, a monetary union is designed to last; opting out of a monetary union after accession entails incalculable economic and political costs. Finally, a monetary zone is unlike a currency area defined by the borders of a single sovereign nation state. Although there is a single monetary policy for the zone, other policy matters, such as budget, tax and social policies, are still largely decentralized. Fiscal policy, in particular, must abide by the rules for monetary union to be effective.

These three characteristics appear straightforward and self-evident, but they have important implications. A monetary union requires lasting economic convergence – convergence in the sense that each country must be able to keep up with the others on a permanent basis, without recourse to national monetary policy or changes in the exchange rate.

A conventional nation state with its own currency has several options available for fostering convergence within its own currency area. There are largely uniform economic and taxation policies to prevent excessive deviations in politically induced conditions for investment. There is a national budgetary policy which can give financial support to regions which are lagging behind the general trend. And there is a largely similar and similarly funded system of welfare. These are not present in a typical monetary union or, at least, not to the same extent as in a nation state.

The key question that subsists in a monetary union is: How can a politically decentralized monetary union safeguard the necessary lasting convergence of all its member states? Ultimately, it appears that there is only one way of doing this. Safeguarding lasting convergence in a politically decentralized monetary union must rest on two pillars: first, on each country's own sustained competitiveness as a result of each country's own efforts, and, second, on a fundamental willingness to accept certain binding rules and to abide by them on a permanent basis. That is the only way in which a monetary union with a decentralized political structure can succeed – not only economically, but also politically without excessive conflict among the participating countries.

The convergence criteria are required as preconditions to entering the monetary union to preclude an end-game problem. An end-game problem occurs whenever the participants in a given institutional regime have an incentive to change their relative position (income or wealth) just before the pre-announced date of the change-over to a new institutional regime (Fratainni *et al.*, 1992). A country that knows that it will be part of a monetary union at some later date may have an incentive to increase its money supply for one last time just before entry into the monetary union. An immediate devaluation of its currency may occur just before the fixing of the irrevocable and irreversible exchange rate vis-à-vis its partner and thus gain a competitive advantage over its partners since future inflation will no longer be determined by national policies. This type of end-game problem is virtually eliminated by convergence criteria, which requires, as a precondition to entry, an inflation rate converging to the inflation rate of other member states. The same explanation holds for exchange rate stability.

The link between monetary and fiscal policy is well articulated in both theory and literature. High debts are an invitation to inflation as contemporary experiences have shown. Even when debts are of short maturity, the temptation to inflate in an effort to reduce at least real interest rates and hence debt accumulation is always present.[1] This conceptual framework fully supports the ideas that went into the inclusion of fiscal criteria in the monetary zone convergence requirement as debt and its mode of financing is a risk factor for sound monetary policy. Therefore limits on debt and deficits are one of the safeguards against inflation. Furthermore, in the spirit of commitment models, unless these rules are firmly institutionalized, the sub-optimal equilibrium cannot be avoided. Therefore, the necessary emphasis on making fiscal criteria an important part of the convergence criteria is appropriate.

The state of macroeconomic convergence

To examine the state of economic convergence in the five member countries during the review period, the West African Monetary Institute (WAMI) adopts a common framework for analysis, which is applied to each country in turn. The common framework is based, essentially, on the WAMZ's Convergence Criteria and the Banjul Action Plan. The analysis also includes backward- and forward-looking economic indicators to help assess the sustainability of convergence.

The convergence criteria are applied in a consistent, transparent and simple manner while it is also underlined that convergence must be achieved on a sustainable basis and not just at a given point in time. The country analyses elaborate on the sustainability of convergence. Economic developments in each country over the past decade are reviewed in order to establish the extent to which current accomplishments are the result of authentic structural reforms and could help sustain economic convergence. Additionally, a forward-looking perspective is adopted. In this regard, scrupulous attention is drawn to the fact that the sustainability of favourable economic developments pivots on proper and

Table 5.1 Convergence criteria in the WAMZ

Primary criteria

Criteria	Target
Inflation single digit	Single digit
Fiscal deficit/GDP ratio	≤–4%
Central bank financing of fiscal deficit as % of previous year's tax revenue	≤10%
Gross external reserves/months of import cover	≥3 months
Secondary criteria	
Non-accumulation of domestic arrears/liquidation of existing domestic arrears	
Tax revenue/GDP ratio	>20%
Salary mass/total tax revenue	<35%
Public investment from domestic receipts	>20%
Real interest rate	>0
Exchange rate stability	±15%

Source: WAMI (2001).

enduring policy responses to current and future challenges. The common framework is applied individually to the five WAMZ member countries.

Compared with the situation depicted in the 2005 State of Preparedness Report, some of the countries have made progress with economic convergence in 2006 and 2007. However, the global economic crisis, epitomized by unprecedented increases in the prices of fuel and food as well as financial crisis, adversely affected the member countries; this resulted in sub-optimal performance of member countries on the convergence scale in 2008. The challenges faced by many countries in 2008 were predominantly in the form of mounting inflation and fiscal constraints.

Primary convergence criteria

The WAMZ's primary convergence criteria include: single-digit inflation; fiscal deficit/GDP ratio of not more than 4 per cent; central bank financing of central government deficits of not more than 10 per cent of the previous year's tax revenue; and external reserves to cover at least three months of normal imports.

Inflation

The requirement for the inflation criterion is to be in single digits. In nominal terms this will be taken as an inflation rate of not more than 9.9 per cent. The WAMZ member countries experienced severe inflationary pressures in 2008, principally due to unprecedented increases in food and fuel prices.

Focusing on the performance of individual countries over the reference period, only one member country (The Gambia, 2.2 per cent) achieved an inflation rate below the reference value. Three countries (Ghana 18.4 per cent; Guinea 24.6 per cent; Sierra Leone 15 per cent) reported inflation rates of at least 15 per cent. Nigeria recorded an inflation rate of 12 per cent, 2.1 percentage

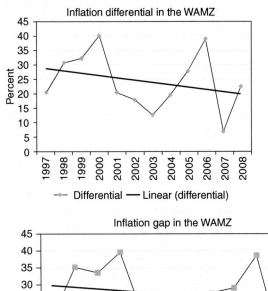

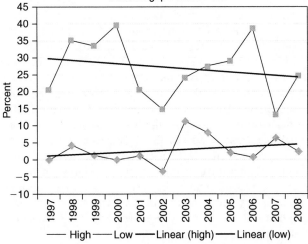

Figure 5.1 Inflation in the WAMZ (source: WAMI (2008)).

points above the reference value. Within the Zone, the differential between the best-performing country (The Gambia) and the worst-performing country (Guinea) was 22.4 percentage points. Member countries' deviation from the mean inflation rate ranged between negative 0.6 per cent in Sierra Leone and 12.2 per cent in The Gambia. Nonetheless, in nearly all countries under review the inflation rate is expected to remain high in the coming months.

Looking back over the past ten years, inflation in most of the countries under review initially declined from relatively high levels in the early and mid-1990s. The Gambia is the only country that has consistently maintained a single-digit inflation rate throughout the last decades (with the exception of 2002 and 2003, when inflation stood at 13 per cent and 17.6 per cent respectively). Ghana has not achieved a single-digit inflation rate in the last ten years; the best performance was in 2006, when 10.9 per cent inflation was recorded. Guinea maintained single-digit inflation from 1997 to 2002; the country consistently recorded a double-digit inflation rate between 2003 and 2008, with the worst performance of 39.1 per cent in 2006. In the last ten years, Nigeria recorded a single-digit inflation rate in three years (1999, 2006 and 2007), and in the other years inflation was mainly in double digits with the highest rate of 23.8 per cent recorded in 2003. Sierra Leone registered double-digit inflation rates in the last three years of the 1990s; from 2000 to 2002, a single-digit inflation rate was sustained; between 2003 and 2005, inflationary pressures heightened resulting in a double-digit inflation rate but in 2006 a single-digit rate of 8.3 per cent was achieved; in 2007 and 2008, respective double-digit rates of 12.2 per cent and 15 per cent were recorded.

These developments in inflation have mostly taken place against the background of dynamic economic conditions, but they also reflect external factors. On the domestic side, buoyant domestic demand has contributed to inflationary pressures in many countries. Private consumption spending has been strong in almost all countries, underpinned by robust growth in disposable income, buoyant credit growth and low real interest rates. Also, investment has increased strongly in most countries under review, supported by strong profits, inflows of foreign direct investment and favourable demand prospects. However, investment has not only contributed to demand pressure (particularly in the construction sector) but has also helped to expand the supply capacity of the economies under review. Not all economies under review have grown rapidly, however. The main exception is Guinea, where economic growth has remained relatively subdued, reflecting the short-term effects of the fiscal profligacy and prolonged macroeconomic imbalances (associated with fiscal and external deficits).

Lastly, periodic changes in administered prices, especially of petroleum products, have had a significant impact on inflation in many countries. In tandem, the most important external driver of inflation has been the increase in energy and food prices, which has had a strong impact in most countries in the WAMZ, including Nigeria, in line with the relatively large weight of these components in the consumption basket in these countries.

Looking ahead, forecasts by WAMI indicate that inflation in most countries could moderate in 2009. Given the declining fuel and food prices coupled with the financial crisis that has resulted in global recession, inflation can be expected to remain low in the short to medium term. There is renewed optimism that recent and expected future one-off price increases in food and energy will ease considerably, although, over longer horizons, it is difficult to assess the resultant effects.

Budget deficits (excluding grants) as a ratio of GDP

The requirement under this criterion is that fiscal operations of the member countries should not result in a deficit that is more than 4 per cent of GDP. In 2008, three countries (The Gambia, Guinea and Nigeria) satisfied this criterion. Two countries (Ghana and Sierra Leone) failed to operate within the defined threshold of the criterion. The difference between the best-performing country, Guinea (0.2 per cent), and Ghana (16.3 per cent) was 16.1 percentage points.

In relation to the zonal mean, the fiscal deficit/GDP ratio for The Gambia was 3.4 per cent below the mean value of 5.2 per cent. Comparative ratios for other countries were: Guinea (5.4 per cent); Nigeria (4.9 per cent) and Sierra Leone (2.6 per cent); Ghana (11.1 per cent). Whereas the deviations from the mean by three countries (Nigeria, Guinea and The Gambia) were negative, those of Ghana and Sierra Leone were positive, indicating that the two countries were the main outliers in the Zone under this criterion.

Looking back at the period from 1997 to 2008, fiscal deficits-to-GDP ratios increased substantially in Ghana (by 13.3 percentage points) and to a considerably lesser extent in Sierra Leone, The Gambia and Guinea. By contrast, in Nigeria the ratio stood clearly below the value of 4 per cent over the same period with the exception of 1998 and 1999, when respective ratios of 4.7 and 7.6 per cent were recorded.

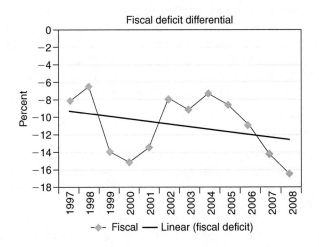

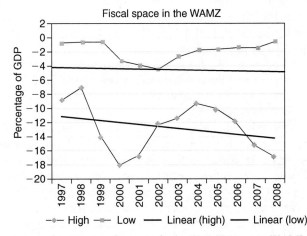

Figure 5.2 Fiscal performance in the WAMZ (source: WAMI (2008)).

In recent years, external debts of most countries in the Zone have reduced considerably due to the various debt relief initiatives administered by international financial institutions in conjunction with several governments. All the WAMZ countries with the exception of Guinea have so far benefited.

Looking ahead, further fiscal consolidation is required in most countries and particularly in those countries still registering excessive deficit. Ghana, which in 2008 had a deficit significantly above 4 per cent of GDP, must reduce it to below the reference value as soon as possible and within the committed time frame. Moreover, sufficiently ambitious consolidation is also highly important in the countries with budget deficits below the reference value, to enable them to achieve lasting compliance with their respective medium-term objectives.

The horizon clearly indicates that, for the countries that rely heavily on grants (The Gambia, Ghana, Guinea and Sierra Leone) for budgetary financing, attaining and sustaining the prescribed benchmark is going to be challenging. However, with the expected production of oil in Ghana in the next few years, it is expected not only that the revenue profile of government will increase but also that the grant components of budgetary support will be reduced. For Sierra Leone and Guinea, appropriate policy measures to attract foreign direct investment into the lucrative mineral sector in an atmosphere of stable democracy should boost the revenue base of government in the medium term.

Central bank financing of budget deficits

This criterion limits the financing of government fiscal operations by the central banks to 10 per cent of the previous year's tax revenue. The countries' performance on this criterion has been generally satisfactory. In 2008, only Ghana failed to satisfy the requirement of this criterion.

Between 1997 and 2008, none of the countries consistently sustained the performance on this criterion. Ghana operated outside the required benchmarks in six of the years in the review period (1997, 1998, 1999, 2000, 2002 and 2008); the corresponding ratios for the years were: 103.5 per cent, 98.0 per cent, 132.1 per cent, 57.9 per cent, 12.1 per cent and 35.1 per cent. The Gambia operated outside the threshold of 10 per cent in three years (2001, 2002 and 2003) where respective ratios of 30.7 per cent, 76.1 per cent and 63.1 per cent were recorded. In the same period Guinea missed the benchmark five times (1999, 2000, 2002, 2003 and 2006), when ratios of 16.6 per cent, 17.6 per cent, 27.1 per cent, 16.1 per cent and 81.6 per cent were registered.

Nigeria's outturn on this criterion during the past 11 years indicate that in 1997, 1998 and 1999, respective ratios of 13 per cent, 56.7 per cent and 141.7 per cent were recorded, but between 2000 and 2008, the country only missed the prescribed threshold once (2003) when 37.6 per cent was the outturn. Sierra Leone faltered on this criterion five times (1997, 1999, 2000, 2003 and 2006) in the past 11 years; however, in the past five years, the country slipped on this criterion only once.

The "zero-financing culture" is gradually gaining ground in the Zone in recent times and there have been positive performances in all the countries, with the

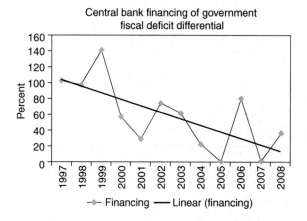

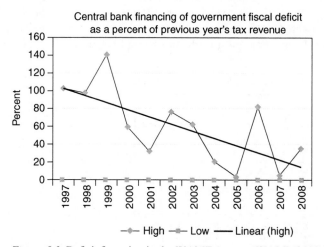

Figure 5.3 Deficit financing in the WAMZ (source: WAMI (2008)).

exception of Ghana, which operated above the ceiling in 2008; this is attributable to the shortfall in domestic revenue owing to the lull in activity during the elections and the lower than expected inflows of donor assistance. Guinea and Sierra Leone significantly improved their performance on this criterion through further fiscal consolidation during the period.

Looking ahead on the medium-term horizon there are bright prospects that the countries will restrain from central bank financing of government.

Gross reserves in months of imports

The performance of the Zone on external reserves (months of import cover) has constantly exceeded the target throughout the convergence period. In 2008, the level of external reserves in the Zone was adequate and substantially above the

three months required by the criterion. However, the influence of Nigeria's performance in the zonal outcome was overwhelming. The country level performance showed that Nigeria consistently satisfied the criterion, from an outturn of
9.6 months in 1997 to 14.2 months in 2008. An impressive reserve build-up was
also registered by The Gambia, where the criterion was only missed in 2002,
when the country suffered severe external shocks affecting the groundnut exports
and tourism sectors.

Ghana consistently met the criterion between 2003 and 2007, but in the earlier
years (1997–2002) the country's external reserves were inadequate to finance up
to three months of imports; again in 2008, the reserves could only finance 2.9
months of imports. In the review period, Sierra Leone satisfied the requirement
of this criterion consistently from 2004 to 2008. Guinea has met this criterion
since 2003.

The major factor that influenced the performance on this criterion was the
price of crude oil on the international oil market. While this development had a
positive impact on Nigeria's external reserves, all other countries in the WAMZ
were adversely affected. However, appropriate policy responses coupled with
positive price developments in most of the other primary commodities exported

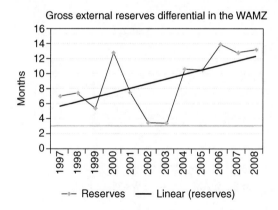

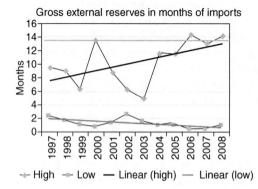

Figure 5.4 Reserves in the WAMZ (source: WAMI (2008)).

from the Zone, particularly gold and cocoa, moderated the impact of escalating crude oil prices.

Looking ahead, there are good prospects for all member countries to attain this criterion in the short to medium term.

Secondary convergence criteria

In addition to the four primary criteria outlined above, member countries were also expected to respect a set of six secondary convergence criteria, including: non-accumulation of domestic arrears; tax revenue as a ratio of GDP of at least 20 per cent; wage bill as a ratio of total tax revenue not to exceed 35 per cent; public investment from tax receipts to exceed 20 per cent; real interest rates to be positive; and exchange rates of domestic currency to remain within a fluctuation margin of ± 15 per cent.

Zero domestic arrears

The requirement under this criterion is that member countries should not accumulate new domestic payment arrears and should have liquidated all arrears by end of 2003. Arrears are defined as expenditure relating to the current budget, which have been outstanding for more than three months. Although consistent data for the assessment of performance on this criterion has remained a challenge to the WAMI as a result of paucity of data from member countries, there are indications that in most of the countries there has been substantial reduction in domestic arrears. However, a definitive statement on this criterion is not possible.

Tax revenue/GDP ratio (greater than 20 per cent)

The obligation under this criterion is that the tax revenue collected by central government as a ratio of GDP (at current market prices) should exceed 20 per cent. In 2008, only Ghana satisfied this criterion. Two countries (The Gambia and Nigeria) recorded ratios in excess of 15 per cent, while the remaining two countries (Guinea and Sierra Leone) registered ratios below 15 per cent. The difference between the best-performing country, Ghana (21.9 per cent), and the worst-performing country, Sierra Leone (9.3 per cent), was 12.6 per cent. In relation to the zonal average of 16 per cent, outturns in three countries (Guinea, Nigeria and Sierra Leone) were 1.5, 0.1 and 6.7 percentage points, respectively, below the mean performance.

In the period from 1997 to 2008, tax revenue/GDP ratios increased substantially in Ghana (by 7.2 percentage points). In The Gambia the ratio ranged between 18.7 per cent in 1997 and 18.2 per cent in 2008. The comparative figures for Guinea during the period were 10.7 and 14.5 per cent. In Nigeria, the ratio declined from 19 per cent to 15.9 per cent during the same period. Also the data for Sierra Leone for 1997 was not available; between 2000 and 2008,

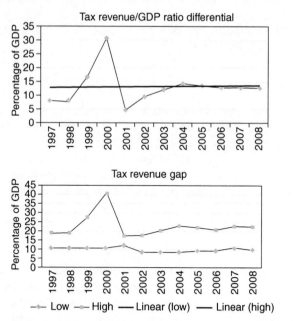

Figure 5.5 Tax revenues in the WAMZ (source: WAMI (2008)).

the ratio was 10.8 and 9.3 per cent, respectively. The real issue on the perform-ance of member countries on this criterion is essentially the low revenue base of the countries and the non-diversification of the production base over time.

Looking forward, the challenge of satisfying this criterion by member coun-tries is formidable. The countries will need to undertake substantial tax reforms, including provision of incentives to the revenue authorities across the countries, to facilitate tax collection. The feasibility of satisfying this criterion by Guinea and Sierra Leone in the short to medium term is slim. However, with minimal additional tax efforts, The Gambia and Nigeria are likely to meet this criterion in the medium term.

Wage bill/total tax revenue ratio (less than 35 per cent)

The requirement of this criterion is that member countries should not expend more than 35 per cent of their tax revenue to pay wages. For the purpose of this criterion, wage bill includes all personnel costs including salaries and wages, fringe benefits and social security contributions by the government. In 2008 only two countries (The Gambia and Guinea) met this criterion, registering respective ratios of 29.2 and 24.8 per cent. Three countries (Ghana, Nigeria and Sierra Leone) recorded respective ratios of 47.3, 41.4 and 59.5 per cent. The average ratio for the five countries in 2008 was 40.4 per cent. Again only two countries that met the criterion also recorded outturns below the zonal mean. The differentials between the best-performing country and the worst-performing country narrowed from 30.5 per cent in 1997 to 28.8 per cent in 1998, but increased to 60.8 per cent in 2000. The difference declined to 29.7 per cent in 2002, but rose consistently to 47.6 per cent in 2005. Between 2006 and 2008, the gap decreased from 45.7 per cent to 34.7 per cent.

In retrospect, Nigeria is the only country that has consistently satisfied this criterion from 1997 to 2008, with the exception of 2002 when 47.2 per cent was registered. Sierra Leone has not satisfied the criterion in any of the years between 1997 and 2008. The Gambia operated within the threshold of the criterion consistently from 2003 to 2008. Ghana's performance has been outside the threshold from 2000 to 2008. It is clear that most of the countries are facing severe challenges on tax revenue generation on the one hand and the increasing wage bill on the other. The countries will need to follow through on tax reforms that are being implemented to ensure that wage bill does not take a disproportionate fraction of the tax revenue.

Looking forward, there are bright prospects for all the countries except Sierra Leone to meet this criterion in the medium term.

Public investment/domestic revenue ratio (greater than 20 per cent)

This criterion requires member countries to spend at least 20 per cent of tax revenue on public investments. The performance of the countries on this criterion has been unsatisfactory. In 2008 none of the countries satisfied this criterion.

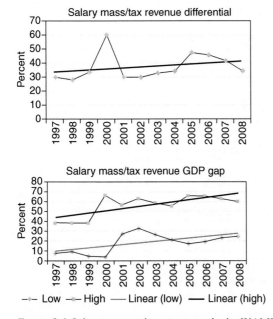

Figure 5.6 Salary mass and tax revenues in the WAMZ (source: WAMI (2008)).

The best-performing country (Nigeria) registered 19.9 per cent, 0.1 percentage points below the required 20.0 per cent. Three countries (The Gambia, Guinea and Sierra Leone) recorded ratios of less than 15 per cent. Ghana registered a ratio of 14.1 per cent. The average for the five countries was 14.2 per cent. Two countries' (The Gambia and Sierra Leone) outturns on this criterion were below the average for the Zone. The difference between the best-performing country and the worst-performing country was 12.2 percentage points.

Retrospectively, between 1997 and 2007, two countries (The Gambia and Sierra Leone) failed to satisfy this criterion in any of the years. One country (Ghana) satisfied the criterion six times, while Guinea met it once. The standard deviation over the period ranged from 0.5 per cent in 1997 to 8.8 per cent in 2007. The country performance on this criterion is predicated on the domestic revenue generation capacity of the countries as well as the policy direction on the provision of required critical infrastructure by government. Given the correlation between infrastructure development and private investment, the countries will need to consciously build up investment through a rigorous revenue drive.

The outlook of country performance is not bright given the increasing wage bill and the relative slow growth rate in domestic revenue generation. However, Ghana and Nigeria have the prospect of attaining and sustaining the threshold in the medium term.

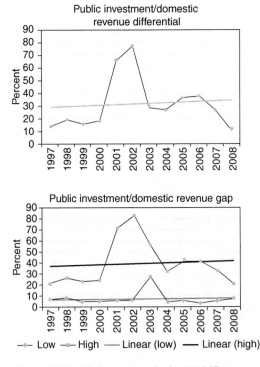

Figure 5.7 Public investment in the WAMZ (source: WAMI (2008)).

Positive real interest rates

This criterion requires the difference between the savings rate and the inflation rate to be positive. That is, the interest rate should be higher than inflation rate. In 2008 only one country (The Gambia) registered a positive real interest rate of 3.3 per cent. Four countries (Ghana, Guinea, Nigeria and Sierra Leone) registered negative real interest rates ranging from 3.2 per cent in Nigeria to 13.2 per cent in Ghana. On average, the real interest rate for the five countries was negative 6.5 per cent.

Real interest rates were largely negative in the Zone in most of the years 1997–2007. The broad patterns observed in member countries are closely related to developments in inflation rates. Other factors underlying this trend were the relative instability of exchange rates in some countries and the relative deterioration in countries' fiscal positions, thereby increasing risk premia.

Looking ahead, countries are striving to put in place monetary frameworks that will check inflationary pressures. Ghana and Nigeria are currently pursuing inflation targeting in their monetary policy frameworks. Sierra Leone, The Gambia and Guinea, though still pursuing monetary targeting frameworks, have put in place monetary policy committees that could enhance the monetary policy formulation and implementation. Inflationary pressure should be largely contained in the medium term in most of the countries and the prospects for positive real interest rates are improving.

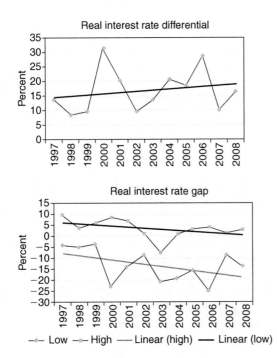

Figure 5.8 Real interest rates in the WAMZ (source: WAMI (2008)).

Nominal exchange rates to fluctuate within ±15 per cent

The requirement of this criterion is that the nominal exchange rate of the various member countries' currencies vis-à-vis the US dollar should be within the margin of ±15 per cent of the WAMZ ERM-II. In 2008 only the leone operated within the band. Four countries' (The Gambia, Ghana, Guinea and Nigeria) currencies operated outside the band. While the dalasi and the naira appreciated by 49.9 and 16.3 per cent respectively, the Guinea franc and the cedi depreciated.

Beginning in 2004, when the ERM-II was instituted, the WAMZ currencies broadly operated within the band. Between 2004 and 2007, three countries' currencies (the dalasi, naira and leone) operated outside the band only in 2007. The Guinea franc operated outside the band throughout the period. The underlying factors that influenced developments in the exchange rates of the various currencies included excessive fiscal deficits by government, increased import demand and dwindling exports. Developments in international commodities markets also impacted on exchange rates.

Looking forward, the prospects of attaining and sustaining stable exchange rates in the region are not too bright. This is essentially because of the global recession that is expected to impact negatively on the demand for the primary commodities produced in the countries in the short to medium term.

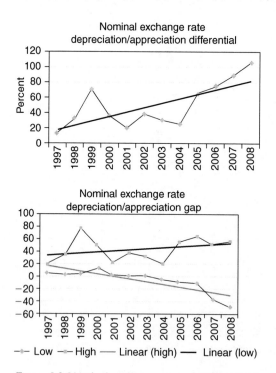

Figure 5.9 Nominal exchange rate and differential (source: WAMI (2008)).

WAMZ and other monetary union convergence criteria: a comparative analysis

All monetary cooperation arrangements have some form of quantitative macroeconomic convergence criteria and structural benchmarks that the member countries are required to observe and comply with prior to the commencement of such union. The structure, number and the quantitative thresholds of the criteria, however, differ from one monetary union to another. Nevertheless, convergence criteria are designed to aid the attainment of a macroeconomic policy environment appropriate for a monetary union. Macroeconomic convergence criteria set by various unions are important preconditions for long-term stability. The achievement of these goals is a major challenge everywhere.

The quantitative convergence criteria are broadly classified into primary and secondary criteria. The quantitative criteria are usually set over a given period of time determined by the relevant institution of the Regional Economic Community (REC). The criteria in most of the RECs are periodically reviewed to assess relevance and the appropriateness of the targets within the context of the regional as well as global economic environment.

All RECs in Africa with the exception of the East African Community (EAC) and Southern African Development Community (SADC) classified their quantitative convergence criteria into primary and secondary. However, there is no differentiation between primary and secondary criteria in the EAC, European Union (EU) and Gulf Cooperation Council (GCC). The EAC has ten criteria, the EU has four and the GCC has four (Table 5.2).

An assessment of selected monetary cooperation arrangements showed that most of the unions, with the exception of the Common Market of Eastern and Southern Africa (COMESA), have at least four primary criteria covering the real, fiscal, monetary and external sectors of the economy.

COMESA has three primary and eight secondary criteria. The three primary criteria cover the real sector, and the fiscal as well as external sectors. The WAMZ and the Economic Community of West African State (ECOWAS) have four primary and six secondary convergence criteria. Two of the primary convergence criteria are related to the fiscal sector, one to the real sector and one to the external sector.

The Economic Community of Central African States (CEMAC) has three secondary criteria of which one is fiscal in nature, one is on real sector issue, while the other relates to the external sector. SADC has four primary and five secondary criteria. The West African Economic and Monetary Union (WAEMU) has four primary and four secondary criteria.

Unlike in the EU and the GCC, public debt and interest rate criteria are not included in the WAMZ primary convergence criteria. Secondary convergence criteria for ECOWAS, WAEMU and WAMZ are similar in definition as well as prescribed reference values. These set of criteria are wide ranging but the composition is largely similar to that of the primary criteria. Inflation, budget deficit, debt and gross external reserves are generally classified as the set of primary criteria. The primary convergence criteria normally form the basis for assessing a country's performance on macroeconomic convergence.

Table 5.2 Primary convergence criteria of selected monetary unions

Primary criteria	WAMZ	ECOWAS	UEMOA	EU	SADC	CEMAC	COMESA	GCC
Inflation	<10% (single-digit) end-period	≤5%	≤3% annual average	Average rate of inflation over the previous 12 months should not exceed by more than 1.5 percentage points of the three best-performing member states	Single-digit by 2008; 5% 2010–2015; 3% in 2018	≤3%	≤5%	Weighted average of the six countries plus 2 percentage points
Budget deficit	≤4% budget deficit (excl. grants) to GDP	4% budget deficit (excl. grants) to GDP	Fiscal balance to GDP ratio of ≥0	Budget deficits should not exceed 3% of GDP	Budget deficit ≤5% of GDP in 2008, 3% of GDP as anchor, with a range of 1% between 2012 and 2018	Budgetary balance must be non-negative	Budget deficit should not exceed 3% of GDP	Not exceeding 3% of GDP although some flexibility will be allowed to account for wild fluctuations in state revenues
Central bank financing of government budget	≤10% of previous year's tax revenue	≤10% of previous year's tax revenue	Not applicable	Not applicable	≤10% of previous year's tax income	Not applicable	Minimize towards 0% target	Not applicable

External reserves	≥3 months of imports	≥6 months of imports	Not applicable	Not applicable	≥3 months in 2008, ≥6 months between 2012 and 2018	Not applicable	≥4% months of imports	Not applicable
Gross public debt	Not applicable	Not applicable	Ceiling on total public debt/GDP ≤0%	≤60% of GDP	Government debt ≤60% of GDP	≤70% of GDP	Not applicable	≤60% of GDP
Interest rates	Not applicable	Not applicable	Not applicable	Average of the lowest six countries plus 2 percentage points	Not applicable	Not applicable	Not applicable	Average of the lowest six countries plus 2 percentage points

Source: Author's compilation.

Inflation

For all the RECs in Africa, WAMZ has the loosest inflation criterion with the highest degree of freedom. WAMZ requires a single-digit headline inflation rate (end-period) while CEMAC requires an annual inflation rate of less than 3 per cent. EAC and ECOWAS prescribe an inflation rate of less than 5 per cent. WAEMU requires an average annual inflation rate maintained at a maximum of 3 per cent. As for SADC, inflation criterion is set at a single digit by 2008, less than or equal to 5 per cent from 2012 to 2015, and 3 per cent by 2018.

In the EU, the inflation criterion is not fixed; it is the average of the three least inflation rates plus 1.5 percentage points. The inflation rate is calculated using the increase in the latest available 12-month average of the Harmonized Index of Consumer Prices (HICP) over the previous 12-month average. This is obtained by using the unweighted arithmetic mean of the rate of inflation in the three countries with the lowest inflation rates; in essence the requirement is flexible from year to year. In the GCC inflation criterion is defined as weighted average of the six member countries plus 2 percentage points. Indeed all the monetary unions have a bench mark for inflation.

Budget deficit

SADC prescribes a wider fiscal space of at most 5 per cent of fiscal deficit-to-GDP ratio as at 2008. However, this is expected to narrow to 3 per cent as anchor with a range of 1 percentage point from 2012 to 2018. WAMZ and ECOWAS prescribe relatively larger fiscal space than other RECs in Africa. WAMZ and ECOWAS target a fiscal deficit (excluding grants)-to-GDP ratio to a ceiling of 4 per cent while WAEMU requires a more stringent threshold, i.e. a balanced budget or surplus budget. In the EU, the ratio of the planned or actual government deficit to GDP is limited to 3 per cent of GDP. Similarly, in the GCC fiscal deficit-to-GDP ratio is fixed at 3 per cent but there is flexibility in the event of wild fluctuation in member states' revenue.

Central bank financing of government budget deficit

ECOWAS, WAMZ and SADC have similar requirements for financing of government fiscal deficit, i.e. central bank financing of government fiscal deficit of not more than 10 per cent of previous year's tax revenue. The rest of the RECs in Africa have no requirement on central bank financing of government fiscal deficit, rather some of them have limits on public debt. They stipulate that government debt-to-GDP ratio should not exceed 60 per cent. However, CEMAC prescribes public debt-to-GDP ratio to 70 per cent.

Gross external reserves

Gross external reserve expressed in months of imports is set at six months for EAC and ECOWAS. WAMZ requires three months of import cover. SADC on the other hand prescribed at least three months of imports as at 2008 and raised the target to a floor of six months of imports from 2012 to 2018. Thus, the SADC target is progressive while the WAMZ is fixed. The GCC has no criterion with respect to gross external reserves.

Overall, the WAMZ set of convergence criteria are comparatively less stringent than other RECs of similar economic conditions. As regards price stability, WAMZ single-digit inflation criterion is more flexible than that of ECOWAS, EAC, CEMAC, WAEMU, GCC and SADC, which require a target of less than or equal to 5 per cent.

On the fiscal deficit criterion, the reference value of 4 per cent gives greater fiscal space to WAMZ member countries compared to the 0 per cent reference value of WAEMU and CEMAC. SADC prescribed less than 5 per cent in 2008 and 3 per cent from 2012 to 2018. The EU and GCC prescribe 3 per cent.

WAMZ prescribed gross external reserve level sufficient to finance three months of imports while others require six months, indicating that WAMZ member countries require fewer months of import. Unlike other RECs, which require public debt-to-GAP ratio of 60 per cent, WAMZ has no prescribed criterion for public debt, rather member countries are not expected to accumulated domestic arrears, and where the arrears existed they are expected to liquidate the arrears. As in the ECOWAS, WAEMU, CEMAC, COMESA and SADC, the WAMZ also has a set of complementary criteria (secondary criteria) designed to support the attainment of the primary criteria.

Alternative methodology

Over the years, the appropriateness of the WAMZ convergence criteria has been called into question by some commentators and academics. The main contention is that, unlike in other monetary unions where convergence criteria are mostly related to the specific yearly performance of the economies in the union, WAMZ criteria appears to stand alone as the thresholds are fixed. For instance, they argue that while other comparable monetary unions restrict inflation for any particular year to certain percentage deviation above the average of two or three best-performing countries, that of the WAMZ is fixed permanently at less than 10 per cent.

Again arguments have been advanced regarding the adoption of fiscal deficit/ GDP ratio of 4 per cent. The key concern has been that, since some countries in the Zone rely heavily on grants for budgetary support, excluding grants components from the revenue without excluding the same from the expenditure constitute a limitation to the ability of the countries to satisfy the criterion. Furthermore, the need to relate the performance in this criterion to the developments in these countries has been advanced. However, the criteria on central bank financing of fiscal deficits of government and the gross external reserves in months of import requirement have not been contested.

In this segment, we adopt the methodology that restricts the criterion to certain percentage points above the three best-performing countries. Specifically, we adopt a deviation of 1.5 per cent from the average of the three best-performing countries in each of the criteria. The 1.5 point deviation is consonant with practice elsewhere in the world, including the European Monetary Union and the GCC. Applying 1.5 percentage points as the maximum allowable deviation from the mean of the three best-performing countries to the primary convergence criteria yields the results presented in Table 5.3.

Inflation

Overall, relating the inflation rate to 1.5 percentage points above the three best-performing countries indicate that the appropriate inflation benchmark fluctuated between 3 per cent in 2000 and 12.7 per cent in 2008. The Gambia satisfied this requirement in all the years with the exception of 2001, 2002 and 2003, when respective inflation rates of 8.1, 13 and 17.6 per cent were recorded.

Ghana failed to meet the criterion throughout the period 2000–2008. The country registered the highest inflation rates of 40.5 per cent (2000) and 10.9 per cent (2006). Guinea's inflation rate was within the threshold in three (2001, 2002 and 2003) out of the nine years under review. Although the country recorded an inflation rate of 7.2 per cent in 2000, it was way above the threshold (3 per cent) for that year. From 2004 to 2008 the rates were perpetually higher than the required threshold, with the highest rate of 39.1 per cent registered in 2006.

Nigeria met the inflation criterion based on the alternative methodology in 2004 and 2007. Although the country recorded a single-digit inflation rate of 8.6 per cent in 2007, the rate was higher than the threshold of 7.3 per cent for that year. The country recorded its highest rate of 23.8 per cent in 2003. In 2008, the rate of 15.1 per cent was 2.4 percentage points higher than the threshold of 12.7 per cent.

Sierra Leone complied with the inflation requirement under the new criterion from 2000 to 2003. Between 2004 and 2008 the country registered inflation rates that were above the threshold. Although a single-digit rate of 8.3 per cent was achieved in 2006, it was 1 percentage point above the required 7.3 per cent for the year.

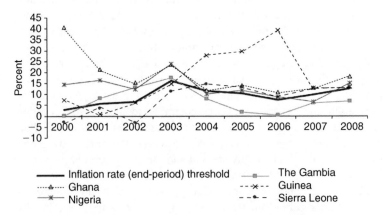

Figure 5.10 WAMZ alternative: inflation (source: WAMI (2008)).

Table 5.3 Alternative primary criteria

Alternative primary criteria	2000	2001	2002	2003	2004	2005	2006	2007	2008
Inflation rate (end-period) threshold	3.0	5.7	6.6	16.1	11.4	10.3	7.3	9.8	12.7
Fiscal balance/GDP (excl. grants) threshold	-3.9	-7.6	-8.2	-7.2	-6.6	-4.5	-3.2	-2.2	-3.2
Central bank financing of fiscal deficit threshold	6.1	1.5	5.5	15.0	1.5	1.5	1.5	1.5	1.5
Gross ext. reserves (months of imports) threshold	9.4	8.0	6.5	6.3	8.6	8.4	9.4	11.5	9.5

Source: Author's calculation from WAMI database.

Applying this methodology, the number of countries that satisfied the inflation criterion in the WAMZ stagnated at two from 2000 to 2004. In 2005 and
2006 only one member country (The Gambia) satisfied the criterion. In the succeeding year, 2007, Nigeria and The Gambia operated within the confines of the
requirement. Again in 2008, only The Gambia satisfied the criterion.

Fiscal deficit/GDP ratio

With the new methodology, the benchmark on this criterion ranged between 2.2
per cent (2007) and 8.2 per cent (2002). The Gambia satisfied the criterion in
three (2000, 2006 and 2007) out of the nine years under review. In 2008, the
ratio of 3.3 per cent achieved was marginally above the benchmark of 3.2 per
cent for the year. The country's best and worst performances were in 2000 (0.3
per cent) and 2001 (10 per cent), respectively.

Ghana's fiscal deficit/GDP ratios were outside the benchmarks for all the
years. The closest the country came to meeting the criterion was in 2002 when
8.3 per cent was achieved against the benchmark of 8.2 per cent for the year. The
country's worst performance was in 2008 when a ratio of 19.7 per cent was
recorded against the threshold of 3.2 per cent. Guinea met the criterion in all the
years with the exception of 2000 (5.5 per cent) and 2003 (10.3 per cent). The best
performance was in 2007 (0.5 per cent) and the worst in 2003 (10.3 per cent).

Nigeria consistently satisfied this criterion between 2000 and 2008. The best
performance was registered in 2008 (0.2 per cent) and the worst in 2002 (3.9 per
cent). Sierra Leone operated outside the benchmark throughout the review period
2000–2008. The country's best performance was in 2007 (5 per cent) and the
worst performance was in 2000 (17.3 per cent).

With respect to central bank financing of government fiscal deficit, the
WAMZ criteria limits it to 10 per cent of previous year's tax revenue. Between

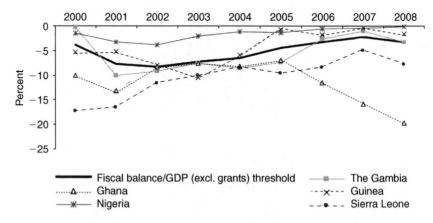

Figure 5.11 WAMZ alternative: fiscal deficit/GDP excluding grants (source: WAMI
(2008)).

2000 and 2008, all the countries operated within the limits of this requirement of the criterion. Three countries met it in 2006, while two countries satisfied the requirement in 2000 and 2002. The worst performance was in 2003 when only one country operated within 10 per cent. Juxtaposing the performance onto the proposed criterion of the average of the three best-performing countries plus 1.5 per cent, the outcome for 2005 and 2007 remained unchanged as all the countries satisfied the criterion.

Central bank financing of government deficit

Applying the new methodology to this criterion reveal that the benchmarks ranged from 1.5 per cent (2001, 2004–2008) to 15 per cent (2003).

The Gambia satisfied the criterion in all the years, excluding 2001, 2002 and 2003 when respective ratios of 80.7, 22.4 and 63.1 per cent were recorded. Ghana met the requirement in six out of the nine years. In 2000, 2002 and 2008, the country recorded 57.9, 12.1 and 35.1 per cent, respectively. Guinea met the criterion in 2005 and 2007, but operated outside the threshold in all other years, with the worst performance recorded in 2006 (81.6 per cent). Nigeria met it in all the years with the exception of 2003, when the financing was 37.6 per cent against the benchmark of 15 per cent for that year. Sierra Leone's performance on this criterion was satisfactory in six out of the nine years. However, in 2000, 2003 and 2006 the country recorded financing ratios of 13.7, 24.3 and 17.9 per cent, respectively, against the respective benchmarks of 6.1, 15 and 1.5 per cent.

Gross external reserves (months of imports)

With the new methodology, the benchmarks for fulfilling this criterion ranged between 6.5 months (2003) and 11.5 months (2007).

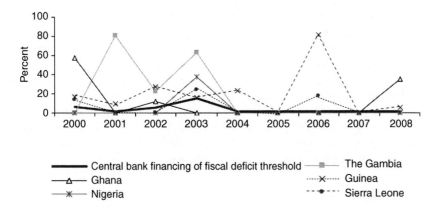

Figure 5.12 WAMZ alternative: central bank financing of fiscal deficit (source: WAMI (2008)).

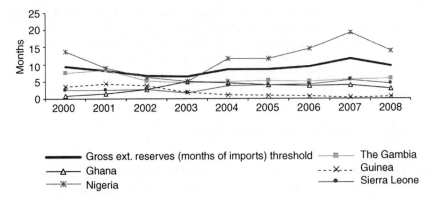

Figure 5.13 WAMZ alternative: gross external reserves (months of imports) (source: WAMI (2008)).

The Gambia satisfied this criterion only once (2001) over the nine-year period. Ghana, Guinea and Sierra Leone did not satisfy it in any of the years. Nigeria met the criterion in all the years with the exception of 2002 and 2003, when respective ratios of 6.2 and 4.9 months were recorded against the benchmark of 6.5 and 6.3 months, respectively.

WAMZ convergence criteria: a comparison of old and new

Inflation

A comparative analysis of the country performance on the two scales indicates that in 2000 and 2001, three countries satisfied the single-digit requirement as stated in the WAMZ criterion, against two countries using the new methodology. In 2002, the number remained unchanged on the two scales, two apiece. Whereas no country satisfied single-digit inflation in 2003, two countries met it in that year based on the new methodology. In 2004 and 2005, one country was compliant with single-digit inflation compared to two and one, respectively, on the new methodology scale. In 2006 three countries met the single-digit requirement against one country on the proposed scale, while in 2007 two countries apiece met the criterion on both scales. In 2008, one country satisfied the inflation criterion based on the single-digit requirement compared to two countries based on the new scale.

Overall, there is no significant improvement on the performance on the inflation criterion with the introduction of the new methodology. The requirement is in fact tighter in five out of the nine years reviewed.

Fiscal deficit/GDP ratio

Utilizing existing criterion to assess countries' performance reveals that between 2000 and 2008, three countries (The Gambia, Guinea and Nigeria) satisfied the criterion in three out of the nine years (2006, 2007 and 2008). Only one country (Nigeria) met the criterion consistently throughout the nine years. Assessing the performance on the criterion based on the alternative methodology indicated a deteriorating trend. The proposed measurement resulted in the threshold that ranged from 2.2 per cent (2007) to 8.2 per cent (2002). The same set of countries (The Gambia, Guinea and Nigeria) satisfied the criterion in 2006 and 2007, but the outturn for 2008 showed that The Gambia failed to meet the criterion, leaving Guinea and Nigeria as the only countries that satisfied the criterion in that year. Nigeria was also the only country that consistently satisfied the criterion throughout the nine years, with the same performance as in the existing scale.

Overall, although the application of the proposed measurement on this criterion whittled down the threshold in five of the nine years under consideration, it tightened the requirement in four of the nine years.

Central bank financing of government deficit

The outturn for 2003, 2004 and 2006 remained the same on both scales as one, four and three countries met the criterion, respectively. The main difference in outcome on countries' performance was in 2001 and 2008; whereas four countries met the requirement in those two years on the existing scale, three countries operated within the threshold when the methodology is applied.

Clearly, there was no significant improvement on the performance on the fiscal deficit financing criterion when the proposed criterion was applied. Indeed, the new methodology resulted in tighter requirements in eight out of the nine years of the convergence process.

Gross external reserves (months of imports)

A comparative analysis of the country performance on the two scales with regard to gross external reserves/months of import cover criterion indicated that three countries consistently met the criterion from 2000 to 2003 and four countries met it from 2004 to 2007, while three countries met it in 2008. However, applying the methodology increased the requirement from three months of import cover to at least six months over the review period. Consequently, on the proposed scale, two countries satisfied the requirement in 2001 and one country in all the other years except 2002 and 2003, when no country met the requirement.

Undoubtedly, the application of the new methodology on the criterion resulted in a significant deterioration in country performance. Obviously, it tightened the requirement in all the nine years of the convergence process.

What is apparent from this exercise, with regard to the alternative methodology, is that the issue is not necessarily the tightness of the criteria but the political will to adopt the needed policies and programmes that are required to firm up the revenue base and the discipline to ensure prudence in the expenditure profile.

Conclusions

Attempts have been made to reflect the zonal economic development in the interpretation and measurement of the WAMZ convergence criteria, by adopting similar definitions as applied by the EU and GCC. This involved limiting the member countries' performance to 1.5 percentage points above the mean of the three best-performing member states. This methodology was applied to all the four primary convergence criteria; inflation, fiscal deficit/GDP ratio, central bank financing of government fiscal deficit and gross external reserves in months of imports.

With regard to inflation, there is no significant improvement on the performance with the introduction of the new methodology. Indeed, using the average of the three best-performing results in a tighter requirement in five out of the nine years reviewed. Concerning fiscal deficits/GDP ratio, although the application of the new measurement on this criterion whittled down the threshold in five of the nine years under consideration, it tightened the requirement in four of the nine years. With respect to central bank financing of government deficits, there was no significant improvement on the performance. The new methodology resulted in tighter requirements in eight out of the nine years of the convergence process. Regarding gross external reserves in months of imports cover, the application of the new methodology resulted in a significant deterioration in country performance. Obviously, it tightened the requirement in all the years of the convergence process.

One thing that stands out from the analysis is that the WAMZ convergence criteria are achievable. The need for the economies to converge before the commencement of the monetary union cannot be overemphasized. Overall, the WAMZ convergence criteria as presently constituted are adequate and appropriate to deliver on a single currency for the Zone. All that is required is the application of political will to adopt and implement policy and programmes that will foster convergence in the member states.

The outstanding policy implication of this exercise with the new methodology is that convergence requirements have become more stringent and given that the WAMZ monetary union is a sub-set of the ECOWAS monetary union, the adoption of the new methodology will take the WAMZ countries further away from the ECOWAS convergence criteria. This might create problems in the future when the ECOWAS Single Monetary Zone is due to commence. Furthermore, a change in the measurement of the criteria in the face of the inability of member states to meet the criteria would definitely send a wrong signal to the international community and thus impinge on the credibility of the union.

Note

1 Consider an application of the Barro–Gordon paradigm. In the present rendition the government loss function includes real debt accumulation and inflation. For purposes of illustration the primary deficit ratio θ is given as the real interest rate, r. Let Π and

Π* denote actual and expected inflation, b the debt ratio, y the growth rate of GDP and the relative aversion to inflation versus debt accumulation.

$$L= [(r + Π* - Π - y]b - \theta]2 + \alpha Π2 \tag{1}$$

The authorities optimize for given expected rate of inflation. The Nash equilibrium inflation rate is proportional to the growth and inflation-adjusted interest budget deficit ratio.

$$Π = (b/\alpha)[(r - y)b - \theta] \tag{2}$$

With a real interest rate in excess of the growth rate, the higher the level of debt, the higher the rate of inflation. Though inflation is fully anticipated and hence does nothing to reduce real debt service, inflation aversion of policy-makers helps dampen inflation, as do primary surpluses.

References

Artigues, A. and Vignolo, T. (2001). "Long-run Equilibria in the Monetary Policy Game", paper presented at the Policy Modelling for European and Global Issues, Brussels, 5–7 July.

Barro, R. and Gordon, D. (1983). "Rules, Discretion, and Reputation in a Model of Monetary Policy", *Journal of Monetary Economics*, December.

Blair, T., Branson, R., Hawking, S., Naipaul, V., Violante, L. and. Murdoch, R. (1999). Lecture Delivered in the Series *Builders of the Millennium*, in celebration of the 750th anniversary of the foundation of University College, Oxford, 3 June.

Fratianni, M., Hagen, J.V. and Waller, C. (1992). "The Maastricht Way to EMU", *Princeton Essays In International Finance* (June).

WAMI (2001). *Convergence Report*. Online: www.wami-imao.org.

WAMI (2008). *Convergence Report*. Online: www.wami-imao.org.

6 Fiscal sustainability in the WAMZ

Temitope W. Oshikoya, Abu Bakarr Tarawalie and Rohey Khan

Introduction

Fiscal sustainability is considered in the literature to be a key ingredient for monetary union between different countries. Achieving fiscal sustainability at the national level allows the authorities to attain low inflation, exchange rate stability, an increase in foreign reserves, a reduction in the fiscal deficit and a decline in public debt, among other things. This chapter, therefore, explores the sustainability of fiscal policy in the WAMZ member countries, using both the accounting and present value budget constraint (PVBC) approaches.

Rationale for fiscal sustainability

Fiscal sustainability analysis is central to establishing the extent to which a monetary union can be sustained. Sustainability is usually discussed in the context of a non-drastic shift in fiscal policy to satisfy debt obligations. The analysis of fiscal sustainability focuses on the ability of the government to generate an adequate level of primary budget surplus in order to stabilize its debt ratio, without a significant adjustment in the fiscal policy stance (Gunter, 2003). Furthermore, sustainability is usually defined as a situation in which a borrower is expected to be able to continue servicing its debt without an unrealistically large correction to the balance of income and expenditure (IMF, 2002, p. 4). In other words, the country must be able to produce a level of primary surplus that, over the medium term, would maintain or lower the ratio of debt to GDP. Debt sustainability is an essential condition for macroeconomic stability and sustained economic growth. Most often, high public debt levels create repayment flows that can crowd out much-needed public spending, and can generate adverse incentives for private investors to engage in activities that spur long-term growth. An excessive level of public debt can make a nation vulnerable to interruption in aid flows or to sudden shifts in domestic financial market conditions. These problems can be aggravated by a narrow export and production base and various structural, political and institutional factors that reduce returns on investment.

Drastic adjustment creates outcomes that may compromise the objectives of a monetary union. Long-term fiscal sustainability plays an important role in a monetary union because of the spill-over effects that spread the negative consequences of one member state's fiscal excessiveness and unwarranted public debt to the others. A fiscal deficit that is financed through external borrowing will increase the external debt burden and directly reduce external sustainability. The accumulation of large debts naturally generates a debt overhang that can create a permanent climate of financial fragility for member countries. For countries in a monetary union this is crucial, as debt-servicing obligations tend to crowd out resources for social services and therefore exacerbate poverty situations.

Protracted fiscal imbalances by one member state would produce negative externalities on the entire monetary union through an increase in real interest rates, a reduction in public investment and the consequent deterioration of growth potential for all members. In addition, a fiscal policy (budgetary course) that is not sustainable in the long run would eventually undermine the ability of the central bank to maintain monetary stability. This would result in high inflation engendered through central bank financing of the fiscal deficit (monetization of the deficit). An expansion in domestic credit would increase imports and thereby reduce the amount of foreign exchange available to the domestic economy, resulting in a fall in months of import cover. Domestic financing may also increase pressure for exchange rate depreciation. Thus, maintaining fiscal sustainability is seen as a sine qua non for the establishment of monetary union in the WAMZ, since an unsustainable fiscal policy is likely to impede the achievement and sustainability of the primary convergence criteria.

The West African Central Bank (WACB), when established, is expected to take over the formulation and implementation of a common monetary policy for the countries in the Zone. This would entail zero financing of national governments by the WACB. The major question that this chapter seeks to answer is: are WAMZ countries' fiscal policies sustainable in the short to medium term, given their debt profile? The purpose of analysing fiscal sustainability is usually to show the difference between the fiscal position resulting from current policies and the sustainable position in a certain moment in future. The general intuition of fiscal sustainability is self-evident: sustainable policies are those that can be continued on current trends, while unsustainable policies will ultimately have to be modified. Given that in a monetary union, monetary policy does not lie within the domain of member countries, it suffices for member countries to maintain a sustainable fiscal policy in order to achieve both internal and external equilibrium. Thus, this fiscal sustainability analysis for WAMZ member countries provides an insight for assessing member countries' fiscal policies, while examination of the sustainability of public debt helps to ascertain whether the debt burden of WAMZ countries can be satisfied continuously without significant adjustment in their fiscal policies.

Public finances in the WAMZ: developments and trends

With the adoption of the convergence criterion aimed at ensuring budgetary discipline to underpin the stability of the planned common currency of the WAMZ

86   *T.W. Oshikoya* et al.

(the eco), fiscal imbalance is being tackled with renewed vigour across the WAMZ countries. From a theoretical standpoint, in a monetary union where member countries no longer have an independent monetary policy, fiscal policy becomes the only instrument available to them to protect themselves against exogenous shocks. On these grounds, it can be argued that a strict budgetary rule may impose a heavy burden on countries in the event of large, idiosyncratic shocks. The trends in government revenue, expenditure and fiscal deficits[1] for the countries of WAMZ are captured in Figures 6.1 to 6.5.

The Gambia's fiscal outturn during the period 1980–2008 was characterized by a fiscal deficit, which was prominent in the early 1980s, arising from excessive government expenditure amid declining revenue. Increased debt repayment on government loans, arising from high inflation and excessive depreciation of the dalasi, as well as increased expenditure on wages and salaries, informed the huge expenditure outlay during this period. Similarly, the decline in earnings from the country's main export[2] partly accounted for the fall in revenue during the 1980s.[3]

However, prior to the military take-over in 1994, the country experienced a decline in the fiscal deficit, arising from increased revenue from the tourism sector and a slowdown in government expenditure. There was a large fiscal deficit rebound in the late 1990s and early 2000s. The increase in fiscal deficit in the late 1990s was ascribed to the military take-over in 1994, which resulted in the suspension of new project aid and cancellation of budgetary assistance by the country's traditional donors.[4] Revenue from tourism fell in 2000 and 2001, following the collapse of a major German tour operator and the fall-out from the 11 September 2001 attacks on the United States. This had a damaging effect on total government revenue and hence the overall fiscal deficit. Since 2005, the country has recorded a drop in the fiscal deficit, mainly engendered by the execution of a cash budgetary management that resulted in a cut in government expenditure and an increase in revenue mobilization.

Ghana's fiscal position remained weak during the review period, informed by persistent fiscal deficits. Government expenditure accelerated between 1980 and

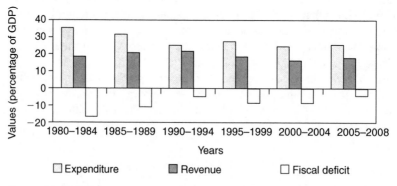

Figure 6.1 Trends in government expenditure, revenue and fiscal deficit (% of GDP) – Gambia (sources: IMF (2008a) and Gambia (2008)).

2008 due to a loose expenditure outlay, especially on wages and salaries. However, the adoption of the Economic Recovery Programme (ERP) in the mid-1980s helped cushion the increase in government expenditure. Since the 1990s, government expenditure has experienced an increasing trend, partly on account of increased capital spending, especially in the foreign finance component as well as the HIPC fund, and high interest payments on government loans. Furthermore, the substantial increase in salaries and other benefits to civil servants in the run-up to the presidential and parliamentary elections in 1992 and 1996 also accounted for the huge expenditure outlay during the 1990s.

Government revenue accelerated steadily during the review period owing to tax reforms, leading to a broadening of the tax base, and the introduction of value added tax (VAT). The sale of the Ashanti Goldfields company also increased government revenue in the 1990s, resulting in a narrowing of the budget deficit. However, despite the increase in government revenue, the budget deficit widened during the period, owing to increased expenditure in excess of revenue.

The *Guinean* economy experienced a persistent fiscal deficit during the period under review. The country was under military rule for over two decades. There was increased expenditure in excess of revenue, leading to a persistent fiscal deficit. Despite the adoption of a Structural Adjustment Programme (SAP), the country's fiscal policy remained relatively weak in the mid-1980s and 1990s, engendered by the excessive spending of the military regime. However, since 2005, the country has maintained a fiscal deficit as a ratio of GDP below the threshold of the WAMZ criterion of 4 per cent.

Since the early 1980s, *Nigeria*'s fiscal position has remained resilient despite a persistent budget deficit. The country recorded a decline in fiscal deficit during the review period. A fall in oil prices, coupled with a reduction in excise and import duties on essential items during the military regime, caused a decline in revenue mobilization during the 1980s and early 1990s. However, despite exceeding government revenue during the same period, government expenditure

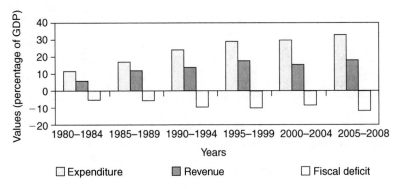

Figure 6.2 Trends in government expenditure, revenue and fiscal deficit (% of GDP) – Ghana (sources: IMF (2008a) and Ghana (2008)).

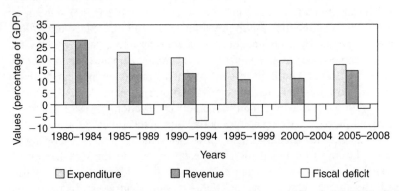

Figure 6.3 Trends in government expenditure, revenue and fiscal deficit (% of GDP) –
Guinea (sources: IMF (2008a) and Guinea (2008)).

remained low. The constraint on government expenditure was informed by the
weak revenue mobilization from oil exports and low donor support. The restora-
tion of civilian rule in the late 1990s witnessed an upsurge in government
expenditure in order to promote general economic development. Oil prices and,
hence, government revenue increased during the same period, leading to a narrowing of the budget deficit.

Sierra Leone's fiscal performance in the review period was weak, characterized by a persistent fiscal deficit, due to a large expenditure outlay. Amid a deteriorating economic situation in the mid-1980s, the country adopted a SAP that
was associated with removal of subsidies on basic items, and this subsequently
reduced government expenditure during the period 1986–1990. Increased
expenditure on arms during the country's civil war of the 1990s accounted for
high spending over the decade. During the post-war period (2001–2006), in
order to rebuild the economy and achieve macroeconomic stability, government
expenditure increased significantly. Amid the prolonged high expenditure

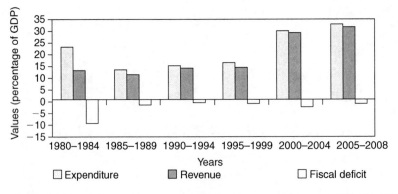

Figure 6.4 Trends in government expenditure, revenue and fiscal deficit (% of GDP) –
Nigeria (sources: IMF (2008a) and Nigeria (2008b)).

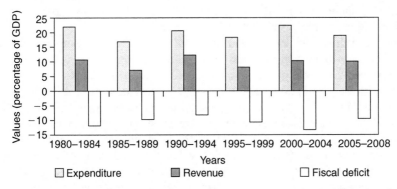

Figure 6.5 Trends in government expenditure, revenue and fiscal deficit (% of GDP) –
Sierra Leone (sources: IMF (2008a) and Sierra Leone (2008)).

throughout the review period, revenue mobilization remained relatively weak.
The drop in official diamond exports and reduction in the country's tax base
informed the decline in revenue between 1976 and 1985, resulting in high fiscal
deficit. Furthermore, the war period (1991–2000) was marred by unstable security and disruption of economic activities, which resulted in a decline in government revenue and a widening of the budget deficit.

Literature review

In the literature, public debt sustainability has been analysed in a number of
ways, albeit in a context appropriate for assessing fiscal sustainability in large
economies. Empirical studies involving sustainability of fiscal policy became an
important issue in economic policy mainly after the 1980s, stimulated by the
increasing US fiscal deficits as well as the debt crisis that affected Latin American countries. There is a diverse body of studies on fiscal sustainability. For
example, Hamilton and Flavin (1986) employed the PVBC methodology, involving tests of stationarity and cointegration on real primary surplus, seignorage and
real debt stock. Applying this methodology to the US data from 1960 to 1981,
these authors found that the US budget balance presented a long-run sustainable
path, despite its systematic budget deficits. Using similar methodology and data
requirements, Trehan and Walsh (1991) also explored a fiscal sustainability test
for the US economy using annual data spanning 1960 to 1984. Their results
showed that fiscal policy in the United States is sustainable.

Following Hamilton and Flavin (1986), many studies such as Tanner and Liu
(1994), Liu and Tanner (1995), Makrydakis *et al.* (1999), Issler and Lima
(2000), Green, Holmes and Kowalski (2001) and Bravo and Silvestre (2002)
have tested the sustainability of budget deficits using the intertemporal budget
constraint of the government. While Hamilton and Flavin (1986), Trehan and
Walsh (1988, 1991) and Tanner and Liu (1994) tested the sustainability of US

government deficits, Makrydakis *et al.* (1999) analysed it for Greece, Issler and Lima (2000) analysed it for Brazil, Green, Holmes and Kowalski (2001) for Poland and Bravo and Silvestre (2002) for 11 European countries.

Using US data for the period 1960–1984, Wilcox (1989) also employed the PVBC approach to investigate fiscal sustainability in the US economy. His results revealed that fiscal policy was not sustainable during the review period. Hakkio and Rush (1991) also employed the PVBC techniques to test for fiscal sustainability in the United States using quarterly data for the period 1950Q1 to 1988Q4. Data used included real government revenue and spending inclusive of real interest. Their empirical results showed that fiscal policy is not sustainable. Cuddington (1996) presented an approach based on the steady state debt–income ratio condition.[5] Intuitively, the sustainability condition implies that the growth rate of the economy (g) must be larger than the real interest rate (r). The contributions of Bohn (1995) and the IMF (2002, 2003) further developed the debt-stabilizing primary surplus approach with fiscal policy reactions functions that can be used to assess if the debt process is mean-reverting or not.

However, these methodologies have been found to be lacking in some important respects, especially in the context of low-income countries. In the first place, these approaches disregard the differences between external and domestic debt for the purposes of evaluating relative costs or overall public debt sustainability. This distinction is particularly important for Low Income Countries (LICs) where external debt has dominated in the past, but domestic debt might be important for the future. Second, the differences between the recorded stock of debt and its market value are ignored in the traditional approaches. While it might be a reasonable omission in the context of rich countries, it is flawed in HIPCs where domestic debt is often non-marketable and most external debt, by definition, is concessionary.

Given the peculiarities of the WAMZ economies, an eclectic approach that combines both methodologies will be adopted in the analysis of debt sustainability in the Zone. Thus, with the PVBC approach, public debt is decomposed into both domestic and external debt. To ensure that volatility in yearly data does not adversely affect the results, eight-year averages (2001–2008) of the variables are used in the accounting approach, while time series data are used in the PVBC approach. Unlike the principles applied in the HIPC Initiative, debt and debt service is not limited to public and publicly guaranteed external debt, but also includes domestic debt. The evaluation of debt sustainability in the WAMZ is undertaken through analysis of key ratios universally applied in measurement of the debt burden, including solvency and liquidity indicators.

Analysis of fiscal sustainability

In analysing fiscal sustainability within the WAMZ countries, two conceptual approaches are pursued: the accounting approach and the PVBC approach. The first section deals with the accounting approach to fiscal sustainability. In this section, four ratios were considered, which include: primary balance, total debt/ GDP, total debt/domestic revenue and total debt/export for each of the countries.

The second section deals with the PVBC approach, using econometric techniques of unit root and cointegration and also considering the sustainability of fiscal policy in the medium term.

Accounting approach

The accounting approach involves the use of a number of indicators of fiscal sustainability, along the lines suggested by Miller (1983), Buiter (1985, 1987), Blanchard (1990) and Buiter *et al.* (1993). These indicators include debt-to-GDP ratio, debt-to-export, total revenue to GDP, among others. According to the accounting approach, a primary deficit (or surplus) is defined as sustainable if it generates a constant (rather than ever-increasing) debt/GDP ratio, given a specified real GDP growth target and constant real interest rate. The indicators are discussed in turn.

Primary balance

The primary balance is defined as excluding interest payment from the fiscal balance to reflect current fiscal stance. The primary balance (or the non-interest component of the fiscal balance) measures how the current fiscal policy stance affects the net indebtedness of the public sector. That is, since interest payments are the result of past deficits, excluding them from the fiscal balance provides a clearer picture of current behaviour. The significance of this measure is that it is useful in determining the long-term sustainability of fiscal policy. If an economy is to sustain high long-run growth above the real rate of interest, the primary balance must at some point become positive to allow repayment of interest on current government debt.

In GDP terms, the government of *The Gambia*, at the initial period of the convergence process, recorded primary deficits of 3 and 2.4 per cent in 2001 and 2002, respectively (Table 6.1). The primary balance subsequently improved from 0.9 per cent in 2003, peaking at 4.2 per cent in 2007 and declined thereafter. The average primary surplus stood at 1.04 per cent during the 2001–2007 period. However, despite the improved performance in the last five years, the surpluses were not adequate to meet interest payments on outstanding debt obligations during these periods.

Despite recording positive fiscal balances between 2001 and 2005, *Ghana*'s primary balance decelerated from 3.4 per cent in 2001 to 2.8 per cent in 2005. This performance was reversed in 2006, with a primary deficit of 3.4 per cent. The deficit situation further worsened in 2007 and peaked at 9.4 per cent in 2008. On average, the country registered a primary deficit of 1.1 per cent during the review period.

An assessment of the fiscal operations in *Guinea* showed that the country recorded primary surpluses during most of the periods under review. With the exception of 2003 and 2004, the primary balance registered surpluses, ranging from 0.2 per cent in 2002 to 5 per cent in 2005. This indicated that substantial

Table 6.1 Debt sustainability indicators

Primary balance (% of GDP)

	2001	2002	2003	2004	2005	2006	2007	2008
The Gambia	−3.0	−2.4	0.9	0.6	3.2	3.8	4.2	0.7
Ghana	3.4	1.3	2.7	1.1	2.8	−3.4	−7.4	−9.4
Guinea	0.5	−5.6	1.7	−1.0	16.2	18.9	15.4	13.9
Nigeria	−3.2	−16.9	−17.7	−24.5	−27.8	−22.8	−15.3	−17.9
Sierra Leone	−6.7	−4.3	−3.8	−2.2	−2.6	−2.6	−2.7	−4.8
Total debt/GDP ratio								
The Gambia	151.2	181.4	163.1	142.0	160.9	153.5	117.3	108.2
Ghana	145.9	133.8	126.0	97.5	83	41.9	50.1	52.2
Guinea	109.8	106.7	96.4	94.2	114.8	114.3	92.3	82.8
Nigeria	60.7	58.9	56.4	53.9	33.4	12.2	12.6	11.7
Sierra Leone	195.1	129.2	128.2	130.9	125.6	109.4	38.3	43.3
Total debt service/domestic revenue								
The Gambia	26.9	31.7	41.3	26.4	24.8	22.3	18.8	20.5
Ghana	44.4	23.2	9.2	10.3	9.3	6.5	5.6	6.4
Guinea	25.1	19.5	18.8	17.4	11.7	8.0	7.8	5.8
Nigeria	15.1	8.2	9.1	6.0	20.8	14.5	2.2	0.8
Sierra Leone	84.0	40.8	37.3	33.9	18.1	10.3	5.0	4.1
Total debt service/export								
The Gambia	15.2	14.9	20.8	17.5	19.6	17.3	21.3	26.8
Ghana	16.4	10.1	4.9	7.2	7.7	4.5	4.6	5.8
Guinea	23.4	21.0	18.5	21.5	22.5	18.8	16.4	13.0
Nigeria	16.4	18.0	7.6	8.1	7.6	15.3	1.6	0.6
Sierra Leone	301.8	80.7	41.2	29.2	6.9	6.9	3.3	1.4

Source: Author's calculation from WAMI's database.

adjustments in revenue were not needed to meet the country's debt service requirement during the review period. Indeed, since 2005, the primary surpluses have exceeded the interest payments on outstanding debt obligations.

Nigeria's fiscal operations of the federal government resulted in a deficit of N103.8 billion in 2000, representing 1.5 per cent of GDP. The fiscal deficit maintained an upward trend which peaked at N301.6 billion or 2 per cent of GDP in 2003 before slowing down to N47.6 billion or 0.2 per cent of GDP in 2008. Wide swings in revenue performance, insufficient expenditure control, as well as steady deterioration in the structure of expenditure contributed to the deficit. The observed downward trend in the government deficit from 2003 to 2008 was attributed to a number of reform measures taken by the government which strengthened the budgetary process.

As a ratio of GDP, the fiscal operations of the government of *Sierra Leone* generally resulted in primary deficits, which improved from 6.7 per cent in 2001 to 2.2 per cent in 2004. The ratio subsequently deteriorated to reach 2.7 per cent in 2007. Sierra Leone needed to generate surpluses to meet the outstanding debt obligations throughout the review period.

Assessment of country performance during the period 2001–2008, as evident in Table 6.1, indicates that all the countries recorded primary deficits in at least one year. For most of the countries, even in the year where surpluses were recorded, the magnitudes were not adequate to offset the debt service payments. Thus, the countries would need to reform their current fiscal policies to achieve the levels of primary surpluses that are consistent with debt servicing requirements.

Total debt/GDP ratio

An indicator of a country's debt problems is the performance of the total debt-to-GDP ratio which is a key measure of a country's vulnerability. An increasing ratio is indicative of vulnerability.

As of end 2008, the stock of public external debt of *The Gambia* was estimated at US$667.9 million representing US$534.32 million in Net Present Value (NPV) terms and 22 per cent of GDP. The Gambia reached HIPC completion point under the Enhanced HIPC Initiative and qualified for debt relief under the Multilateral Debt Reduction Initiative (MDRI) in 2007. On reaching completion point and the subsequent flow of HIPC resources, the country's debt profile improved due to the combined effect of the decline in new borrowing, revealed preference for highly concessional loans as well as fiscal consolidation. NPV of debt-to-GDP ratio dropped from 24 per cent in 2007 to 22 per cent in 2008 (IMF, 2008b). This ratio is projected to remain fairly stable at an average of 25 per cent through 2013. Despite the improvement in the external debt situation, due mainly to the receipt of HIPC and MDRI debt relief, The Gambia's external debt will likely remain above the debt burden threshold. The country's debt sustainability outlook depends on export growth, fiscal outcome as well as new borrowing terms and conditions. The major risk to the country's debt sustainability include slowing of export growth, fiscal expansion and borrowing at commercial terms. A slow down in exports will have a negative effect on the country's debt sustainability as this will worsen the denominator of the indebtedness ratios.

The domestic debt-to-GDP ratio trended downwards in the past three years from 30.9 in 2006 to 25.5 per cent in 2008. In 2006, the present value of domestic debt-to-domestic revenue ratio was 198.8 per cent, above the sustainable reference threshold of 88–127 per cent. This was attributed to the domestic debt structure being concentrated in the short term and mainly in the 364-day tenor. The ratio trended downwards to 107.8 and 105.8 per cent in 2007 and 2008, respectively. Although the ratio remains above the sustainable threshold, the declining trend indicates improvement in the domestic debt situation. This was as a result of payments of domestic arrears and government bonds within five years coupled with the policy of no new issuance and strong projected revenue growth.

The total public debt-to-GDP ratio increased from 151.2 per cent in 2001 to 181.4 per cent in 2002. The ratio fluctuated between 163.1 per cent in 2003 and 124.5 per cent in 2008.

Ghana qualified for debt relief under the MDRI in 2006 that resulted in huge reduction of external debt from US$6,384 million (59.2 per cent of GDP) in 2005 to US$2,177 million (17.1 per cent of GDP) in 2006. However, since 2006, the country's external debt experienced an increasing trend and was estimated at US$3,982.6 million (24.9 per cent of GDP) in 2008, up from US$3,590.2 million (23.7 per cent of GDP) in the previous year. The upsurge in external debt was meant to finance higher public investment, especially the expansion of the country's electricity generation capacity and the development of the road network. Furthermore, the Debt Sustainability Analysis (DSA) showed that the country's external debt burden indicators remained below the established Country Policy and Institutional Assessment (CPIA)-dependent threshold during the review period, as the NPV stood at 20 per cent in 2008 and is expected to increase to 35 per cent by 2028 (IMF, 2006c). However, the result showed that Ghana's debt dynamic is subject to moderate risk of distress in the medium to long term as the total public debt is expected to increase from 50 per cent of GDP in 2007 to 81 per cent of GDP by 2028.

The major risk to debt sustainability in the medium to long term includes moderate GDP and export growth performance, high current account deficit and protracted fiscal adjustment due to high government expenditure in spite of projected strong tax revenue performance. Ghana's domestic debt has shown an increasing trend since 2005, increasing from 18.6 per cent of GDP in 2005 to 34.7 per cent of GDP in 2008. Furthermore, the present value of the domestic debt/domestic revenue ratio increased from 77.2 per cent in 2007 to 130.9 per cent in 2008. Debt owed to the banking system constitutes the largest share of domestic debt. Ghana's total debt/GDP ratio has experienced a declining trend since 2001. Available data showed that the total debt/GDP ratio, which stood at 145.9 per cent in 2001, declined to 83 per cent in 2005, attained its lowest value of 41.9 per cent in 2006, but gradually increased to 52.2 per cent in 2008.

Guinea reached enhanced HIPC decision point in 2000, and was expected to qualify for US$545 million (in NPV terms) in debt relief after attaining the completion point in 2009. Debt sustainability analysis conducted on Guinea in 2004 estimated the country's NPV of debt-to-exports ratio at 191.5 per cent (IMF, 2004; Guinea, 2004), well above the relevant policy-based indicative threshold suggesting that the country's export earnings were insufficient to service external debt. Guinea's stock of public external debt stood at US$3,102.11 million as at end 2008, representing US$2,635.83 million in NPV terms and 68.6 per cent of GDP. Guinea was in debt distress, and the country may be vulnerable into the medium term under the baseline scenario unless new borrowings are highly concessional, export growth strengthened and domestic revenue mobilization enhanced. However, the external debt service ratio is expected to fall gradually below the relevant threshold once HIPC debt relief is received in full at completion point, but this may not be enough to remove the risk of debt distress. Looking ahead, it is estimated that NPV of debt-to-exports ratio will fall below the 100 per cent threshold in 2015 under the baseline scenario.

As at end 2004, the government's domestic debt represented about 22 per cent of GDP and included advances from the central bank (15 per cent); treasury bills held by commercial banks (4 per cent) and accumulated arrears to the private sector (3 per cent). The present value of domestic debt-to-domestic revenue stood at 216 per cent as at end 2008 which remained above the sustainable threshold of 88–127 per cent, suggesting that domestic debt level was unsustainable. For domestic debt to decline within the sustainable threshold, the government should undertake fiscal reforms aimed at increasing domestic revenue mobilization as well as improving export growth. The ratio of total debt to GDP followed a mixed trend, declining from 109.8 per cent in 2001 to 96.4 per cent in 2003, before rising to 114.8 and 114.3 per cent in 2005 and 2006, respectively. In 2008, the ratio improved to 82.8 per cent.

At the end of December 2008, *Nigeria*'s stock of external debt stood at US$3,720.36 million, representing US$3,522.7 million in NPV terms. The stock of external debt was equivalent to 2 per cent of GDP in 2008, compared to 46 and 48.1 per cent of GDP in 2001 and 2002, respectively. The observed low external debt profile resulted from the implementation of a comprehensive economic reform programme which helped towards reducing the country's debt stock drastically. Specifically, in April 2006, the country paid the last instalment on the US$30 billion it owed to the Paris Club of creditors, which accounted for more than 85 per cent of its external debt. As part of the initial agreement, Nigeria paid US$6 billion in arrears, with the remaining US$24 billion restructured on Naples Terms – the Paris Club's concessionary terms for restructuring poor countries' external debt. This resulted in a substantial decline in the country's debt profile, coupled with prudent borrowing and debt management strategies.

The domestic debt-to-GDP ratio experienced a downward trend in the past seven years from 14.8 per cent in 2001 to 9.7 per cent in 2008. In 2000, present value of domestic debt-to-domestic revenue ratio stood at 41.6 per cent, below the sustainable reference threshold of 88–200 per cent. The ratio sustained a downward trend from 37 per cent in 2001 to 30.7 and 29 per cent in 2004 and 2008, respectively. The ratio of NPV of debt to GDP and revenue remain sustainable over the period. The ratio of NPV of debt to GDP stood at 2.5 per cent in 2008 (Nigeria, 2008a), which remained far below the threshold of 30 per cent, while the ratio of NPV of debt to revenue and grants is below 40 per cent during the same period against the threshold of 200 per cent.

In 2008, a National Debt Sustainability workshop was conducted in order to assess the sustainability of Nigeria's debt position in the medium to long term. The result of the analysis showed that Nigeria's debt, which includes both external and public debt, was sustainable throughout the projected period 2008–2028, on the assumption of sustainable macroeconomic reforms, prudent borrowing and fiscal responsibility. The external debt-to-GDP ratio was projected to remain low and fairly stable over the period 2008–2028 and was expected to grow at an annual average ratio of 2.5. Similarly, the external debt to export and external debt to revenue were also well within their respective threshold levels. The debt service-to-export ratio decreased over time from 1.6 per cent in 2007 to less than 1 per cent through the projected period. The debt service to revenue was also at a sustainable level, declining from of 1.6 per cent in 2008 to 0.1 per cent in 2028, which remained below their respective thresholds of 15 and 25 per cent.

In 2002, *Sierra Leone* was in line to benefit from a comprehensive debt reduction package under the Enhanced HIPC Initiative. Debt relief was estimated at nearly US$950 million or US$600 million in NPV terms, equivalent to 80 per cent of the country's debt. At end 2004, Sierra Leone's nominal external debt including arrears stood at US$1,720 million (161 per cent of GDP) (IMF, 2006a). Two-thirds of the debt was owed to multilateral creditors and the remainder to bilateral and commercial creditors. The domestic debt stock fell to 33 per cent of GDP in 2005 from 57 per cent of GDP in 2000. This was attributed to high GDP growth at the end of the country's civil war.

Domestic borrowing was costly, with interest rates on treasury bills ranging between 15 and 28 per cent from 2000 to 2005. Interest payment on domestic debt consumed a sizeable portion of government revenues: approximately 30 per cent in 2004. The debt stock was predominantly short term in nature and subject to significant roll-over risk. Sierra Leone reached HIPC completion point in 2006 and qualified for debt relief worth US$600 million in NPV terms. By end 2007 the full effect of the debt relief was evident, with the external debt trending downwards to US$536.7 million (US$442.5 million in NPV terms) or approximately 27.7 per cent of GDP. As at end December 2008, Sierra Leone's stock of external public debt had increased to US$620.2 million (US$325.4 million in NPV terms) or 31.5 per cent of GDP. Risk to Sierra Leone's debt sustainability stems from a shock to the export base as evidenced in 2008, with a decline in exports of diamonds and rutile, an increase in domestic debt and lower GDP growth.

Domestic debt-to-GDP ratio fell from 11.9 per cent in 2006 to 10.9 per cent in 2007 but increased to 11.9 per cent in 2008. In 2006, the present value of domestic debt to domestic revenue was 101.5 per cent, which lies within the threshold. The ratio further declined to 97.3 per cent and 55.1 per cent in 2007 and 2008, respectively. This result showed that domestic debt was sustainable. The improvement in domestic debt was attributed to improvements in domestic revenue generation.

Total debt service/domestic revenue

The ratio of total debt service to domestic revenue is an indication of how much of a country's domestic revenue will be used up in servicing its outstanding level of total debt. A declining ratio below 25 per cent shows that the country's revenue generation is efficient and can accommodate total debt service payments.

In *The Gambia*, the debt service-to-domestic revenue ratio stood at 20.5 per cent in 2008. Overall, debt service-to-domestic revenue ratio trended downward during the reference period. However, in the earlier years of the convergence process, the ratio rose sharply from 26.9 per cent in 2001 and peaked at 41.3 per cent in 2003. The ratio increased between 2001 and 2003, partly because of the high rates of interest as well as modest revenue performance arising from a narrow revenue base and relatively weak tax administration system during the period. Macroeconomic performance generally deteriorated between 2002 and 2003 occasioned by a short episode of drought, which resulted in high inflation and stunted growth. However, the situation was reversed in 2004, as the period recorded strong growth engendered by good rain and enhanced revenue mobilization. The ratio nearly halved in 2004, reaching 26.4 per cent from a high of 41.3 per cent in the previous year. Between 2005 and 2007 the ratio continued to decline, and stood at 20.5 per cent in 2008. Thus, despite prudent efforts in revenue generation, the high total debt service-to-revenue ratio was an indication that the country may have problems in meeting its obligations in future through the use of domestic revenue to service its debt.

Ghana's liquidity ratios displayed a declining trend during the review period. From an average of 44.4 per cent in 2001, total debt service as a percentage of domestic revenue declined to 9.2 per cent in 2003, increased to 10.3 per cent in 2004 and gradually declined to 5.6 per cent in 2007. Total debt as a percentage of domestic revenue stood at 6.7 per cent in 2008. During the review period, total debt service to domestic revenue remained below the threshold of 25 per cent with slippages observed in 2001. The decline in total debt to domestic revenue during the period can be explained by the country's efforts in generating domestic revenue through prudent fiscal management. The debt relief enjoyed by the country after the attainment of the HIPC completion point also accounted for the declining trend after 2006.

Debt service-to-domestic revenue ratio in *Guinea* declined from 25.1 per cent in 2001 to 5.8 per cent in 2008 and averaged 14.9 per cent during the period. The decline in the ratio was due to the robust domestic revenue mobilization effort as well as modest donor support. Projections indicate that the ratio would experience a declining trend given that the country reached the HIPC completion point in 2009 which would make it eligible for HIPC and MDRI resources. The trend in debt service-to-domestic revenue indicates that domestic revenue is adequate to service total debt.

Nigeria's external debt stock in 2000 stood at US$28.3 billion. The stock of external debt increased to US$35.9 billion in 2004 before falling sharply to US$3.7 billion in 2008. The decline in the level of external debt in 2008 was due to the settlement of Paris Club debt between 2005 and 2007 which accounted for about 85 per cent of the country's external debt. Total external debt service payments declined from US$3.1 billion in 2000 to US$1.8 billion in 2004. Debt service payments between 2000 and 2004 were low compared to 2005 and 2006. The debt service payments for 2007 and 2008 were considerably lower than the previous two years. Total debt service payments as a ratio of domestic revenue, which stood at 15.1 per cent in 2001, declined to 6 per cent in 2004. The ratio, however, rose to 20.8 per cent in 2005, reflecting the period of high payments of Paris Club debt. In 2008 the debt service-to-domestic revenue ratio fell significantly to 0.8 per cent, mainly because there were no debt service obligations to the Paris and London Clubs. The result indicates that Nigeria was able to generate adequate revenue to service its debt obligations.

In 2001, *Sierra Leone*'s debt service-to-domestic revenue ratio was 83.9 per cent. The low ratio was attributed to low domestic revenue mobilization following the end of the civil war. As normal economic activities resumed, domestic revenue mobilization improved which led to a declining trend of the ratio to 40.8 per cent in 2002; it further declined to 7.8 per cent in 2006. After reaching HIPC completion point in late 2006, the country benefited from debt relief worth approximately US$600 million in NPV terms. This resulted in a lower debt service-to-domestic revenue ratio of 5 per cent in 2007. The ratio further decreased to 4.1 per cent in 2008, because of the improved domestic revenue mobilization.

Total debt service/export

Total debt service-to-export ratio indicates how much of a country's export revenue will be used up in servicing its outstanding level of total debt. An increasing trend in the ratio is an indication that revenue from export is not sufficient to service total debt.

As of end 2008, the ratio of debt service to exports in *The Gambia* stood at 26.8 per cent. The growth pattern of the debt service to exports was uneven over the reference period but generally trended upward. Between 2000 and 2003, the ratio stood at 16.1 per cent, slightly rose to 18.5 per cent during 2004 and 2005, before edging up to 21.8 per cent between 2006 and 2008, an indication of an unsustainable debt level. The general upward trend was attributable to relatively low exports as well as re-exports. The decline in exports was partly due to the appreciation of the local currency, a fall in demand for exports arising from the global economic downturn as well as challenges in the marketing of groundnuts, the main export commodity of the country.

In *Ghana*, debt service as a percentage of total exports declined from 16.4 per cent in 2001 to 4.9 per cent in 2003 and 4.5 per cent in 2006, rising to 5.8 per cent in 2008. The trend in total debt-to-export ratio remained below the threshold of 15 per cent for the entire period, denoting sustainability of the ratio. Increased export earnings from both traditional and non-traditional exports engendered by increased demand greatly accounted for the declining trend in the ratio.

As at end 2008, *Guinea*'s debt service to exports stood at 13 per cent lower than the average of 19.2 per cent during 2000–2008. Between 2001 and 2003, the ratio moved downwards, rose between 2004 and 2005, before declining gradually to reach 13 per cent in 2008. The drop in the ratio during the period was attributed to decline in donor support as well as a drop in the value of exports owing to the cutbacks in foreign demand for some of Guinea's exports that resulted from the global economic downturn and financial crisis.

Nigeria's debt service-to-export ratio stood at 18 per cent in 2001 and declined to 7.6 per cent in 2004. The ratio rose significantly to 15.3 per cent in

2005, reflecting the huge payments of Paris Club debt during the period. The rate, however, fell to 0.6 per cent in 2008 from 1.6 per cent recorded in 2007.

Sierra Leone's debt service-to-export ratio showed a declining trend from an initial high ratio of 30.2 per cent in 2001, to 7.8 per cent in 2006, due to high export earnings. After attaining the HIPC completion point, the ratio further declined to 3.7 per cent in 2007, but increased to 4.3 per cent in 2008, as a result of a decline in export earnings arising from the global crisis and decline in domestic production of diamond and rutile, the two main exports of the country.

PVBC approach

The theoretical notion of fiscal sustainability based on the solvency condition states that the present discounted value of future primary budget balances should at least be equal to the value of the outstanding stock of debt. On this definition, the public sector cannot be a debtor, and the private sector cannot be a creditor, in present value terms. If there is debt at present, the primary balance should become positive at some date in the future in order for the PVBC to be respected. Furthermore, fiscal sustainability is said to exist when government policies satisfy the PVBC. Fiscal sustainability framework focuses on the capacity of the government to generate an adequate level of primary budget surplus in order to stabilize its debt ratio.

The PVBC approach for assessing fiscal sustainability involves econometric testing of the PVBC or of the Non-Ponzi Game (NPG)[6] condition for a set of time series data on government expenditure, revenue, deficits and/or debt. This involves tests of stationarity and cointegration analysis.[7] The starting point for this PVBC approach is the balance sheet of the consolidated public sector or the government budget constraint.[8]

$$B_t - B_{t-1} = -(T_t - G_t) + rB_{t-1} \qquad (1)$$

Where B_t is the stock of public debt at period t, T_t is the public sector revenue, G_t is the primary public expenditure, i.e. public expenditure excluding interest payments on public debt, and r is the return on government debt in period t. This budget constraint ignores public revenues arising from the creation of money (seigniorage revenue). From equation (1), if the government runs a primary surplus equal to zero, the stock of debt will grow at a rate equal to the interest rate. However, if the government runs a primary deficit, the stock of debt will grow at a rate exceeding the interest rate. Also, if the government runs a primary surplus, the stock of debt will grow more slowly than the interest rate. If the surplus more than offsets interest payments on existing debt, then the debt will actually shrink over time.

The PVBC approach to evaluating fiscal sustainability involves econometric testing of the stationarity (unit root) and cointegration properties of primary balance and public debt (Hamilton and Flavin, 1986), while others include both government revenue and expenditure (Hakkio and Rush, 1991). Test for fiscal sustainability involves two steps (see Hamilton and Flavin, 1986); first, we test whether S_t and B_t are I(1).[9] If the null hypothesis is confirmed, we proceed to the second step: testing for cointegration by means of the following regression model:

$$S_t' = \alpha_o + \alpha_1 B_t + \upsilon_t \tag{2}$$

Where S_t', is primary balance excluding grant, B_t is total debt (includes both external and domestic debt), μ_t is the error term, which is identically and independently distributed with mean zero and constant variance. The condition for sustainability is that both variables must be integrated of order one, I(1), and should be cointegrated. If there is no cointegration, the PVBC does not hold and the fiscal balance is not sustainable.

The intuition behind this is that although government debt and fiscal balance may grow over time, a stable equilibrium (cointegrating) relationship should exist between them. If S_t', for example, is non-stationary (I(1)) while B_t is stationary (I(0)), then there is no long-term or equilibrium relation between them. This implies that government is violating its intertemporal budget constraint because S_t' tends to grow while B_t does not.

Empirical result

Unit root tests

In order to test for fiscal sustainability, we pursue the standard procedure to find out if two time series are cointegrated. First, we check for unit roots using the Augmented Dickey–Fuller (ADF) and Phillips–Perron (PP) tests and second, we verify cointegration with the Johanssen maximum likelihood test.

The data set comprises annual data on fiscal deficit (surplus), domestic debt, external debt and total debt, over the period 1980–2008. All variables are expressed as a ratio of GDP. The results of the unit root tests for the WAMZ countries are presented in Table 6.2.

The results showed that the ADF and PP statistics for all variables in levels for all the countries did not exceed their critical values. However, when all the variables were differenced once and subjected to ADF and PP tests, the test statistics exceeded their critical values at least at the conventional level of significance. These results suggested that all the variables for all the countries were integrated of order one, I(1), that is they were non-stationary in levels but became stationary after taking their first difference.

Cointegration tests

Having established that all the variables in all the countries were integrated of order one, i.e. I(1), tests of cointegration among the variables was then carried out using the Johansson maximum likelihood technique. In the Johanssen

Table 6.2 Results of unit root tests

Country	Variable	ADF test with drift and trend		PP test with drift and trend		Order of Integration
		Level	1st diff.	Level	1st diff.	
The Gambia	Fiscal surplus/deficit	−1.013	−4.626	−2.264	−4.437	I(1)
	Total debt	−1.760	−5.414	−2.180	−7.274	I(1)
	Domestic debt	−2.204	−5.761	−1.964	−4.420	I(1)
	External debt	−1.937	−4.414	−2.006	−7.274	I(1)
Ghana	Fiscal surplus/deficit	−1.028	−4.427	−0.759	−3.989	I(1)
	Total debt	−1.481	−4.427	−1.400	−4.473	I(1)
	Domestic debt	−1.836	−4.745	−1.751	−4.832	I(1)
	External debt	−0.986	−3.674	−1.051	−3.671	I(1)
Guinea	Fiscal surplus/deficit	−1.608	−7.743	−2.117	−5.718	I(1)
	Total debt	−1.958	−5.264	−0.341	−5.2384	I(1)
	Domestic debt	−1.478	−7.744	−2.194	−5.718	I(1)
	External debt	−2.095	−4.195	−1.264	−5.2384	I(1)
Nigeria	Fiscal surplus/deficit	−2.341	−5.947	−3.166	−8.623	I(1)
	Total debt	−1.901	−3.449	−1.981	−3.284	I(1)
	Domestic debt	−1.896	−3.480	−1.991	−3.330	I(1)
	External debt	−1.681	−5.364	−0.697	−5.379	I(1)
Sierra Leone	Fiscal surplus/deficit	−3.087	−7.041	−3.038	−7.616	I(1)
	Total debt	−0.469	−4.279	−0.698	−4.280	I(1)
	Domestic debt	−2.388	−3.292	−1.284	−3.292	I(1)
	External debt	−0.949	−6.239	−0.761	−6.239	I(1)

Notes
Critical values: 1%=−4.324 and 5%=−3.587.

maximum likelihood procedure, tests for the optimal lag lengths of the related Vector Auto-regression (VAR) were first conducted. This is because the method is preceded by estimating a VAR model which must have the appropriate lag length. The likelihood ratio test, Akaike Information Criterion, Schwartz Information Criterion, Hannan Quin test and Final Prediction Error test were used in the lag length selections. The lag length supported by most of the five criteria was chosen as the appropriate lag length. In order to save the degrees of freedom, the highest lag length in the testing-down procedure of the lag length tests was taken to be one for each of the countries. The Johanssen procedure tests the null hypothesis of no cointegration, and rejection of the null hypothesis implies the data series are cointegrated. The results of the Johanssen tests are shown in Appendix 2.

Both the Trace Statistics and maximum Eigen values rejected the null hypothesis of no cointegration between fiscal deficit (surplus) and total debt in the case of *The Gambia*. This result indicates that fiscal policy is sustainable during the review period. Furthermore, the result showed the existence of cointegration between fiscal deficit (surplus) and domestic debt, indicating sustainability of domestic debt. Decline in new borrowing, decline in inflationary pressures and lower interest rates on domestic debt were the main driving force for the sustainability of domestic debt during the review period. However, the null hypothesis of no cointegration between fiscal deficit (surplus) and external debt cannot be rejected. The implication of such a result is that external debt was found to be unsustainable, arising mainly from depreciation of domestic currency and increased interest rate on external debt.

In *Ghana*, the result showed the existence of cointegration between fiscal deficit (surplus) and total debt. This result indicates the existence of fiscal sustainability during the review period. Furthermore, the result revealed that external debt was sustainable during the reference period as indicated by the existence of cointegration between fiscal deficit (surplus) and external debt. The sustainability of external debt was partly attributed to the huge debt relief accorded the country after attaining the HIPC completion point. In addition, export earnings increased due to a growth in the volume and value of traditional exports during the review period. However, the result further revealed that domestic debt was unsustainable, as evidenced by the existence of no cointegration between domestic debt and fiscal deficit (surplus). High inflationary spiral and high interest rate resulted in an increased interest payment on government domestic debt. The country was plagued by huge domestic borrowing by government for fiscal deficit financing, which impacted negatively on domestic debt sustainability. The huge domestic debt servicing crowded out private sector investment and thereby resulted in decreased output growth.

The result for *Guinea* revealed that the null hypothesis of no cointegration between fiscal deficit (surplus) and total debt was rejected, indicating that external debt was sustainable during the review period. Furthermore, the results establish the existence of cointegration between fiscal deficit (surplus) and external debt. However, the results further revealed the non-existence of cointegration between fiscal deficit (surplus) and domestic debt, indicating that domestic debt was unsustainable, arising mainly from high inflation, increased interest payments on domestic debt and accumulation of new debts.

The Johansson results in the case of *Nigeria* showed the existence of cointegration between fiscal deficit (surplus) and total debt indicating fiscal sustainability. Furthermore, the cointegration results showed sustainability between fiscal deficit (surplus) and external debt as well as between fiscal deficit (surplus) and domestic debt. Fiscal sustainability during the review period was partly due to prudent fiscal policy that resulted in a decline in government budget deficit arising from a decline in government borrowing. Furthermore, earnings from oil exports increased significantly as a result of higher world oil prices over the years. In addition, the relative stability of the exchange rate amid low inflation also reduced government debt service payment. The sustainability of the domestic debt implies increased private sector credit and hence increased investment and output growth.

In *Sierra Leone*, both the Trace and Maximum Eigen statistics results revealed the existence of no cointegration between fiscal surplus/deficit and total debt. Also, no cointegration existed between fiscal surplus/deficit and domestic debt, as well as between fiscal surplus/deficit and external debt. Intuitively, the results indicate that Sierra Leone's fiscal performance was unsustainable during the review period. Evidently, the country experienced an increasing trend in domestic debt due to high interest payment informed by high interest rate and high inflation rate. Furthermore, despite debt relief, the external debt position of the country remained poor during the review period, partly informed by the persistent exchange rate depreciation which increased the external value of the stock of external debt, as well as increased disbursement from multilateral creditors. In addition, the civil war in the 1990s also caused a decline in export earnings, moderation in revenue mobilization due to disruption in economic activities, increased expenditure outlay on defence and basic utilities, which resulted in a huge fiscal deficit that was financed through domestic and external borrowing.

Conclusions

The evolution of public debt in WAMZ countries requires some form of monitoring. The present chapter proposes a simple strategy that enables one to integrate the use of indicators and econometrics tests of fiscal sustainability. Indicators are *forward looking*, in the sense that they are based on published forecasts, thereby reacting to a set of current and expected future conditions in fiscal policy. Tests, on the other hand, are *backward looking*, in the sense that they are based on a sample of past data to see if the stock of real government debt follows a stationary process. Our integrated approach allows testing the consistency of fiscal plans over the relevant sample period.

In synthesis, the findings of sustainability tests, under both the accounting and the PVBC approaches, indicate that fiscal policy in The Gambia was weakly sustainable. It was evident from the results that the indicators of fiscal sustainability under the accounting approach revealed a weak performance of The Gambia's fiscal policy, and this result was re-echoed by the PVBC. In the case of Ghana, both the accounting and PVBC approaches indicate that the country's fiscal policy was sustainable. Specifically, with the PVBC, the result showed that total debt and external debt were sustainable arising from the existence of cointegration between these two variables respectively and primary surplus. However, domestic debt was found to be unsustainable due to the lack of cointegration between domestic debt and primary balance. Finally, the debt indicators under the accounting approach showed that Ghana's fiscal policy is sustainable.

Both the accounting approach and PVBC revealed that Guinea's fiscal policy was sustainable during the review period. However, the country's domestic debt was found to be unsustainable arising from high interest payments, while both external and total debts were found to be sustainable. Nigeria also posed a similar picture in which both the accounting and PVBC approaches confirmed the sustainability of fiscal policy during the reference period. The PVBC result showed that total debt, external debt and domestic debt were sustainable. In addition, the debt indicators also revealed similar results. For Sierra Leone, it was evident from both the accounting and PVBC approaches that the country's fiscal policy was unsustainable during the review period.

The issue of sustainability is critical for debt relief initiatives, since one of its targets is to avoid a new build-up of unsustainable public debts. Thus, the policy implication arising from this study is that fiscal policy should not be contemplated in a vacuum, but rather it must be seen within the wider context of overall macroeconomic sustainability. In this regard, policy-makers in the WAMZ countries must coordinate fiscal policy with other policy areas, so as to maintain an environment of low inflation, exchange rate stability and external account equilibrium, as well as fiscal sustainability. Furthermore, in the case of Ghana, Guinea and Nigeria, policy-makers need to ensure that future policy decisions continue in the tradition of prudent fiscal management. However, for The Gambia and Sierra Leone, policy-makers must reschedule their debt profile in order to access highly concessional loans, reduction in new borrowing as well as fiscal consolidation. In addition, these countries must step up robust fiscal policies aimed at increasing revenue generation and tailoring expenditure towards growth enhancing and poverty reduction activities.

Appendix 1

The PVBC model

The initial analysis of the PVBC is the government budget constraint given in the following equation

$$G_t - R_t + r_t B_{t-1} = B_t - B_{t-1} \qquad (1)$$

Where B_t is the stock of public debt at period t, R_t is the public sector revenue, G_t is the primary public expenditure, i.e. public expenditure excluding interest payments on public debt, and r is the return on government debt in period t. This budget constraint also ignores, to ease the analysis, public revenues arising from the creation of money. From equation (1), if the government runs a primary surplus equal to zero, the stock of debt will grow at a rate equal to interest rate. However, if the government runs a primary deficit, the stock of debt will grow at a rate exceeding the interest rate. Also, if the government runs a primary surplus, the stock of debt will grow more slowly than the interest rate. If the surplus more than offsets interest payments on existing debt, then the debt will actually shrink over time.

$$\text{Let } S_t = R_t - G_t \tag{2}$$

Substitute equation (2) into equation (1) and rearrange to get equation (3):

$$B_{t-1} = B_t (1+r)^{-1} + S_t (1+r)^{-1} \tag{3}$$

Substituting recursively forward for N periods gives the intertemporal budget constraint in equation (4):

$$B_t = (1+r)^{-N(-1)} B_N + \sum_{i=1}^{N} (1+r)^{-i} S_{t+i} \tag{4}$$

By letting $N \to \infty$, the limiting value of equation (4) can be expressed as follows.

$$B_t = Lim_{N \to \infty} \left[(1+r)^{-N(-1)} B_N \right] + \sum_{i=1}^{N} \left[(1+r)^{-1} S_{t+i} \right] \tag{5}$$

Equation (5) states that the current debt stock is equal to the present value of the debt stock in the limit plus the present value of its future primary surplus. A sustainable fiscal policy should ensure that the NPG condition holds, i.e. the present value of the stock of public debt goes to zero in the limit. It is also worth noting that the hypothesis of fiscal policy sustainability is related to the condition that the trajectory of the main macroeconomic variables is not affected by the choice between the issuance of public debt and the increase in taxation. Under such conditions, it would therefore be irrelevant how the deficits are financed, which also implies the assumption of the Ricardian Equivalence hypothesis.[10]

Thus,

$$Lim_{N \to \infty} \left[(1+r)^{-N(-1)} B_N \right] = 0 \tag{6}$$

Equation (6) represents the NPG condition, and the implication of this equation is that in the long run, debt cannot grow at a rate equal to or higher than the interest rate. Assuming that the NPG is satisfied, then substituting equation (6) into (5) gives the PVBC equation as follows:

$$B_t = \sum_{i=1}^{N}\left[(1+r)^{-1}S_i\right] \tag{7}$$

Equation (7), which represents the PVBC, showed that government debt at any point in time must equal the present value of its future primary surplus. The implication is that public sector debt cannot be continuously rolled over, that is, repayment of the principal must take place at some point and, while the PVBC does not rule out large fiscal deficits or debt ratios, government is required to run some primary surplus in the future by increasing revenue through taxes or grants, reduction in expenditure, monetization of the debt or shifting between debt sources to take advantage of lower interest rates.

The PVBC approach to evaluating fiscal sustainability involves econometric techniques in stationarity and cointegration analysis. The starting point for these tests is to take the first difference of equation (5) to get an empirical testable representation of the intertemporal government budget constraint.

$$\Delta B_t = Lim_{N \to \infty}\left[(1+r)^{-N(-1)}\Delta B_{N+1}\right] + \sum_{i=1}^{N}\left[(1+r)^{-1}\left(\Delta R_{t+i+1} - \Delta G_{t+i+1}\right)\right] \tag{8}$$

Assuming the real interest rate is stationary, with mean, r, and defining $E_t = G_t + (r_t - r)B_{t-1}$ and an additional definition, $GG_t = G_t + r_t B_{t-1}$, and assuming the NPG in equation (6) is satisfied, the intertemporal budget constraint may also be written as:

$$GG_t - R_t = \sum_{i=1}^{N}\left[(1+r)^{-1}\left(\Delta R_{t+i+1} - \Delta E_{t+i+1}\right)\right] \tag{9}$$

Equation (9) forms the basis for testing the sustainability hypothesis where GG_t and R_t must be cointegrated variables of order one. Assuming that R_t and E_t are non-stationary variables, and that the first differences are stationary variables, this implies that the series R_t and E_t in levels are I(1). Then, for equation (9) to hold, its left-hand side will also have to be stationary. If it is possible to conclude that GG_t and R_t are integrated of order 1, these two variables should be cointegrated with cointegration vector (1, −1) for the left-hand side of equation (9) to be stationary. The conditions for sustainability is that both variables must be integrated of order one, I(1), and should be cointegrated.

Appendix 2

Johansson cointegration test results

Panel (i): Fiscal deficit (surplus) and total debt (Ghana)

Date: 29/03/09 Time: 15:35				
Sample (adjusted): 1993 2008				
Included observations: 16 after adjustments				
Trend assumption: Linear deterministic trend				
Series: FD TD				
Lags interval (in first differences): 1 to 2				
Unrestricted Cointegration Rank Test (Trace)				
Hypothesized		Trace	0.05	
No. of CE(s)	Eigenvalue	Statistic	Critical Value	Prob.**
None *	0.655022	20.04395	15.49471	0.0096
At most 1	0.171777	3.015573	3.841466	0.0825

Notes
Trace test indicates 1 cointegrating eqn(s) at the 0.05 level.
* Denotes rejection of the hypothesis at the 0.05 level.

Panel (ii): Fiscal deficit (surplus) and external debt

Date: 29/03/09 Time: 15:38				
Sample (adjusted): 1993 2008				
Included observations: 16 after adjustments				
Trend assumption: Linear deterministic trend				
Series: FD ED				
Lags interval (in first differences): 1 to 2				
Unrestricted Cointegration Rank Test (Trace)				
Hypothesized		Trace	0.05	
No. of CE(s)	Eigen value	Statistic	Critical value	Prob.**
None *	0.679119	22.72281	15.49471	0.0034
At most 1 *	0.246849	4.535831	3.841466	0.0332

Notes
Trace test indicates 2 cointegrating eqn(s) at the 0.05 level.
* Denotes rejection of the hypothesis at the 0.05 level.

Panel (iii): Fiscal deficit (surplus) and domestic debt

Date: 29/03/09 Time: 15:40				
Sample (adjusted): 1993 2008				
Included observations: 16 after adjustments				
Trend assumption: Linear deterministic trend				
Series: FD DD				
Lags interval (in first differences): 1 to 2				
Unrestricted Cointegration Rank Test (Trace)				
Hypothesized		Trace	0.05	
No. of CE(s)	Eigen value	Statistic	Critical value	Prob.**
None	0.504311	13.88984	15.49471	0.0860
At most 1	0.153215	2.660939	3.841466	0.1028

Notes
Trace test indicates no cointegration at the 0.05 level.
* Denotes rejection of the hypothesis at the 0.05 level.

Panel (iv): Fiscal surplus/deficit and total debt (Nigeria)

Date: 11/03/09 Time: 15:12				
Sample (adjusted): 1983 2005				
Included observations: 23 after adjustments				
Trend assumption: Linear deterministic trend				
Series: FS TD				
Lags interval (in first differences): 1 to 2				
Unrestricted Cointegration Rank Test (Trace)				
Hypothesized		Trace	0.05	
No. of CE(s)	Eigen value	Statistic	Critical value	Prob.**
None *	0.591852	21.56218	15.49471	0.0054
At most 1	0.040517	0.951303	3.841466	0.3294

Notes
Trace test indicates 1 cointegrating eqn(s) at the 0.05 level.
* Denotes rejection of the hypothesis at the 0.05 level.

Panel (v): Fiscal surplus/deficit and external debt

Date: 11/03/09 Time: 15:19				
Sample (adjusted): 1983 2005				
Included observations: 23 after adjustments				
Trend assumption: Linear deterministic trend				
Series: FS ED				
Lags interval (in first differences): 1 to 2				
Unrestricted Cointegration Rank Test (Trace)				
Hypothesized		Trace	0.05	
No. of CE(s)	Eigen value	Statistic	Critical value	Prob.**
None *	0.581803	20.87253	15.49471	0.007
At most 1	0.035069	0.821063	3.841466	0.3649

Notes
Trace test indicates 1 cointegrating eqn(s) at the 0.05 level.
* Denotes rejection of the hypothesis at the 0.05 level.

Panel (vi): Fiscal surplus/deficit and domestic debt

Date: 31/03/09 Time: 15:49				
Sample (adjusted): 1982 2005				
Included observations: 24 after adjustments				
Trend assumption: Linear deterministic trend				
Series: FS1 RESID				
Lags interval (in first differences): 1 to 1				
Unrestricted Cointegration Rank Test (Trace)				
Hypothesized		Trace	0.05	
No. of CE(s)	Eigen value	Statistic	Critical value	Prob.**
None *	0.465808	16.34175	15.49471	0.0372
At most 1	0.052478	1.293734	3.841466	0.2554

Notes
Trace test indicates 1 cointegrating eqn(s) at the 0.05 level.
* Denotes rejection of the hypothesis at the 0.05 level.

Notes

1 Fiscal deficit excluding grants.
2 Revenue from the export of groundnuts fell due to a combination of low world prices, inconsistent sector.
3 See The Gambia's "Diagnostic Trade Integration Study", Gambia (2007).
4 The Gambia's presentation to the Third United Nation Conference on the Least Developed Countries, May 2001.
5 $Ps = \dfrac{r_t - g_t}{1 + g_t} b$, where Ps is primary surplus (deficit) to GDP ratio, b is the debt to GDP ratio, r_t is real interest rate and g_t is growth rate in GDP, while t is time period. From the equation, Ps is the level of primary surplus that would be required each year to keep the debt/GDP ratio constant at its current level b.
6 Non-Ponzi Game is the impossibility of government issuing new debt to pay interest on the outstanding debt. The NPG condition is that the present value of the stock of public debt goes to zero in the limit.
7 A stationary time series is one whose statistical properties such as mean, variance, autocorrelation, etc. are all constant over time. If two or more series are themselves non-stationary, but a linear combination of them is stationary, then the series are said to be cointegrated.
8 See Appendix 1 for detailed analysis of the PVBC framework.
9 A variable is said to be I(1) when it is non-stationary, but became stationary after differencing the variable once.
10 Afonso (2005) provides evidence of overall Ricardian behaviour on the part of EU15 governments.

References

Blanchard, O.J. (1990). "Suggestions for a New Set of Fiscal Indicators", *OECD Economics Department Working Paper*, no. 79.
Bohn, H. (1995). "The Sustainability of Budget Deficits in a Stochastic Economy", *Journal of Money, Credit and Banking*, 27(1), 257–71.
Bravo, A. and Silvestre, A. (2002). "Intertemporal Sustainability of Fiscal Policies: Some Tests for European Countries", *European Journal of Political Economy*, 18(3), 517–28.
Buiter, W.H. (1985). "A Guide to Public Sector Debt and Deficits", *Economic Policy*, 1(1), 4–79.
Buiter, W.H., Corsetti, G. and Rubini, N. (1993). "Excessive Deficits: Sense and Nonsense in the Treaty of Maastricht", *Economic Policy*, 8, 57–100.
Cuddington, J. (1997). "Analyzing the Sustainability of Fiscal Deficits in Developing Countries", *World Bank Working Paper*, no. 1784.
Gambia (2007). "Diagnostic Trade Integration Study for the Integrated Framework for Trade-related Technical Assistance to Least Developed Countries", July.
Gambia (2008). Ministry of Finance Fiscal Report.
Ghana (2008). Ministry of Finance Fiscal Operation Report.
Government of The Gambia (2001). "Country Presentation on the Third United Nations Conference on the Least Developed Countries", Brussels, 14–20 May, A/Conf. 191/ CP/35.
Green, C.J., Mark, J.H. and Tadeusz, K. (2001). "Poland: A Successful Transition to Budget Sustainability?", *Emerging Markets Review*, 2, 160–82.

Guinea (2008). Ministry of Finance Fiscal Data Set.

Gunter, B. (2003). "Achieving Long Term Debt Sustainability in All Heavily Indebted Poor Countries (HIPC)", discussion paper, XVI Technical Group Meeting, Trinidad and Tobago.

Hakkio, C.S. and Rush, M. (1991). "Is the Budget Deficit 'Too Large'?" *Economic Inquiry*, 29, 429–45.

Hamilton, J.D. and Flavin, M.A. (1986). "On the Limitations of Government Borrowing: A Framework for Empirical Testing", *American Economic Review*, 76(2), 353–73.

IMF (2002). "Assessing Sustainability", policy paper prepared by the Policy Review and Development Department, May, Washington, DC.

IMF (2003). "Public Debt In Emerging Markets: Is it Too High?", *World Economic Outlook 2003*, III, 49–88.

IMF (2006a). "Sierra Leone: Joint Bank–Fund Debt Sustainability Analysis", May.

IMF (2006b). "Gambia: Joint Bank–Fund Debt Sustainability Analysis", December.

IMF (2006c). "Ghana: Joint Bank–Fund Debt Sustainability Analysis", December.

IMF (2008a). *International Financial Statistics Year Book*, Washington, DC: IMF.

IMF (2008b). "Update on Joint IMF/IDA Debt Sustainability Analysis in the Gambia", August 20.

Issler, J.V. and Lima, L.R. (1997). "Public Debt Sustainability and Endogenous Seignorage in Brazil: Time-Series Evidence from 1947–92", *Ensaios Econômicos da EPGE*, 306.

Makrydakis, S., Tzavalis, E. and Balfoussias, A. (1999). "Policy Regime Changes and Longrun Sustainability of Fiscal Policy: An Application to Greece", *Economic Modelling*, 16(1), 71–86.

Miller, M. (1983). "Inflation Adjusting the Public Sector Financial Deficit", in J. Kay (ed.), *The 1982 Budget*, Basil Blackwell, London.

Nigeria (2008a). "Report of the Annual National Debt Sustainability Analysis (DSA)", Debt Management Office, Nigeria.

Nigeria (2008b). Ministry of Finance and Economic Planning Report.

Sierra Leone (2008). Ministry of Finance and Economic Development Fiscal Report.

Tanner, E. and Liu, P. (1994). "Is the Budget Deficit Too Large? Some Further Evidence", *Economic Inquiry*, 32, 511–18.

Trehan, B. and Walsh, C. (1991). "Testing Intertemporal Budget Constraints: Theory and Applications to U.S. Federal Budget and Current Account Deficits", *Journal of Money, Credit and Banking*, 23, 210–23.

WAMI (2008). *Convergence Report*. Online: www.wami-imao.org.

Wilcox, D.W. (1989). "The Sustainability of Government Deficits: Implications of the Present-Value Borrowing Constraints", *Journal of Money, Credit and Banking*, 21(3), 291–306.

Part II

Market integration in the WAMZ

7 Trade integration and a common market

Temitope W. Oshikoya, Lanto Harding and Cyprian K. Eboh

Introduction

As discussed in Chapter 3, the theory of the Optimum Currency Area posits that countries that trade substantially with each other would benefit from a common currency, which would minimize transaction costs due to exchange rate fluctuations. This chapter examines progress made towards a common market by the member countries of the WAMZ. It assesses the extent of trade integration of the member countries in the creation of a WAMZ common market and the institutional arrangements. In addition, labour mobility, infrastructure development and provision of logistics to support trade facilitation are also discussed.

In recognition of the importance of trade integration as an important element for the success of a monetary union, the Banjul Action Plan (BAP) expanded the WAMZ programme to include issues relating to the actualization of a single economic space through a free trade area within a common market. The common external tariff regime for the customs union in WAMZ/ECOWAS was adopted in June 2009.

A common market is a form of trade integration between a number of countries in which members eliminate all trade barriers between themselves on goods and services and establish a uniform set of barriers against trade with the rest of the world, in particular a common external tariff. A common market provides for the free movement of labour and capital across national boundaries with the aim of securing the benefits of specialization, thereby improving member states' real living standards. The short- and medium-term impact of the formation of a common market is mainly felt through an increase in trade between member countries. Trade creation is typically associated with a reallocation of resources within the market, favouring least-cost supply locations and a reduction in prices, resulting in the elimination of tariffs and lower production costs. In addition, a common market can be expected to promote longer-term (dynamic) changes conducive to economic efficiency through a combination of the following benefits:

- competition: the removal of tariffs and import duties can be expected to widen the area of effective competition; high-cost producers are eliminated, while efficient and progressive suppliers are able to exploit new market opportunities;

- economies of scale: a larger home market enables firms to take advantage of economies of large-scale production and distribution, thereby lowering supply costs and enhancing comparative advantage;
- technological progressiveness: a common market widens market opportunities. Exposure to greater competition can be expected to encourage firms to invest and innovate new techniques and products;
- investment and economic growth: a virtuous circle of rising income per head, growing trade, increased productive efficiency and investment may be expected to combine to produce higher growth rates and real standards of living.

In general terms, the WAMZ common market will be expected to remove the barriers to intra-WAMZ and ECOWAS trade flows as the Zone is exposed to greater regional competition and as there is closer ECOWAS-wide convergence towards a common regional trade policy than hitherto.

Regional trade among member countries of the WAMZ

The process of trade liberalization that has been promoted across ECOWAS, in particular through the ECOWAS Trade Liberalization Scheme (ETLS) since 1990, has not, in general, contributed significantly to trade diversification for the countries of the WAMZ. There has been low intra-WAMZ trade, except between Ghana and Nigeria, which resulted in significant trade biases towards non-members of the WAMZ in ECOWAS and other regions. Intra-ECOWAS trade patterns indicate that WAMZ member countries' exports to ECOWAS have been comparable to those of the WAEMU.

In 2007, the WAMZ contributed 48.7 per cent to intra-ECOWAS exports, while the share of WAEMU was 51.3 per cent (Figure 7.1). The total value of the WAMZ's export to ECOWAS was US$2.95 billion, while total intra-ECOWAS export trade was US$6.05 billion in 2007, compared to US$7.05 billion in 2006. Intra-WAMZ export trade in 2007 was US$953.8 million, constituting 32 per cent of total exports to the rest of ECOWAS, compared to 38 per cent in 2006 (Figure 7.2). Intra-WAMZ exports were much lower, being primarily affected by supply capacity, distance and the weak transportation network.

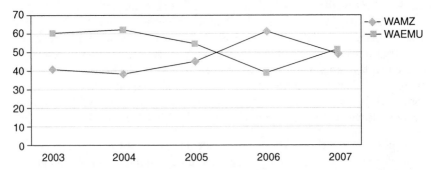

Figure 7.1 Percentage contributions of WAMZ and WAEMU to total exports in ECOWAS (sources: WAMI (2008) and ECOWAS Commission (2008)).

In 2007, The Gambia's merchandise exports to ECOWAS countries amounted to US$3.29 million, of which 3.52 per cent went to the WAMZ compared to 3.12 per cent in 2006. Ghana's exports to ECOWAS in 2007 totalled US$610.62 million, of which 9.61 per cent went to the WAMZ, while Guinea's exports to ECOWAS were US$11.98 million, of which 24.41 per cent were made to the WAMZ against 23.85 per cent in 2006. Nigeria's merchandise exports to ECOWAS were US$2.32 billion in 2007, of which 38.4 per cent went to the WAMZ, compared with 42.07 per cent in 2006. Sierra Leone's merchandise exports to ECOWAS in 2007 were US$2.73 million, of which 49.63 per cent went to the WAMZ in relation to 54.51 per cent in 2006.

WAMZ member countries' regional trade openness and trade integration

Based on the ratio of intra-regional trade to GDP,[1] The Gambia's average trade openness in the WAMZ was 0.39 per cent, Ghana's was 3.79 per cent, Guinea's 0.20 per cent, Nigeria's 0.76 per cent and Sierra Leone's 0.32 per cent (Table 7.2). The implication is that Ghana could be perceived to be more open to intra-WAMZ trade, followed, in order of openness, by Nigeria, The Gambia, Sierra Leone and Guinea. However, in terms of trade openness in the ECOWAS, Sierra Leone was found to be more open to intra-ECOWAS trade, followed by Ghana, The Gambia, Guinea and Nigeria.

As to the degree of trade integration of the member countries in the region, Ghana was found to be more integrated in the WAMZ, followed by Nigeria, Sierra Leone, The Gambia and Guinea (Table 7.4). In ECOWAS, trade integration was highest for Sierra Leone, followed by Ghana, Guinea, The Gambia and Nigeria (Table 7.5).

WAMZ member countries' (excluding Sierra Leone) trade with ECOWAS averaged 8.2 per cent. Sierra Leone's trade with ECOWAS on average was 63.8 per cent, indicating a heavy dependence on trade with other West African countries. This was attributed to a major slowdown in formal exports of diamonds and other commodities to the rest of the world, and relatively high imports of oil from ECOWAS during the period.

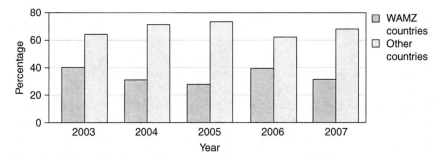

Figure 7.2 Percentage of WAMZ's total ECOWAS exports to WAMZ and non-WAMZ countries (sources: WAMI (2008) and ECOWAS Commission (2008)).

Table 7.1 Percentage contributions of member countries' total ECOWAS exports to the WAMZ

Year	The Gambia	Ghana	Guinea	Nigeria	Sierra Leone
2003	–	16.23	16.76	41.75	0.00
2004	41.43	24.67	21.20	30.45	72.37
2005	87.16	19.43	8.16	28.33	69.70
2006	3.12	10.74	23.85	42.07	54.51
2007	3.52	9.61	24.14	38.40	49.63

Sources: WAMI (2008) and ECOWAS Commission (2008).

The Gambia's major export destination in the WAMZ in 2006 and 2007 was Ghana, while Ghana and Nigeria remained each other's major export destinations in the Zone. Guinea and Sierra Leone were the main export destinations for each other in the WAMZ. Merchandise exports among WAMZ member countries include mainly processed and non-processed agricultural products, manufactured products, processed wood, chemicals, oil and handicrafts.

Re-exports constitute about 80 per cent of The Gambia's exports to ECOWAS, with the largest share destined for the Senegalese market. Ghana's exports to ECOWAS remain diverse with an increasing trend engendered by the use of ECOWAS trade integration for economic growth. Oil constitutes about 90 per cent of Nigeria's exports to ECOWAS, while other commodities exports were relatively low. The country, however, remains the largest WAMZ exporter to ECOWAS. Between 2003 and 2006, Guinea's exports to ECOWAS increased, but then declined in 2007. Sierra Leone's exports to ECOWAS remained relatively high

These trade patterns indicate that, although markets outside the WAMZ and ECOWAS are of more relative importance to the member countries, the significance of the ECOWAS and WAMZ markets to Ghana, Nigeria and Sierra Leone for original manufactured products increased during the reference period. However, the relative importance of intra-WAMZ exports decreased in the case of The Gambia and Guinea, but rose for both countries in relation to exports to ECOWAS.

Export structure of member countries

Primary products, such as minerals, oil and agricultural products, dominated trade between the WAMZ countries and the rest of the world (Table 7.6). The process of trade liberalization that was promoted across ECOWAS did not contribute significantly to trade diversification for most of the countries that participated in the WAMZ (and the WAEMU), by end 2007. Member countries' exports were highly concentrated both in terms of the range of export bundles and in terms of the limited markets which they supply. Comparatively, in the WAMZ, Ghana's exports (0.441) were less concentrated, followed by The Gambia (0.506), Guinea (0.660) Nigeria (0.857) and Sierra Leone (estimated at 0.865). ECOWAS was 0.609, while Europe was 0.063 (Table 7.7).

Table 7.2 Trade openness of member countries in intra-WAMZ trade

Country	2003	2004	2005	2006	2007	Period average (2003–2007)
The Gambia	0.24	0.26	0.73	0.24	0.50	0.39
Ghana	6.35	4.17	5.17	0.94	2.31	3.79
Guinea	0.13	0.22	0.26	0.25	0.16	0.20
Nigeria	0.66	0.57	0.93	1.14	0.50	0.76
Sierra Leone	0.22	0.19	0.33	0.21	0.63	0.32

Sources: WAMI (2008) and ECOWAS Commission (2008).

Table 7.3 Trade openness of member countries in intra-ECOWAS trade

Country	2003	2004	2005	2006	2007	Period average (2003–2007)
The Gambia	4.14	8.87	8.69	7.17	4.59	6.69
Ghana	11.06	6.88	8.84	6.09	7.00	7.97
Guinea	2.13	5.36	9.94	7.51	0.97	5.18
Nigeria	1.91	2.03	2.89	2.79	1.59	2.24
Sierra Leone	4.43	3.98	5.08	35.82	69.42	23.75

Sources: WAMI (2008) and ECOWAS Commission (2008).

Table 7.4 Trade integration of member countries in WAMZ

Country	2003	2004	2005	2006	2007	Period average (2003–2007)
The Gambia	0.30	0.33	0.99	0.32	0.94	0.58
Ghana	8.34	5.28	6.81	1.13	2.77	4.87
Guinea	0.33	0.53	0.48	0.35	0.27	0.39
Nigeria	1.27	0.99	1.11	1.85	0.94	1.23
Sierra Leone	0.76	0.65	0.89	0.57	1.62	0.90

Sources: WAMI (2008) and ECOWAS Commission (2008).

Table 7.5 Trade integration of WAMZ member countries in ECOWAS

Country	2003	2004	2005	2006	2007	Period average (2003–2007)
The Gambia	5.10	11.18	11.78	9.48	8.69	9.25
Ghana	14.51	8.71	11.62	7.27	8.39	10.10
Guinea	5.54	13.13	18.26	10.59	1.65	9.83
Nigeria	3.65	3.51	3.45	4.52	3.01	3.63
Sierra Leone	15.38	13.77	13.91	97.98	177.92	63.79

Sources: WAMI (2008) and ECOWAS Commission (2008).

Imports of member countries (Table 7.7) suggested they heavily relied on man-ufactured goods. However, the shares of manufactured exports were relatively high for The Gambia, Guinea, Ghana and Sierra Leone, when compared with that of Nigeria with a lower share of manufactured exports (Table 7.6 and Figure 7.4). This trend was in response to a national trade policy aimed at increasing the share of non-traditional exports to ECOWAS in particular. Ghana displayed a higher

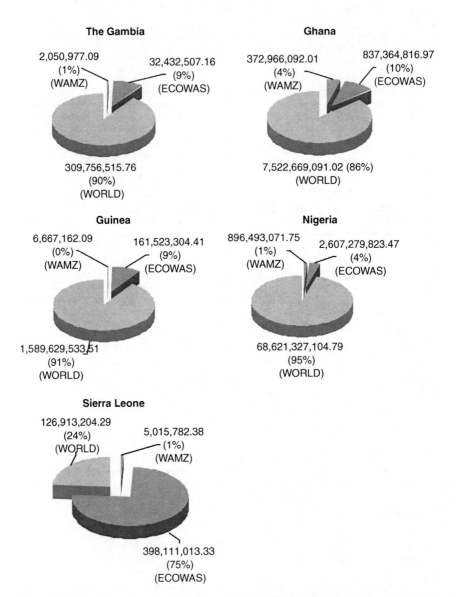

Figure 7.3 Direction of trade with the world in US$, 2003–2007 (source: UNCTAD (2008)).

Table 7.6 Structure of merchandise exports

Country/region	Year	Total value (millions of US$)	Food	Agricultural raw materials	Fuels	Ores and metals	Manufactured goods
The Gambia	1995	19	58.8	0.5	0.2	1.1	36.8
	2000	16	80.8	1.2	0.1	0.3	17.0
	2006	11	81.1	3.9	0.0	0.9	14.1
Ghana	1995	1,754	40.9	10.3	3.4	36.1	9.3
	2000	1,671	30.7	6.5	4.9	48.6	9.3
	2006	3,614	41.9	2.8	0.4	34.1	20.6
Guinea	1995	702	7.4	1.1	0.5	70.3	20.7
	2000	522	2.5	2.4	0.0	70.2	24.7
	2006	976	8.8	2.5	5.5	78.0	3.1
Nigeria	1995	11,877	2.7	2.4	92.5	0.3	2.0
	2000	27,079	0.1	0.0	99.6	0.0	0.2
	2006	46,896	1.5	0.3	95.0	0.3	0.8
Sierra Leone	1995	–	–	–	–	–	–
	2000						
	2006						
Sub-Saharan Africa	1995	76,692	18	7	37	8	28
	2006	231,263	–	–	–		
N. Africa	1995	68,070	6	1	73	2	17
	2006	280,990	5	0	76	2	15
Euro area	1995	1,733,625	11	2	2	2	81
	2006	3,492,756	8	1	5	3	79

Source: UNCTAD (2008).

regional orientation for manufactured products spanning a broad array of product groups. Leading regional manufactured exports from Ghana during the period included perfumes, electric cables, pharmaceuticals, articles of plastics, footwear, wood products, iron and steel products, cotton and printed matter.

Nigeria had registered most products under the ECOWAS Trade Liberalization Scheme (Table 7.8). However, about 0.8 per cent of its manufactures of significant value are exported to ECOWAS and the rest of the world. Petroleum and petroleum by-products constitute about 94 per cent of Nigeria's total exports. The country's manufactured exports include dentifrices, plastic products, paper, paper-making material, footwear, chemical products and textiles.

Exports from The Gambia, Guinea and Sierra Leone were less diversified. The Gambia's exports include groundnuts, fish, detergents and re-exports, while exports from Guinea and Sierra Leone include fish, other agricultural products, other food items and re-exports.

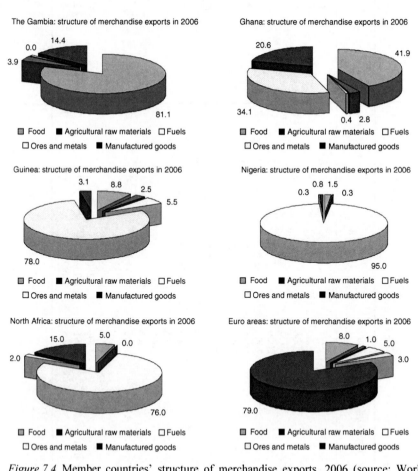

Figure 7.4 Member countries' structure of merchandise exports, 2006 (source: World Bank (2008b)).

Table 7.7 Export and import concentration and diversification indices of member countries and ECOWAS

Region/country	1995			2006		
	Number of products exported* 1	Diversification index+ 2	Concentration index++ 3	Number of products exported 4	Diversification index 5	Concentration index 6
Exports						
ECOWAS	233	0.804	0.458	237	0.755	0.609
The Gambia	22	0.596	0.323	9	0.593	0.506
Ghana	95	0.848	0.444	117	0.823	0.441
Guinea	39	0.800	0.644	57	0.834	0.660
Nigeria	149	0.892	0.853	174	0.855	0.857
Europe	261	0.156	0.048	260	0.183	0.063
Imports						
ECOWAS	261	0.484	0.216	260	0.433	0.136
The Gambia	127	0.609	0.179	135	0.532	0.180
Ghana	198	0.460	0.103	216	0.439	0.132
Guinea	178	0.557	0.196	182	0.508	0.115
Nigeria	246	0.423	0.059	232	0.452	0.123
Europe	261	0.093	0.047	260	0.108	0.069

Source: UNCTAD (2008).

Notes

* Number of products (at SITC, Revision 3 three-digit group level) exported or imported by country, this figure includes only those products that are greater than US$100,000 or more than 0.3 per cent of the country's total exports or imports.

+ Diversification index that ranges from 0 to 1 reveals the extent of the differences between the structure of trade of the country or country group and the world average. The index value close to 1 indicates a bigger difference from the world average.

++ The lower the index the less concentrated are a country's exports.

The likely success or failure of any proposed regional trade arrangement is contingent on the range of products prospective members have the capacity to export or import (to or from each other). If the members export a wide range of diversified goods, this is a positive factor. If their exports are concentrated, it will limit the prospects of increasing regional trade. The underlying assumption is that the higher the level of export diversification, the better the prospects for a successful regional initiative. The more diversified a country's exports, the greater the range of potential products that can be traded with regional partners. If only a limited number of such goods exist, members of an FTA may have to rely heavily on third countries for a higher share of its key imports (and as a destination for their major exports), and this would be likely to reduce their commitment to perceived benefits from the arrangement (Yeats, 1998).

Box 7.1 Export diversification (concentration[2]) index

Export diversification is held to be important for developing countries because many developing countries are often highly dependent on relatively few primary commodities for their export earnings. Unstable prices for these commodities may subject a developing country exporter to serious terms of trade shocks. Since the covariation in individual commodity prices is less than perfect, diversification into new primary export products is generally viewed as a positive development. The strongest positive effects are normally associated with diversification into manufactured goods, and its benefits include higher and more stable export earnings, job creation and learning effects, and the development of new skills and infrastructure that would facilitate the development of even newer export products. The export diversification (*DX*) index for a country is defined as:

$$DX_j = (\text{sum} |h_{ij} - x_i|)/2$$

Where h_{ij} is the share of commodity i in the total exports of country j and h_i is the share of the commodity in world exports. The related measure used by UNCTAD is the concentration index or Hirschman (*H*) index, which is calculated using the shares of all three-digit products in a country's exports:

$$H_j = \text{sqrt} [\text{sum} (x_i/X_t)^2]$$

Where x_i is country j's exports of product i (at the three-digit classification) and X_t is country j's total exports. The index has been normalized to account for the number of actual three-digit products that could be exported. Thus, the maximum value of the index is 239 (the number of individual three-digit products in SITC revision 2), and its minimum (theoretical) value is zero, for a country with no exports. The lower the index, the less concentrated are a country's exports.

Source: World Bank (2009)

Table 7.8 Number of WAMZ companies and products registered under the ETLS, December 2008

Country	No. of companies registered	No. of products registered	Share of total ECOWAS companies registered under the ETLS (%)	Share of total ECOWAS products registered under the ETLS (%)
The Gambia	7	17	0.74	0.64
Ghana	260	800	27.40	30.00
Guinea	4	6	0.42	0.22
Nigeria	568	1,326	59.90	49.70
Sierra Leone	0	0	0	0
WAMZ	839	2,149	88.50	80.60
Non-WAMZ	109	518	11.50	19.40
ECOWAS	948	2,667	100	100

Sources: WAMI (2007) and ECOWAS Commission (2007a).

Assessment of compliance with ECOWAS trade facilitating institutional arrangements

ECOWAS recognizes the need for institutional policies to enable community members to meet trade integration objectives, assuming that member countries would implement the policies. Thus, among others, for trade integration, the BAP enjoined WAMZ member states to comply with the following:

- a free trade area;
- the ETLS;
- the protocol relating to free movement of persons, residence and establishment;
- the protocol on the establishment of the ECOWAS Brown Card;
- the convention relating to inter-state road transportation between ECOWAS member states;
- the convention relating to inter-state road transit of goods;
- the convention for mutual administrative assistance in customs matters;
- adoption of common external tariffs by end 2007;
- adoption of a Community Customs Code and capital liberalization;
- adoption of a common investment code;
- harmonization of indirect taxes (VAT and excise taxes).

There is also the requirement of member states to ensure constant supply of power for household and industry and to set up Road Transit Facilitation Committees to oversee compliance with the provisions relating to road transportation and road transit consignment of goods.

Status of compliance with the BAP

The free trade area. Insofar as member states are able to determine adherence to the rules of origin of imported goods from the community, such goods are allowed entry without tariffs or quotas.

The ETLS. The promotion of trade in goods originating in member states as well as the collective economic development of the community requires indigenous ownership and participation. According to the ECOWAS Revised Treaty 1993, the claim that goods shall be accepted as originating from a member state in accordance with the provisions of the scheme shall be supported by the appropriate certificate. The Gambia, Ghana, Guinea, Nigeria and Sierra Leone have actively participated in the ETLS. During 2008, five companies and a total of 11 products were approved by the National Approval Committee in The Gambia, thereby increasing the number of companies and products to seven and 17, respectively. In Nigeria, 18 companies and 31 products registered under the ETLS in 2008, which increased the total number of registered companies and product under the scheme to 568 and 1,326 respectively. The number of registered companies and products under the ETLS scheme in Ghana amounted to

260 and 800, respectively, while four companies and six products were registered under the scheme in Sierra Leone.

It is reported that 88 and 80 per cent of ECOWAS-registered companies and products under the ETLS, respectively, originate from the WAMZ, which indicates active participation of WAMZ countries in the scheme (Table 7.8). As a result of a combination of factors, including lack of adequate infrastructure, not all the registered companies have exported the registered products. In 2006, the total number of products exported to all parts of the world by The Gambia, Ghana, Guinea and Nigeria were 9, 117, 57 and 174 respectively (Figure 7.4). It is important to enable such registered companies (most of which fall within the small and medium enterprises (SMEs) and labour-intensive categories) to produce and export to the region since they provide scope for learning by doing, technical progress and sustained growth in living standards. The Gambia, Guinea and Ghana have simple reference sources to check authenticity of participation of companies and products, under the ETLS, at points of entry. Nigeria is yet to institutionalize such a measure. In cases of doubt on the rules of origin, all the member states (excepting Sierra Leone) have instituted arrangements to address the issue.

Protocol relating to free movement of persons, residence and establishment. All five member states have applied the provisions of the protocol. Member states' citizens are allowed free entry and the right of residence based on the provisions. Though citizens of other member states are able to establish businesses either in partnership with citizens of the host country or individually, national laws do not treat non-WAMZ countries' citizens equally. Member states have not moved into Phase III of the Protocol (on the right of establishment).

Protocol on the establishment of the ECOWAS Brown Card. All member states of the WAMZ implemented this scheme, which is a derivation from the protocol on free movement of persons across the ECOWAS sub-region. The scheme compensates inter-territorial third-party motor accident victims in the event of death, injury or property damage. In the absence of the Brown Card Scheme, each motorist had to procure a local insurance cover at the frontier of each member state before entry was allowed, making transiting for truckers and travelling for other commuters very cumbersome and discouraging to cross-border trade. More than 60 per cent of motorists covered under the scheme in almost every ECOWAS member state are commercial drivers of huge cargo trucks and articulators. Truckers are not allowed passage if they do not hold a card.

Convention relating to inter-state road transit of goods (ISRT). The convention allows the transportation of goods from one customs office in a member state to another customs office in another member state free of duties, taxes and restriction while in transit. Four WAMZ countries, namely The Gambia, Ghana, Guinea and Nigeria, ratified the ISRT and appointed a national guarantor to guarantee operations of the ISRT in their countries. For effective implementation, Ghana deployed a satellite tracking system for transit consignments. Absence of the satellite tracking system contributed to unwarranted and costly stoppages, at several checkpoints, of vehicles with transit consignments, in particular on the transit route between Guinea and Sierra Leone, and the Lagos–Badagry route. The number of customs checkpoints on the Lagos–Badagry route was reduced to four. The major transit route in The Gambia, Banjul–Amdallai to Senegal, has two checkpoints, while the Aflao–Elubo transit route also has two customs checkpoints on the coast of Ghana.

Convention for Mutual Administrative Assistance in Customs Matters. The member states agree to render each other assistance with a view to the prevention, detection and punishment of customs infringements, in accordance with the provisions of the convention. The convention also covers mutual administrative assistance in customs matters among member states. This convention was applicable to the entire membership, with regular meetings of their respective customs offices at the ECOWAS level.

Adoption of common external tariff (CET) by end 2007. Adopting CET rates would enhance the integration process in the WAMZ towards a single market. A decision was taken for the adoption of the ECOWAS CET, which provided for a two-year transitional period from 1 January 2006 to 31 December 2007. The categorization and rates of the ECOWAS CET, which became effective on 1 January 2008, are as follows:

Category 0: essential social goods and agricultural inputs and equipment
– 0 per cent;
Category 1: basic raw materials, capital goods and specific agricultural inputs – 5 per cent;
Category 2: intermediate products – 10 per cent;
Category 3: final consumer goods – 20 per cent.

The Gambia adopted the ECOWAS CET rates and aligned some tariff lines, while others still require alignment with the ECOWAS CET. Due to its limited capacity to produce sufficient rice, The Gambia withdrew its participation in the proposed fifth band, while maintaining a zero duty rate on rice. Ghana, Guinea, Nigeria and Sierra Leone reduced their external tariffs to the levels of the ECOWAS CET, with some exceptional lists of products (sensitive products) that were not aligned with the ECOWAS CET bands.

Some 90 per cent of the tariff lines of type B exceptions were agreed upon.

Regarding the remaining products, a number of problems were raised including the creation of a fifth band of 50 per cent required by Nigeria (with the support of Ghana, Côte d'Ivoire and others); processing of the products proposed in the 0 per cent category (inputs and agricultural capital goods, fire-fighting vehicles and other vehicles for special uses, butane, some construction equipment, drugs and some specific inputs for drug manufacture); rice categorization (considering its sensitive nature, requiring consequent tariff protection); products some countries want to classify in a lower category to keep consumer prices low, but which other countries want classified in a higher category to protect their local production; and harmonization of safeguard measures (safeguards allow a country to raise tariffs temporarily to counter a surge in imports that threaten to damage domestic industry). In October 2008, member countries of ECOWAS agreed on a 35 per cent rate for a fifth band.

Adoption of a Community Customs Code. A draft Community Customs Code, aimed at harmonizing customs codes and customs valuation, was completed through the study on the texts and conventions on customs valuation regimes of the member countries. The Gambia has adopted international best practice in customs administrative procedures in the clearance of goods. In the valuation of goods, The Gambia applies the destination inspection approach. Ghana, Nigeria and Sierra Leone also apply international best practice in respect of customs administrative procedures, but Guinea did not apply the destination inspection approach, which had allowed discretionary valuation of imports, resulting, in large part, in significant losses of customs revenue to the country and distortion of prices of same goods across neighbouring countries. The intention of streamlining and harmonizing customs procedures within the ongoing creation of the WAMZ/ECOWAS customs union is to make the union more competitive and attractive to both regional and foreign investors and encourage expansion in exports.

Impact of adoption of the CET on national budgets of member states

Since the adoption of the CET in January 2005 by member countries, the impact on revenue has been mixed. The anticipated spontaneous huge loss in revenue for all the member countries following adoption was not evident. The Gambia (rates were 0 per cent, 5 per cent, 10 per cent and 18 per cent) and Guinea (0 per cent, 5 per cent, 10 per cent and 15 per cent) experienced an increase in revenue and volume of imports over the last two years since the adoption of the CET, while Ghana, whose external tariff rates were also similar (0 per cent, 5 per cent, 10 per cent, 20 per cent and 40 per cent) to those of the ECOWAS CET (0 per cent, 5 per cent, 10 per cent and 20 per cent) recorded an increase in revenue (Table 7.9).

In Nigeria, where the national rates (ranging from 0 per cent to 150 per cent) were significantly higher than those of the CET, no significant decline in revenue was observed (Table 7.10). However, despite the increase in the volumes of import, there was a decrease in customs revenue collected in Sierra Leone, whose rates were 0 per cent, 5 per cent, 10 per cent, 20 per cent and 30 per cent.

Table 7.9 Trend of import revenue collection in Ghana, 2004–2007, in ¢bn and US$

No.	Year	Amount ¢	Amount US$
1	2004	92.93	10,441,573
2	2005	113.16	12,573,333
3	2006	132.57	14,254,838
4	2007	195.38	19,936,735

Sources: Ghana (2008a) and WAMI (2008).

To cushion the expected loss in revenue to member countries owing to the adoption of the CET, the ECOWAS Commission set up a fund to which member countries could submit claims for compensation. However, since the introduction of the fund, no country has submitted claims for compensation.

Cross-border payments. Payments for cross-border trade improved significantly across the Zone. Local banks operating in the Zone and the region established subsidiaries in all the five member states and across the ECOWAS, making settlement of intra-regional trade transactions much easier.

Convention regulating Inter-State Road Transportation between ECOWAS member states. The convention defines the conditions under which transportation by road shall be carried out between the member states of the community with a view to promoting trade. It deals with the road transportation of persons and merchandise between one or several points of the territories of member states by road vehicle or by containers mounted on such vehicles and operating along clearly defined interstate road axes. Member states have largely complied with this provision. Frequently, though, transit vehicles have exceeded authorized axle-load weights, resulting in stoppages at checkpoints.

Adoption of a common investment framework. ECOWAS drafted a Supplementary Act for a Common Investment Code for consideration by all stakeholders in member countries.

Harmonization of indirect taxes (VAT and excise tax). As part of market integration efforts, all member countries of ECOWAS were expected to apply a harmonized VAT and excise tax. A study was carried out on the harmonization of member states' VAT legislations and excise duties, and the main conclusions of the study were discussed at a regional seminar in March 2007 in Cotonou. In this regard, Ghana, Guinea and Nigeria have introduced VAT, although at different rates, while The Gambia and Sierra Leone have not introduced VAT.

Standardization of sanitary and phyto-sanitary (SPS) measures. The West African Quality Programme support for competitiveness and harmonization of Technical Obstacles to Trade (TOT) and sanitary and phyto-sanitary measures (SPS) for ECOWAS member states (non-WAEMU members) and Mauritania was due for execution. The Gambia worked through its National Codex Committee, in collaboration with the ECOWAS Commission and other partners, under the West African Quality Programme, to improve on its standardization

Table 7.10 Trend of customs revenue collections in Nigeria, 2002–2006, in naira and US$

S/No.	Year	Amount (naira)	Amount (US$)
1	2002	5,613,298,950.24	43,853,898
2	2003	6,961,593,252.42	54,387,447
3	2004	7,575,210,053.92	59,181,328
4	2005	9,229,518,231.29	72,105,611
5	2006	11,105,495,067.50	86,761,680

Source: Nigeria (2007).

procedures and SPS measures to meet regional standards. Ghana and Nigeria are two of three regional centres for standard certification in the sub-region. That notwithstanding, the authorities are committed to achieving international best practice in standardization and SPS measures. Guinea and Sierra Leone are expected to upgrade their standardization practice in the mode of the Regional Quality Programme.

Road Transit Facilitation Committees (RTFCs). In all the member countries of the WAMZ and ECOWAS, an RTFC was required to be established to monitor and promote adherence by relevant agencies of measures put in place by the community to ensure smooth passage of goods at ports and border posts and along the transit corridors. An RTFC was established in all the member countries but most lack sufficient financial support to carry out expected activities.

The harmonized customs regime

Much progress was achieved in the harmonization of a number of customs mechanisms and instruments (Rules of Origin, Certificate of Origin, customs nomenclature, Single Customs Declaration and automated customs clearing procedures through the computerization of member states' customs departments) thereby enabling the latter to be incorporated in national laws.

Although customs nomenclature and criteria of origin were standardized, customs regimes and clearance procedures were not. In view of the slow pace of standardization, the ECOWAS Commission engaged the services of a consultancy firm to carry out a study on the imperatives of harmonizing customs procedures and customs regimes with a view to formulating an ECOWAS Community Customs Code. The Code would ensure that, while enabling customs to exercise all of its duties and controls necessary for the accomplishment of its tasks, there would be established a common system of application of customs procedures that conform to the requirements of international trade and which facilitate intra- and extra-Community trade.

Status of compliance by member countries with current Customs Harmonized Measures

The Gambia

The Gambia printed and introduced harmonized customs documents, namely, the certificate of origin, the Harmonized System (HS) of customs nomenclature and declaration form. The transit certificate of the ISRT was never introduced, but a guarantor was designated for transit operations.

Ghana

The harmonized customs documents, the certificate of origin, the HS of customs nomenclature and the customs declaration have all been introduced. Average clearing time of trucks at border posts is three hours while ship waiting time is stable, at two days (Table 7.11) and three days clearing time at the ports. Quick clearing time was made possible by the installation of the GCNet (Ghana Community Network), a far more advanced system than the ASYCUDA (Automated System for Customs Data), to expedite the capture of data, quick clearance of goods and determination of customs revenue received in real time. The ISRT was ratified and a National Guarantor (State Insurance Company) oversees its application. Application of the ISRT started in October 2007. The country discontinued the use of customs officers to escort transit vehicles to the next exit points, and was replaced by a satellite tracking system. Ghana reduced the number of checkpoints to just two in its eastern corridor, from the Côte d'Ivoire–Ghana border to the Ghana–Togo border, and in the northern corridor, from Tema (on the coast) to Paga (Ghana–Burkina Faso border) in the north, all in compliance with ECOWAS decisions.

Guinea

Guinea has applied the ECOWAS Harmonized System. It takes on average about four hours for a truck-load of goods to be cleared at any of its border posts and ports. In order to facilitate transit, the country established a Transit Office at the National Directorate of Customs with a view to reducing customs formalities for transit goods. Guinea Port Authority gives priority to ships carrying goods in transit with a 50 per cent fee reduction for freight goods in transit. However, port entry charges still rank among the highest in the ECOWAS region (Table 7.13). The country grants VAT exemption on all goods in transit. The average time taken for transit formalities is 24 hours.

A national guarantor for transit operations was designated. Guinea had set up a National Committee on ISRT and a Transit Facilitation Committee, with the Guinea Chamber of Commerce, Industry and Crafts serving as guarantor. In order to allow for free flow of transit goods all road security checkpoints were removed. The average flow of goods in transit through the country's seaport showed a noticeable increase between 2002 and 2005 (Table 7.12).

Table 7.11 Ship waiting times for container berths at Lagos and other ports, 2005

Port	Days waiting for berth	Trends
Efficient international ports	Minimal	
Lagos	7–14	Not improving
Cotonou	3	Worsening
Luanda	1–3	Improving
Tema	2	Stable
Durban	2	Fluctuating
Abidjan	0	Stable

Source: Nigeria (2005).

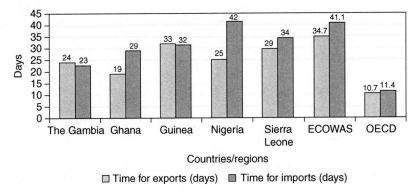

Figure 7.5 Trading across borders: transit time (source: World Bank (2008a)).

Nigeria

Nigeria introduced the HS of customs nomenclature and the transit certificate. However, flow of trade was hampered by numerous checkpoints on some transit routes (45 checkpoints on the Lagos–Seme transit route). Customs clearance and freight forwarding costs vary widely, but were extremely high, with average delays of 21 days. Nigeria adopted the ASYCUDA, and the ASYCUDA ++ was deployed at six major sites in the country. Ship waiting time at ports ranges from seven to 14 days (see Table 7.11). According to the World Bank *Doing Business Report* (2006), services are characterized by long waiting times, low handling speeds and high costs of moving a container through the ports. Port entry charges at Lagos are the highest in the region (Table 7.13).

The federal government embarked on reforms at the ports in order to provide more efficient and less expensive services. Completing the four remaining port concessions was critical for further improvements in port efficiency and trade facilitation. The Nigeria Customs Service runs a weekly interactive programme, *Customs Duty*, on nationwide TV to educate the public on their rights and responsibilities and to solicit information for improvement on services provided.

Table 7.12 Transit traffic in Guinea

Year	Freight in port	Transit traffic	% transit
2002	4,774,140 t	22,620 t	0.47
2003	5,280,528 t	68,664 t	1.30
2004	5,675,962 t	46,433 t	0.81
2005	6,088,888 t	127,638 t	2.09

Source: Guinea (2007).

Table 7.13 Comparison of port entry charges at selected West African ports

Port	Index of port charges per 1,700 TEU Abidjan = 100
Abidjan	100
Dakar	125
Tema	131
Cotonou	155
Douala	490
Conakry	530
Lagos	689

Source: Nigeria (2002).

Sierra Leone

Sierra Leone adopted the HS and a single declaration form but never employed the ASYCUDA or any other technology to capture data electronically. In 2007, however, the country sought to improve its trade competitiveness by reducing scanning and manifest fees and port charges, and increased the demurrage period from five to ten days excluding weekends.

By the end of 2008, member countries' efforts to facilitate trade across borders showed that the average cost of exporting a container from The Gambia was US$831; US$1,003 in Ghana; US$720 in Guinea; US$1,179 in Nigeria; and US$1,450 in Sierra Leone. The WAMZ average of US$1,037 compared favourably with the OECD average of US$1,069.1 and the ECOWAS' US$1,878 (Figure 7.6). The much higher average cost of exporting a container from ECOWAS was due to the high cost of shipments from Burkina Faso, Mali and Niger (landlocked countries), and port inefficiencies in some member countries. On the number of days required for exports, the WAMZ average was 26 days, while it was 34.7 in the ECOWAS and 10.7 in the OECD. The days required in The Gambia, Ghana, Guinea, Nigeria and Sierra Leone were 24, 19, 33, 25 and 29 respectively. Efforts at reduction in the number of documents required for exports resulted in seven days for The Gambia; eight for Ghana; nine for Guinea and Nigeria; and seven for Sierra Leone (Figure 7.7). In ECOWAS, the average was 8.8 days and in the OECD countries it was 4.5 days.

Labour market integration

The concept of labour integration in most literature is limited to the movement of labour from one country to another. However, labour integration also means the ability of businesses to access the pool of migrant labour in different ways in a bid to achieve economic efficiency. Although labour migration is a key factor in economic integration, the paucity of data makes analysis difficult.

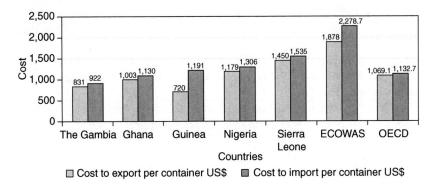

Figure 7.6 Trading across borders: cost (source: World Bank (2008a)).

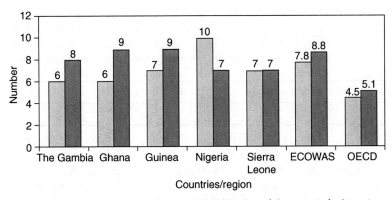

Figure 7.7 Trading across borders: number of documents required (source: World Bank (2008a)).

Generally, labour market integration can be evaluated on the basis of a broad set of basic indicators including the following:

• Labour mobility. This is particularly important where wage flexibility is not sufficient. Labour mobility helps the economy re-establish previous equilibrium through regulating the demand for and supply of labour (labour migration) rather than the relative input price. High labour mobility can offset inadequate flexibility of wages. Indicators include the participation rate of immigrants, for example, the percentage of working-age immigrants who are employed in the national labour market and the unemployment rate of immigrants as compared to the general unemployment rate.

• Residential integration. The environment in which migrants live provides information about the level of residential integration. The area of settlement and the nature and quality of the housing itself show to what extent migrants are separated from the host society, and whether their housing standard is below, equal to or higher than the average housing standard of the host society.

- Integration within the education system. This is an important condition for the economic integration of migrants, as well as mutual recognition of diplomas and qualifications.
- Language is a fundamental basis for any interaction within society. A high degree of linguistic homogeneity will facilitate national labour.

Labour mobility

Cross-border mobility of labour would become an important factor of adjustment mechanism after the formation of a monetary union. Such mobility would equilibrate demand and supply of factors of production by shifting resources from surplus areas to deficit areas in the monetary zone. This could stabilize the wage rate and reduce the incidence of frictional unemployment. ECOWAS explicitly recognized that enhancing mechanisms of labour mobility is key to advancing economic integration by ensuring that labour and skills are available when and where needed within the larger West African economic space. Recognizing the centrality of labour migration to moving forward the regional integration process and development in the sub-region resulted in the abolition of visas and entry permits, while endorsing the right of residence and establishment and instituting a community insurance scheme (ECOWAS Brown Card).

The ECOWAS Protocol on Free Movement of Persons and the Right of Residence and Establishment was adopted on 29 May 1979, and is expected to span a 15-year period. The implementation of the first phase over the first five years abolished requirements for visas and entry permits. Community citizens in possession of valid travel documents and an international health certificate were permitted to enter member states without a visa for up to 90 days. Member states can, however, refuse admission into their territories to so-called inadmissible immigrants under its laws. Where a citizen of the community is to be expelled, states undertake to guarantee the security of that citizen, his/her family and his/her property.

The second phase (Right of Residence) of the Protocol came into force in July 1986, when all member states ratified it. In 1993, the Revised ECOWAS Treaty, among others, affirmed the right of citizens of the community to entry, residence and settlement and enjoined member states to recognize these rights in their respective territories. It also called on member states to take all necessary steps at the national level to ensure that the provisions are duly implemented. All the five member countries of the WAMZ applied the provisions of the protocol relating to free movement of persons, residence and establishment. Citizens of member states were allowed free entry and the right of residence based on the provisions.

Box 7.2 Ghana's unique GCNet system for port clearance

The GCNet system was introduced in response to stakeholder concerns for the removal of constraints to legitimate trade development and facilitation, and to enhance Ghanaian business competitiveness. It was also geared at ensuring that the facilitation of trade processes did not compromise the mobilization of trade-related revenue.

The system is presently made up of a front-end electronic messaging platform (the TradeNet) and a back-end system (the Customs Management System) that process all customs operations electronically, such as electronic submission and integration of manifests by carriers, access of the manifest details by authorized agencies, elimination of several manual interventions and the inherent duplications, selective targeting of high-risk consignments via the system's risk management module, customs payment and revenue accounting. The system has been deployed at Customs, Excise and Preventive Service (CEPS) headquarters and all relevant border posts and ports.

In addition to the customs system, linkage of other back-end applications (e.g. a system for port cargo management, automated registration of vehicles and income tax assessments and payments) is possible.

The system also has an electronic permit, licence and exemptions module that enable agencies such as the Ghana Free Zones Board, Standards Board, Mineral Commission and the Investment Promotion Centre to issue permits, licences or exemptions electronically when applied for by importers/exporters to facilitate trade and customs clearances.

Among the other unique features of the system is a valuation module that enables customs to access transactional values that have been collated in a Transactional Pricing Database (TPD). Another valuation feature is an electronic valuation application that automatically assesses the value of an imported used vehicle, and the corresponding duty and taxes payable on it once the vehicle's chassis number or vehicle identification number or engine number is entered into the system.

An enhanced transit tracking module has also been introduced, with features that include deployment of electronic transit bonds, seals, IPA surveillance cameras along the transit corridor, as well as electronic GPS tracking devices to ensure effective monitoring of all transit consignments and minimize revenue leakages associated with the diversion of transit goods.

The GCNet system has contributed significantly towards the realization of trade facilitation with improved revenue mobilization goals. Customs clearances at Kotoka Airport, for instance, have improved from a pre-GCNet situation of 1–2 days to an average of four hours. Takoradi Port also has 71 per cent of consignments being cleared within one day, while Tema Port has averaged 2–5 days instead of the pre-GCNet average of two weeks. Clearances at the border posts are also taking on average 2–3 hours as compared to the pre-GCNet average of two days.

CEPS have also recorded significant annual growth in revenue at its stations connected to the system (e.g. nearly 40 per cent in the first year, 30 per cent in the second year and an average 25 per cent annual growth subsequently). The GCNet allows customs to know in real time, at any time, the amount of revenue collected.

Source: Ghana (2007)

A major challenge for the ECOWAS Commission is the effective implementation of free movement of people in the sub-region. In spite of their efforts, compliance remains frustrated by numerous roadblocks on highways and extortion by officials mostly at border posts. ECOWAS is investing in other complementary initiatives to ease free movement of goods and services through the construction of joint border posts to expedite immigration formalities. There is a need to enhance the interconnection of rail networks to facilitate the movement of people in the region to boost intra-regional trade and enable citizens to avail themselves of business opportunities in member states.

Labour market dynamics

There remains a dearth of consistent labour market data for the WAMZ countries. Despite this difficulty, there are some important deductions that can be made concerning the nature and characteristics of the labour market. Table 7.14 depicts the population dynamics in the WAMZ countries. WAMZ countries are characterized by high population growth averaged at 2.5 per cent in 2005.

Table 7.14 showed wide disparities in the populations of the countries, with Nigeria posting the largest number of people and The Gambia the smallest.

The rapid growth of the population and the labour force coupled with decades of stunted development rendered high proportions of the work force unemployed, while wages for those in employment plummeted dramatically. The sub-region's rapidly growing population placed tremendous strains on the development process, creating conditions for migration through linkages with labour force growth and unemployment. Table 7.15 also provides the labour force participation rates for the WAMZ countries and the results indicate disparities in the participation rates across the Zone.

Integration within the education system

Integration within the education system is an important condition for the economic integration of migrants, as well as mutual recognition of diplomas and qualifications.

ECOWAS adopted a General Convention on the recognition and equivalence of Degrees, Diplomas, Certificates and other qualifications in ECOWAS member states.

Table 7.14 Population dynamics in the WAMZ, 2005

	Total (million)	Male (% of total)	Female (% of total)	Annual growth rate (%)
The Gambia	1.5	49.6	50.4	2.6
Ghana	22.1	50.6	49.4	2.0
Guinea	9.4	51.2	48.8	1.9
Nigeria	131.5	50.6	49.4	2.4
Sierra Leone	5.5	49.3	50.7	3.5

Source: World Bank (2007).

Table 7.15 Labour force participation, 2005

Country	Participation rate (%)							
	Total		Male			Female		
	Ages 15–64	Ages 65 and older	Ages 15–64	Ages 65 and older		Ages 15–64	Ages 65 and older	
The Gambia	72.6	58.6	86.0	76.8		59.8	43.0	
Ghana	73.2	56.1	75.7	65.1		70.7	48.0	
Guinea	83.7	50.6	88.3	68.9		79.5	34.7	
Nigeria	67.1	46.5	86.2	69.5		48.3	27.3	
Sierra Leone	73.4	50.7	93.8	87.1		54.3	21.9	

Source: World Bank (2007).

Box 7.3 Human resources

Under the Revised Treaty of ECOWAS, Article 60, Human Resources, member states agreed to cooperate in the full development and use of their human resources. They undertook measures to:

- strengthen cooperation among themselves in the fields of education, training and employment; and to harmonize and coordinate their policies and pro-grammes in these areas;
- consolidate their existing training institutions, improve the efficiency of their educational systems, encourage exchanges between schools and universities, establish equivalences of academic, professional and technical qualifications, encourage literacy, promote the teaching and practice of the official languages of the community, and establish regional centres of excellence in various disciplines;
- encourage the exchange of skilled manpower between member states.

Source: Revised ECOWAS Treaty 1993

On a national level, different countries were at different stages in tackling the issue of recognition of qualifications. While some countries were involved in regional collaboration, others were not, resulting in great diversity. In addition, the nature of national bodies in charge of recognition differs in the sub-region.

Regional infrastructure

Infrastructure – such as air and sea ports, roads, railways, electricity supply and water provision – is generally inadequate in all the member countries and does not constitute an effective means of lowering trade costs and promoting trade growth. It is expected that improving the infrastructure would play a key role in regional trade flows. Without the creation of good basic infrastructure in sectors such as electricity, water, telecommunications and transport, the objective of an economically developed ECOWAS/WAMZ, through intra-community trade, would remain a mirage.

Supply of power

Efforts were made by member countries to address the energy situation. Table 7.17 shows the programme of energy activities that was undertaken to improve energy supply.

In member countries, installed generation capacity was higher than available energy output. For instance, installed generation capacity in Nigeria was 6,000 MW compared to available energy output of only 3,000 MW. Actual demand was estimated to be 10,000 MW. The transmission network is not appro-priately configured for reliability and lines extend over distances that were too

Table 7.16 Infrastructure situation in member countries

Country	Quality of overall infrastructure	Quality of roads	Quality of railroad infrastructure	Quality of port infrastructure	Quality of air transport infrastructure	Available seat Kilometres	Quality of electricity supply	Telephone lines
The Gambia	4.1	3.9	n/a	4.1	4.6	5.5	4.4	3
Ghana	3.4	3.4	1.3	3.5	4.1	71.4	3.2	1.6
Guinea	n/a	n/a	n/a	n/a	n/a	n/a	n/a	n/a
Nigeria	2.4	2.3	1.4	2.6	4.2	213.0	1.6	1.3
Sierra Leone	n/a	n/a	n/a	n/a	n/a	n/a	n/a	n/a

Source: World Economic Forum (2009).

Table 7.17 Regional energy programme

Programme	Activity purpose	Period of implementation	Beneficiary country	Stage of completion
West African Gas Pipeline Project	Gas supply from Nigeria through Benin, Togo to Ghana	2003–2007	Benin, Togo and Ghana	Near completion. Full production scheduled for March 2009
West Africa Power Pool Programme: Transmission line projects – Ghana, Burkina Faso, etc. Transmission projects – Ghana Interconnection projects – Nigeria, Benin, etc. Restoration of power systems – Gambia, Guinea, Sierra Leone, etc. Hydroelectric scheme	Provision of mechanism and institutional framework for integrating national power systems of member countries	2005–2011	Benin, Burkina Faso, The Gambia, Ghana, Guinea, Guinea-Bissau, Liberia, Mali, Nigeria, Senegal, Sierra Leone, Togo	None of the projects has been completed; about US$350m of the needed US$1.5bn has been secured towards execution of the projects
Ratification of ECOWAS Energy Protocol Establishment of a regional regulatory body for the electricity sector	The Energy Protocol is intended to attract and protect private capital, ensure protection of the environment and enhance energy efficiency in member states	2006–2007	All member countries of the ECOWAS	Protocol has been ratified Funds secured for the establishment; body yet to be operational

Source: ECOWAS Commission (2007b).

long for efficient and reliable load flows. Poor transmission and distribution networks result in frequent financial losses. On average, a representative business enterprise in Nigeria was believed to have spent close to N50,703 (about US$350) for electricity (in 2002), of which 31 per cent was payment for public-sector electricity and 69 per cent was the running cost of the business-owned generator. Similar situations exist in Ghana, Guinea and Sierra Leone.

In 2006, Ghana's consumption of power supply per capita kWh was 266, while in Nigeria it was 127.[3] The average in sub-Saharan Africa was 542; it was 6,926 in Europe and 2,678 for the rest of the world (World Bank, 2008).

Provision of power supply in the Zone remains mixed. In The Gambia, there is stable but limited supply in the capital Banjul, while the rest of the country experiences limited but predictable supply at regular intervals. Since the beginning of 2008, Ghana has enjoyed a relatively stable power supply across the country, with limited power failures. Power supply in Guinea and Nigeria is relatively unstable. In Sierra Leone, while the capital Freetown enjoys regular supply, the electricity situation in the other parts of the country is unstable.

Road transport

Roads constitute the dominant type of intra- and inter-country transport in the region, but non-compliance with transit road usage regulations and lack of up-to-date standard construction of the roads contributes to the poor conditions of the highways. The axle-load limit of 11.5 tonnes for all types of vehicles is flouted in all the countries, resulting in faster deterioration of the roads. In The Gambia, the community road axis – Banjul–Karang (Senegal) – underwent reconstruction. In Ghana, the road axes were largely passable, however, the last stretches of the Accra–Aflao (Togo) axis, on the eastern coastal corridor, and the northern road axes, Accra–Dormaa–Ahenkro (Côte d'Ivoire) and Accra–Paga (Burkina Faso), were in a deplorable state. The Conakry–Pamelap–Freetown axis was also in a bad state, due to poor road maintenance. The Lagos–Badagry–Cotonou (Benin) and Lagos–Port Harcourt road axes in Nigeria were in a very good condition.

In general, the percentage of paved roads (Figure 7.8), during the period 2000–2005, was: 19.3 in The Gambia, 17.9 in Ghana, 9.8 in Guinea, 15 in Nigeria and 8 in Sierra Leone. In sub-Saharan Africa, it was 11.9 per cent, while it was 70.2 per cent in the Middle East and North Africa and 100 per cent in the euro area.

All member countries have a National Facilitation Committee set up to ensure compliance with transportation rules and to facilitate implementation of ECOWAS regional programmes. However, the committees do not function effectively (WAMI, 2008).

Rail transport

In The Gambia and Sierra Leone, there is no railway service. In Ghana, Guinea and Nigeria the railway systems are inefficient, with about 3–5 per cent of freight handled by railways.

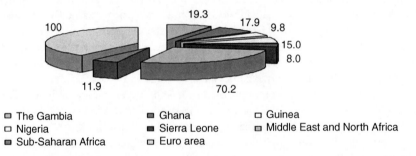

Figure 7.8 Quality of road network: percentage of paved roads (source: World Bank (2008b)).

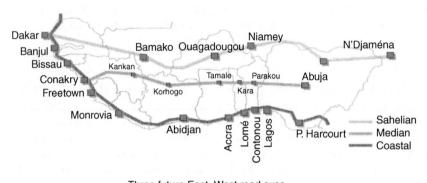

Three future East–West road axes

Figure 7.9 Future road axes (source: ECOWAS and Sahel Club Report (2006)).

Air transport

Airline connections between the WAMZ capitals are limited. A proposal has been developed on common air transport economic regulations by the Commission to the Authority of ECOWAS on passenger compensation, ground handling and airport slot allocation.

Telecommunications

As specified in the Revised ECOWAS Treaty of 1993, the main objectives of the telecommunications sub-sector are as follows: development of a reliable and modern regional telecommunications infrastructure through the execution of INTELCOM I and II programmes; harmonization of telecommunications policies and legal and regulatory frameworks for the establishment of a single liberalized telecommunications market within the Community. In line with these Treaty provisions, the Council of Ministers adopted a harmonization model based on "Centralized Policies with Individual National Implementation", a roadmap for the implementation of a single liberalized telecommunications system within the Community and a roadmap for the implementation of effective GSM roaming within the region. Regional guidelines on the harmonized regional telecommunications market on licensing, interconnection, spectrum management and numbering, tariffs, universal access and competition were adopted by stakeholders. Further, a programme was also executed for the facilitation of West African countries' transition to the Meteorological Satellite Second Generation (MSG) installation in ECOWAS member states for the purpose of gathering meteorological data for monitoring the environment for sustainable development.

The implementation of the INTELCOM II Programme by the ECOWAS Commission identifies 32 telecoms inter-state links to form a regional broadband backbone infrastructure which would be connected to the international network via the SAT 3 submarine fibre optic and three other fibre-optic submarine cables.

Telecommunications were provided by both state and private operators in the member states. Member states are relatively effectively connected to the Internet (Figure 7.11), but access to phones and computers remains low. As at end 2006, for fixed line and mobile phones (Figure 7.10), for every 100 people, in The Gambia there were three and 24 people; Ghana two and 23; Guinea almost none and two; Nigeria one and 22; data for the period were not available for Sierra Leone. Since 2007, Sierra Leone has had six mobile-phone network providers. As at end 2008, there were three providers in The Gambia, five in Ghana, two in Guinea and four in Nigeria. In 2006, for every 100 people in the WAMZ region, one person had access to a fixed line phone and 14 people to a mobile phone. In the euro area 54 people had access to fixed lines, while 99 used mobile phones.

With regard to access to personal computers and the Internet (Figure 7.11), out of every 100 people in The Gambia, there was a ratio of almost two people to a personal computer and four people to the Internet, while Ghana had one

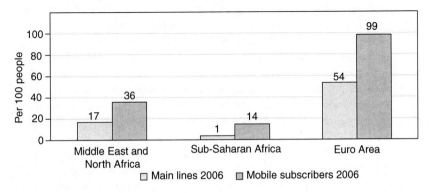

Figure 7.10 Access to telephones, 2006 (source: World Bank (2008b)).

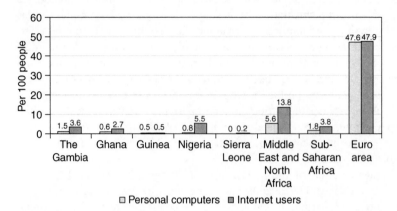

Figure 7.11 Personal computers and Internet use (source: World Bank (2008b)).

person and three people, respectively. Guinea had one person each to a computer and Internet, while Nigeria had one person to a computer and six people to the Internet. In Sierra Leone, computer and Internet usage was limited as there were 0 and 0.2 people with access to computer and Internet respectively. For sub-Saharan Africa, the ratio was two people to a computer and four to the Internet, while that for Europe was 48 people each to a computer and Internet.

Conclusions

The above analysis, using various definitions of the "natural trading partner"[4] hypothesis, demonstrated that WAMZ countries were characterized only moderately as natural trading partners. The following points provide supporting evidence for such an assertion.

First, the "volume of trade" criterion for natural trading partners[5] suggests that the WAMZ countries fell short of this characterization. Ghana and Nigeria were exceptions to the overall low shares of intra-regional trade. The Gambia, Guinea and Sierra Leone do not trade "disproportionately" within the region.

Evidence from the WAMZ/ECOWAS trade patterns also does not strongly support the hypothesis that characterizes natural trading partners on the basis of geographical proximity (Wonnacott and Lutz, 1989; Deardorff and Stern, 1994. The countries of the WAMZ (and ECOWAS) region demonstrated an increasing tendency to trade with partners *outside* the region, due to either pure endowment differences (vis-à-vis industrial countries) or due to longstanding historical affiliations.

In terms of "trade complementarity"[6] – a third criterion of the natural trading partner hypothesis (Schiff, 1999; Michaely, 1996) – the evidence on the WAMZ/ ECOWAS was mixed. Ghana and Nigeria's exports complement the import demands of a number of countries including Niger, Togo, Burkina Faso, Benin and Côte d'Ivoire. However, The Gambia, Guinea and Sierra Leone displayed efficiencies in a limited range of products that fulfilled Ghana and Nigeria's (as well as other regional members') major import requirements. The ETLS in the emerging ECOWAS customs union encouraged some countries in the WAMZ (Ghana and Nigeria), and ECOWAS (Côte d'Ivoire and Senegal) to produce and export more local manufactures to the region.

The ETLS helps some member countries to refine their incentive environments by reducing distortions and improving the region's competitiveness in some manufactured products.

Available statistics also showed that infrastructure is weak across the Zone and sub-region. In this regard, the provision of quality infrastructure would enhance intra-regional trade flows. Hence, policy must be intensified in all member countries to implement regional infrastructure programmes. Similarly, if the institutional framework is complied with, trade barriers would be eliminated or reduced to the barest minimum, and there would be greater trade flows.

In order to mitigate the consequence of delays in the integration process, reduce long-term costs of trade restructuring and encourage trade within the WAMZ and ECOWAS, member countries should seek to eliminate institutional barriers to trade. The continuous and faster implementation of structural reforms is a necessary precondition for an increase in openness in trade.

Notes

1 The ratio of intra-regional trade to GDP is an indicator that measures the degree of openness. It is measured as the total trade of a member country with the regional or zonal grouping over the GDP of the member country.
2 This means exports on a narrow range of categories of goods and services, or exports to a narrow range of countries. The higher the degree of export concentration, the more liable are a country's balance of trade and national income to disruption by fluctuations in the sectors of concentration.
3 Data were not available for The Gambia, Guinea and Sierra Leone.
4 A natural trading partner is a country with whom another country's trade is likely to be large, because of low transport or other trade costs between them (Deardoff and Stern, 1994).
5 See Lipsey (1960) and Summers (1990) for the volume of trade criterion for natural trading partners.
6 The trade complementarity (TC) index can provide useful information on prospects for intra-regional trade in that it shows how well the structures of a country's imports and exports match. It also has the attraction that its values for countries considering the formation of a regional trade agreement can be compared with others that have formed or tried to form similar arrangements. The TC between countries k and j is defined as:

$$TCij = 100 - \text{sum } (|mik - xij|/2)$$

where xij is the share of good i in global exports of country j and mik is the share of good i in all imports of country k. The index is zero when no goods are exported by one country or imported by the other and 100 when the export and import shares exactly match.

148   *T.W. Oshikoya* et al.

References

Deardorff, A. and Stern, R.M. (1994). "Multilateral Trade Negotiations and Preferential Trade Arrangements", in *Analytical and Negotiating Issues in the Global Trading System*, Ann Arbor: University of Michigan Press.

ECOWAS Commision (2007). Report on Trade.

ECOWAS Commission (2007b). Infrastructure Department Report.

ECOWAS Commission (2008). Statistics Dept Report.

Gambia (2008). Ministry of Trade, Industry and Employment, Desk Reports.

Ghana (2007). GCNet (Ghana Limited) pamphlet, www.ghanatradenet.com/home.

Ghana (2008a). Customs, Excise and Preventive Service Report.

Ghana (2008b). Ministry of Trade and Industry, Desk Reports.

Guinea (2007). Ministry of Transport Report.

Guinea (2008). Ministry of Trade, Guinea, Desk Reports.

Lipsey, R. (1960). "The Theory of Customs Unions: A General Survey", *Economic Journal*, 70, 498–513.

Nigeria (2002). Port Reform Progress Report.

Nigeria (2005). "Port Reform Draft", *Containerisation International*, 2 November.

Nigeria (2007). Customs Service, Report on Revenue Outcome.

Schiff, M. (1993). "Small is Beautiful: Preferential Trade Agreements and the Impact of Country Size, Market Share, Efficiency and Trade Policy", Washington, DC: World Bank. Online: http://ideas.repec.org/p/wbk/wbrwps/1668.html.

Schiff, M. (2001). "Will the Real 'Natural Trading Partner' Please Stand Up?", *Journal of Economic Integration*, 16(2).

Summers, L. (1991). "Regionalism and the World Trading System: A Symposium on Policy Implications of Trade and Currency Zones", in Nihal Pitigala (ed.), *What Does Regional Trade in South Asia Reveal about Future Trade Integration? Some Empirical Evidence World Bank International Trade Division*. Online: http://papers.ssrn.com/sol3/papers.cfm?abstract_id=654524.

UNCTAD (2008). *Handbook of Statistics*. Online: www.unctad.org/Templates/Page.asp?intItemID=1890&lang=1.

WAMI (2007). *Report on Recent Developments and Status of the Emerging Common Market in the West African Monetary Zone (WAMZ)*, Accra, Ghana: WAMI.

WAMI (2008). *Convergence Report*. Online: www.wami-imao.org.

Wonnacott, P. and Lutz, M. (1989). "Is there a Case for Free Trade Areas?", in J.J. Schott (ed.), *Free Trade Areas and U.S Trade Policy*, Washington, DC: Institute of International Economics, pp. 59–84.

World Bank (2008a). *Doing Business Report*. Online: www.doingbusiness.org/EconomyRanking.

World Bank (2008b). *World Development Indicators*, Washington, DC: World Bank.

World Bank (2009). *International Economics and Trade in East Asia and Pacific*, Washington, DC: World Bank.

World Economic Forum (2009). *Global Competitiveness Report*. Online: www.weforum.org/en/initiatives/gcp/Global%20Competitiveness%20Report/index.htm.

Yeats, A. (1998). "What Can Be Expected from African Regional Trade Arrangements? Some Empirical Evidence", *Policy Research Working Paper*, no. 2004, World Bank.

8 Financial integration

Temitope W. Oshikoya, Abdoulaye Barry and Emmanuel Adamgbe

Introduction

Financial integration is an important element of any regional integration process, especially for a monetary union. According to Wakeman-Linn and Wagh (2008), "regional financial integration refers to a process, market driven and/or institutionalized, that broadens and deepens financial links within a region". The financial sector must be adequately prepared to promote financial inclusion[1] and to sustain a changeover to a new currency. The sector itself is at the heart of the market economy, playing a major role in intermediating savings and investments. This can be facilitated by "eliminating barriers to cross-border investments and differential treatment of foreign investors" (Wakeman-Linn and Wagh, 2008, p. 2). The depth and quality of an integrated financial market can also enhance a broad range of choices for savings, investments, thereby facilitating economic growth within the currency area.

Integration of the financial markets in the WAMZ, in particular, would allow adjustment to asymmetric shocks.[2] In other words, as noted by De Grauwe (2000), an integrated market provides a risk-sharing mechanism for risks occasioned by a negative shock. Negative shocks in one area of the Zone could be mitigated by a compensating variation in the other parts.

The financial sector, in particular the money market, is also an important transmission mechanism for implementing monetary policies. An integrated financial market is, therefore, essential for an efficient and effective monetary policy, as it ensures an even distribution of liquidity and similar levels of short-term interest rates across the currency zone. A well-integrated financial market could also promote financial stability, since financial risks could become easily shared.

However, on the side of caution, financial integration poses the challenge of engendering financial contagion arising from the pass-through effect of an external shock (Wakeman-Linn and Wagh, 2008). Anecdotal evidence suggests that the economies of WAMZ member countries were anything but insulated from the impact of the 2007–2009 global financial crisis.[3]

The WAMZ programme for financial integration encapsulates: full capital account liberalization; cross-listing of stocks; regional currency convertibility/

quoting and trading in WAMZ currencies; harmonization of banking supervision practices; and cross-border payments systems.[4] The WAMZ programme is consistent with a certain minimum set of pre-requisites associated with functioning regional markets (Addo, 2007; Wakeman-Linn and Wagh 2008[5]).

In the WAMZ, cross-border transactions have been hampered by fragmented regulatory regimes. Banking markets are still expanding with limited use of banking products across borders.[6] Insurance markets are localized within country boundaries. Capital markets are not yet integrated[7] and bond markets are underdeveloped. Elimination of these obstacles is not impossible as "over time, cohesion of regulatory frameworks, operational structures, and information systems, and convergence of prices and risk assessments mean that national financial markets within the region effectively function as one" (Wakeman-Linn and Wagh, 2008, p. 2).

The regional financial structure

This section provides a detailed picture of the financial structure in the WAMZ with the aim of putting into perspective the fragmented nature of the region's financial structure.

Evolution of the financial sector in the WAMZ

In the era prior to the late 1990s, the WAMZ financial sector was generally repressed as a result of controls that were intended to bring about development in certain preferred sectors. The financial sectors were characterized by state-owned financial institutions, which dominated the banking industry. These institutions became distressed following the accumulation of non-performing assets and bailout failures. Privatization programmes were instituted in the aftermath of financial sector reforms that embodied liberalization. The phenomenon saw a rapid growth in the number of institutions, especially in banking.

Although the financial sector is thin[8] in *The Gambia*, even this small country by 2008 had 11 banks, including an Islamic development bank with a total of 44 branches. The majority of the banks are foreign-owned. With provisional approval given to additional banks, the total number of banks is expected to increase in future. As of 2008, the insurance sector had nine insurance companies, while microfinance is becoming more prevalent, with about 62 microfinance institutions (MFIs) – five finance companies (FCs) and 57 credit unions and village savings and credit associations (VISACAs) – operating in the country.[9]

In *Ghana*, reforms (Brownbridge and Gockel, 1996; Lawfields Consulting, 2009) resulted in a shift of the financial sector away from a shallow[10] and distressed banking system dominated largely by foreign and public banks. Private banks emerged to foster and enhance financial intermediation, while insurance business is burgeoning into an important source for risk mitigation and as an alternative investment outlet. According to the Bank of Ghana (BoG) Annual

Report 2007, the total number of major banks by 2007 stood at 24, and all met the minimum capital requirement for universal banking business. Rural and community banks[11] stood at 126 at the end of 2007. There were 35 insurance companies, 41 non-bank financial institutions (NBFIs) in operation, comprising 21 FCs, 14 savings and loans companies, four leasing companies, one mortgage finance company and one discount house (DH) which was granted approval to change its status to a finance house.

In *Guinea*, there are eight commercial banks but services are concentrated in the capital, Conakry, with contributions from branches and subsidiaries of foreign or regional banks.

In *Nigeria*, the number of banks grew from just over ten banks in 1980 to over 100 banks by 1995. Buoyed by reforms in 2007, the Nigerian financial system comprised, among other institutions, 24 deposit money banks (DMBs), five DHs, 709 microfinance banks (MFBs), 112 FCs, 93 primary mortgage institutions (PMIs), five development finance institutions (DFIs) and 77 insurance companies (CBN Annual Report, 2007).

In *Sierra Leone*, the banking and financial landscape has expanded, with 13 commercial banks (ten are subsidiaries of foreign banks) with a total of 58 branches, two DHs, six community banks, about ten insurance companies and several other financial outfits including eight MFIs and a recently opened mortgage finance institution fully owned by the National Social Security and Insurance Trust (NASSIT) (BSL, 2007). MFIs in Sierra Leone are, however, not licensed by the Bank of Sierra Leone (BSL) but are monitored by Microfinance Investment and Technical Assistance Facility (MITAF) and there are no prescribed capital requirements.

Box 8.1 Recreating the financial system in post-conflict Sierra Leone

The Financial Sector Assessment Programme (FSAP) prepared in 2006 by the International Monetary Fund (IMF) and World Bank had revealed that the financial system in Sierra Leone was inadequately prepared to provide adequate support to the private sector, there was a significant level of financial exclusion and the obstacles transcended the financial sector.

Some of the bottlenecks were evident in poor infrastructure as well as institutional, administrative and legal impediments that characterize the conduct of banking and financial transactions. In addition, there was an inadequacy of skilled professionals, insufficient technological resources and financial illiteracy in the products and procedures of a broadened financial system. Thus, the reform as embodied in the Financial Sector Development Programme (FSDP) is intended to recreate the sector through:

- strengthening the commercial banking system;
- building a comprehensive rural financial system comprising MFIs, community banks and a strong commercial bank branch network;
- strengthening short-term financial markets and monetary policy;
- strengthening the enabling environment:

- microeconomic stability
- legal and regulatory
- strengthening contractual and long-term savings – NASSIT; insurance industry;
- strengthening the BSL and its banking supervision function.

The strategy for realizing the financial sector reforms would focus on:

- proper sequencing of the reform programme by taking cognizance of national characteristics as well as initial conditions precedent to the reforms;
- developing long-term financing options that would strengthen rural access to financial services;
- improving financial services technology and infrastructure designed to promote efficiency through real-time funds transfer and to improve monetary policy management and banking supervision;
- enhancing domestic savings mobilization to support investment, and restructuring of payment systems and developing the capital markets;
- strengthening corporate governance in financial institutions by implementing code of ethics for directors and managers;
- strengthening and/or creating institutions (i.e. commercial courts, credit bureaux) that support financial reforms; and
- developing comprehensive public debt management strategies and deepening financial markets.

It is expected that the reform programme will quickly prepare the financial sector for better intermediation.

Source: Bank of Sierra Leone (2006)

The banking sector in West Africa has always been localized and cross-border movements have not been evident. Although foreign ownership of banks was prevalent by the late 1980s, banks in the ECOWAS member countries availed themselves of the opportunities created by the promotion of trade and economic integration by ECOWAS to bolster their competitiveness by establishing an expanded branch network.[12]

The upsurge in the number of financial institutions in some countries provided linkage effects to the development of capital markets as alternative sources of financing investments. Insurance markets also evolved as a means for galvanizing synergy for risk mitigation and, recently, as a counterfactual investment source to the banking and stock markets.

Obviously, the growth of these financial institutions has not been symmetrical across the member countries. For instance, the domestic bonds market as well as the equities segment is shallow at the regional level.[13] Where they exist these markets are fragmented even with a regional arrangement in place. Participants include the regulators, the stock and insurance brokers and companies.

Structure of the WAMZ financial sector

Financial depth and size of the banking system

The distribution of deposit-taking (commercial) banks in the WAEMU and WAMZ that constitute the 15 ECOWAS member countries as of December 2007 is shown in Table 8.1a.

The rapid growth of the industry had been largely informed by the regulatory reforms that engendered cross-border establishment of bank subsidiaries and the consolidation in the Nigerian banking industry arising from increased capital requirements which have engendered the synergy for these banks to seek additional markets in other West African countries.

The location dynamics of the cross-border subsidiaries had been influenced mainly by perceived market interest. Table 8.1b indicates that, with the exception of Standard Chartered and Stanbic Banks, nine banks within the Zone have a cross-border presence. GT Bank, Zenith Bank and United Bank for Africa have subsidiaries in three other member countries.[14] Other banks with a growing presence in the sub-region include Intercontinental Bank, Skye Bank, Access Bank, Bank PHB and Oceanic Bank.

The actual size of the banking industry in the two regions[15] in West Africa is significantly different as the minimum capital base of the banks differs among the countries, ranging from Nigerian banks with a minimum of approximately US$200 million to US$2 million in the WAEMU member countries,

---

Box 8.2 Ghana's quest to become a financial services hub

The Financial Sector Strategic Plan (FINSSP) is the government of Ghana's blueprint for reforming Ghana's financial sector development for the period 2004–2008. The vision of FINSSP is to establish "a financial sector that is efficient in the mobilization and allocation of funds, fully integrated with the global financial system and supported by an effective regulatory system that promotes a high degree of confidence". To realize this vision, five key objectives were identified in FINSSP. Each objective drives a set of strategic initiatives designed to facilitate achievement of the objective.

The objectives of FINSSP were to:

- make Ghana the preferred source of finance for domestic companies;
- promote efficient savings mobilization;
- enhance the competitiveness of Ghana's financial institutions within a regional and global setting;
- ensure a stronger and more facilitative regulatory regime;
- achieve a diversified domestic financial sector within a competitive environment.

A stakeholder Forum was held in December 2007 to develop a roadmap for the preparation of an updated FINSSP document to guide financial sector development for the next five years. The Forum agreed on the following next steps:

- • an impact analysis of FINSSP would be carried out, to provide the empirical basis for an updated FINSSP;
- • preparation of a strategic framework, recommendations and action plans for stakeholder consideration and adoption by government.

A new strategic plan, FINSSP II, will soon be put in place to consolidate the gains achieved under FINSSP which ended by 2008 and generally reflect the government broad policy objectives for the financial sector.

Source: Ghana (2008b)

Nigerian banks dominate the banking industry in the WAMZ – seven in The Gambia, five in Ghana, one in Guinea and five in Sierra Leone, as shown in Table 8.1b. They are growing their subsidiary network across the region, predominantly in the English-speaking countries where language is not a limitation and traditional affiliations are stronger. The majority of the banks in the WAMZ member countries have their branch networks within national boundaries.

In spite of the significant growth of the banking sector, financial depth has largely remained steady over the last decade, as shown in Table 8.2. With increased growth in the economies of most of the WAMZ countries, numbers suggest weak intermediation in the banking sector. At this level, further efficiency in the intermediation process is expected, especially for Guinea, Nigeria and Sierra Leone. The traditional intermediation roles of banks had been subdued in favour of lucrative arbitrage gains in the foreign exchange markets. Recent anecdotal evidence points to room for cross-border arbitrage in the Zone and calls for a review of various exchange rate arrangements within the Zone to stem volatility in the markets.

Ultimately, the integration of West Africa demands a synthesis of the financial system of the WAMZ with that of the WAEMU. It is expected that the two zones will merge to form a single economic bloc. With regional banks springing up across the West African sub-region, the introduction of a single currency will be a further catalyst to the integration of the financial sector in the sub-region.

Table 8.1a Distribution of commercial banks in West Africa

WAEMU		*WAMZ plus Liberia and Cape Verde*	
Benin	22	Cape Verde	23
Burkina Faso	13	The Gambia	11
Guinea Bissau	2	Guinea	8
Mali	14	Liberia	5
Niger	9	Nigeria	24
Côte D'Ivoire	18	Ghana	24
Senegal	14	Sierra Leone	13
Togo	11		
Total	103	Total	108

Sources: World Bank (2007) and WAMI (2008).

Table 8.1b Cross-border banking in WAMZ – locations of subsidiaries

	Home supervisor	The Gambia	Ghana	Guinea	Nigeria	Sierra Leone
Stanchart	UK	✓	✓		✓	
Ecobank	TOGO	✓	✓	✓	✓	✓
GT Bank	NGN	✓	✓		✓	✓
Intercontinental	NGN		✓		✓	
First International	GMB	✓		✓		✓
Stanbic	ZAF	✓	✓		✓	✓
Zenith	NGN	✓	✓		✓	✓
United Bank for Africa	NGN	✓	✓		✓	
Oceanic Bank	NGN	✓	✓		✓	
Access Bank	NGN	✓			✓	✓
Skyle Bank	NGN	✓			✓	✓
Bank PHB	NGN	✓			✓	

Sources: World Bank (2007) and WAMI (2008).

Table 8.2 Level of financial depth in the WAMZ

	2000	2001	2002	2003	2004	2005	2006	2007	2008	*Average*
Broad money supply (in % of GDP)										
The Gambia	36.8	36.1	43.5	45.9	44.3	44.3	44.3	44.3	44.3	42.2
Ghana	26.7	26.9	31.4	32.0	32.7	33.1	32.9	32.9	32.9	30.8
Guinea	10.8	11.3	12.6	15.0	17.4	16.2	14.8	13.0	11.6	14.0
Nigeria	22.1	19.4	23.4	21.5	20.7	18.9	21.0	22.1	22.9	21.0
Sierra Leone	16.4	18.2	19.3	20.2	18.3	17.6	17.5	17.6	17.8	18.2

Source: WAMI (2008).

Financial soundness indicators

Evidence from financial soundness indicators suggest that financial vulnerabilities have been significantly lessened in recent times. In *The Gambia*, the financial sector has remained resilient and sound (WAMI, 2008). The banks were generally well capitalized with a capital adequacy ratio (CAR) of 21.6 per cent. The risk-weighted CAR improved by 12.8 percentage points from its level of 23.69 per cent in December 2007 to 35.87 per cent in December 2008. The increase was mainly occasioned by the addition of a new bank to the industry, which is yet to hold risky assets.

Evidence of declining profitability is observed as the annual return on assets (ROA) fell by 0.53 percentage points from the level in December 2007 to 1.22 per cent in December 2008. The developments perhaps reflected the intense competitive climate of the sector following new entrants into the industry.

The quality of assets also improved with the ratio of non-performing loans (NPL) to total loans declining to 9.45 per cent in 2008 relative to 13 per cent recorded in the previous year. This reflected the recovery of some previously non-performing loans, loan restructuring as well as enhancement of court orders by the Sheriff's department. NPL at 9.45 per cent are satisfactory by regional standards. However, the loan-to-deposit ratio (41 per cent) is relatively low in part due to high risk associated with the weak legal system.

In the case of *Ghana*, according to the BoG Annual Report 2007, the banking industry had generally been sound except in 2007 when one bank failed to comply with the required minimum CAR of 10 per cent. The industry average stood at 14.8 per cent as shown in Table 8.3. Although the banking industry is still profitable, the trend has been declining as a result of the rise in average total assets without a compensating growth in profit levels, due mainly to narrowing net interest spreads. The expenditure by banks on ICT re-engineering also subdued earnings performance. Asset quality improved with NPL to gross loans falling from 16.3 per cent in 2004 to 6.4 per cent in 2007, while banks' exposure to foreign exchange risks was stable. *Guinea*'s NPL have remained stable around 12 per cent per annum.

In *Nigeria*, the observed credit expansion in 2008 to the private sector raised credit quality concerns. Nigeria's NPL fell from 21.6 per cent in 2004 to 7.7 per cent (Table 8.4). Measured by Tier 1 Capital, *The Banker Magazine* reported that in 2007, 11 Nigerian banks ranked in the top 1,000 in the world, up from

Table 8.3 Ghana – financial soundness indicators

	2004	2005	2006	2007
Capital adequacy				
Regulatory capital ratio	13.9	16.2	15.8	14.8
Regulatory tier 1 capital ratio	17.3	16.2	15	13.6
Asset quality				
Non-performing loans to gross loans	16.3	13	7.9	6.4
Earnings and profitability				
ROA before taxes	5.8	4.6	4.8	3.7
ROE before taxes (average)	33.7	23.6	39.6	35.8
Interest margin to gross income	62.9	64	51.8	46.1
Liquidity				
Core liquid assets to total assets ratio	25.4	20.7	23.5	23.4
Exposure to foreign exchange risk				
Share of foreign liabilities in total liabilities	2.8	2.4	4	8.1

Sources: IMF (2008) and Bank of Ghana (2008).

seven in 2006. Afrinvest (2008) reported that by end 2007, capital of up to seven Nigerian banks was in excess of US$1 billion, while over ten banks had a total market value exceeding US$2 billion each. In terms of profitability, the banking industry recorded ROA of 3.89 in 2007, the highest since 2004 and return on equity of 23.8 per cent, the highest in the last three years. The market value of these banks, however, plummeted in 2008 following the collapse of the stock exchange due to shocks emanating from the global financial crisis.

Table 8.4 Nigeria – financial soundness indicators

	2004	2005	2006	2007
Capital adequacy				
Regulatory capital ratio	14.7	17.8	22.6	18.6
Regulatory tier 1 capital ratio	13.4	16.5	21.8	17.5
Asset quality				
Non-performing loans to gross loans	21.6	18.1	8.8	7.7
Earnings and profitability				
ROA before taxes	3.1	1.85	1.6	3.89
ROE before taxes (average)	27.4	12.97	10.6	23.84
Interest margin to gross income	54.37	55.9	10.6	23.84
Liquidity				
Core liquid assets to total assets ratio			61.1	62.2
Exposure to foreign exchange risk				
Share of foreign currencies deposits in total liabilities	–	–	–	–
Share of foreign liabilities in total liabilities		5.9	12.5	6.7

Source: IMF (2008) and Central Bank of Nigeria (2008).

In *Sierra Leone*, as shown in Table 8.5, the banking industry's NPL rose from 26.8 per cent in 2005 to 31.7 per cent in 2007. However, relative soundness of the banking system has been achieved due to the improvement in the regulatory environment and the attempts by the central bank to comply with Basel Core Principles (BCPs).

Box 8.3 Nigeria financial sector reforms: a catalyst for growth

In line with Nigeria's goal to become one of the top 20 economies in the world by 2020, the Central Bank of Nigeria (CBN) initiated a strategy to implement a financial system that would transform Nigeria into an international financial centre and provide the safest and the fastest-growing financial system among emerging economies.

The strategy, known as the Financial System Strategy 2020 (FSS 2020), is the blueprint for achieving the goals of developing and transforming Nigeria's financial sector into a growth catalyst, and propelling Nigeria into an international financial centre (IFC). Nigeria's large population makes the country one of the largest markets in the world and is one of the identified 'Next 11' (N11) countries with the potential to become like Brazil, Russia, India and China (BRIC). In addition, Nigeria is centrally located in the middle of Africa and midway between the United States and Asia. Nigeria's GDP is about 80 per cent of the total GDP of the 15 countries that make up ECOWAS.

To accomplish these goals, it has been recognized that there is a need for the concurrent strengthening of the domestic financial markets and enhancement of the sector's integration with external financial markets. The objective is to successfully develop the financial sector such that Nigeria would be the natural destination in West Africa for financial products and services, and also the ideal point for channelling investments to other parts of the economy. The FSS 2020 is an outgrowth of the various reforms of the federal government and the financial sector of Nigeria.

The objectives of FSS 2020 are to:

- develop a shared vision and an integrated strategy for the nation's financial system;
- develop market and infrastructure strategies that would align fully with the strategic intent of the overall system;
- create a performance measurement framework and evolve a partnership of all key stakeholders to implement the strategy; and
- establish a harmonious and collaborative environment for the development and delivery of the strategy.

The CBN under the FSS 2020 intends to transform Lagos into an IFC by creating the Lekki International Financial Corridor (LFC). With no African city occupying the top 46 IFCs, as reported by the Global Financial Centre Index (GFCI), there is a clear opportunity for the LFC to be a successful IFC.

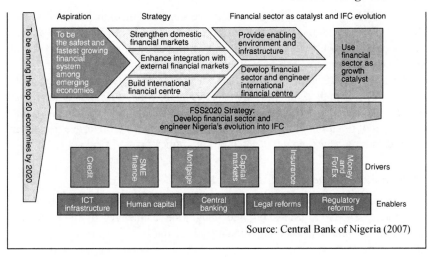

Source: Central Bank of Nigeria (2007)

The non-bank financial sector in the WAMZ

The institutions in the non-bank financial sector of the WAMZ are widespread and bridge the gap between the formal and informal sectors in the Zone. Regulation of the non-bank financial sector is generally influenced by the level of complexities of the financial system. The supervisory oversight on these institutions is not homogeneous and is exercised by central banks, finance ministries or a specialized agency set for this purpose. Measures were initiated and implemented to streamline the activities of these institutions from the hitherto weak growth due to low capitalization.

Table 8.5 Sierra Leone – financial soundness indicators

	2004	2005	2006	2007
Capital adequacy				
Regulatory capital ratio	–	–	–	–
Regulatory tier 1 capital ratio	38.13	35.73	36.02	38.74
Asset quality				
Non-performing loans to gross loans	16.52	26.83	27.1	31.69
Earnings and profitability				
ROA before taxes	9.9	8.12	5.84	3.05
ROE before taxes (average)	32.92	27.95	21.09	10.28
Interest margin to gross income	–	–	–	–
Liquidity				
Core liquid assets to total assets ratio	35.9	38.89	32.07	26.77
Exposure to foreign exchange risk				
Share of foreign currencies deposits in total liabilities	20.83	23.31	24.57	27.47
Share of foreign liabilities in total liabilities	21.07	23.79	25.19	27.97

Source: Bank of Sierra Leone (2007).

The NBFIs are the financial bedrock of the small and medium-scale enterprises (SMEs). SMEs are important drivers for growth and a conduit for poverty alleviation. Deepening the financial sector with improved savings per household and significant reduction of cash in circulation through the introduction of innovative products would strengthen the financial industry. For instance, the upsurge in the number of MFIs in the Zone is clearly an attestation to the robustness of the contributions of this sector. With the expansion in the banking industry, commensurate absorption of the informal sector into the formal sector would improve the gathering of data for a better economic and monetary policy management.

The non-bank financial markets in the WAMZ

This section essentially presents a detailed review of the capital, inter-bank and insurance markets. It brings out the integration challenges of these markets within the overall financial integration agenda of the Zone.

Box 8.4 Moves towards financial sector soundness: credit information markets in the WAMZ

In order to maintain financial sector soundness, member countries in the WAMZ are in the process of facilitating the establishment of credit reference bureaux. The bureaux would be expected under the enabling law to collate and maintain data for the formation of credit histories, process credit-related data and deliver credit reports based partly or fully on information not in the public domain. Credit bureaux are essential elements of the financial infrastructure that facilitate access to finance. A borrower's credit history provides information for objective decision-making on whether or not to grant credit. There are basically two types of credit bureaux:

- the public credit bureau, which is usually owned and operated by the government through its agent;
- the private sector-owned credit bureau.

In The Gambia, a Credit Reference Bureau has been set up in the Central Bank of The Gambia (CBG) with the aim of eliminating the number of non-performing creditors. This framework is publicly owned and similar to the CBN's Credit Risk Management System (CRMS).

In Ghana, the credit bureau is private sector-driven and is regulated under the Credit Reporting Act 2007 (Act 726), which defines the authority under which any body corporate incorporated in Ghana shall be eligible to apply for a licence to engage solely in credit reference bureau activities in Ghana. No licence would be granted for the operation of a credit reference bureau, if a financial institution or a debt-collection agency has 10 per cent or more of the voting rights in the proposed credit reference bureau. The BoG shall grant a licence to carry on the business of credit reference bureau if the proposed entity:

- has the human, financial and operational resources to enable it to function efficiently and perform its functions effectively in accordance with the Credit Reporting Act 2007 (Act 726);

- has premises suitable for the intended lines of business;
- has put in place adequate security systems to protect data;
- presents plans to adopt mechanisms to gather, input, integrate, update, validate and provide adequate security for data;
- presents a credible plan to develop and adopt procedures to ensure that:
- questions, concerns and complaints of credit information subjects, or
- data providers are treated equitably and consistently in a timely and efficient manner.

In Nigeria, given the legal backing from the CBN Act, the CBN had been operating a CRMS. The *modus operandi* of the CRMS raised a number of concerns regarding coverage, privacy infringement and the morality of CBN's role as well as integrity issues, among others, and led to the need for the establishment of a private credit bureau as an additional tool that would enhance monitoring of credit exposure of banks. Consequently, Section 57 of the CBN Act 2007 empowered the CBN to license and regulate private credit bureaux in Nigeria. Operational guidelines relating to licensing and operational and regulatory requirements for private sector-run credit bureaux in Nigeria have been issued by the CBN with contributions from various stakeholders. Unlike the CBN CRMS, privately run credit bureaux would cover all sectors of the economy and provide credit reports on all individuals or corporate bodies enjoying any type of facility in the country. Thus, the private sector-run credit bureaux complement the CBN CRMS in the monitoring of credits in the financial system.

Source: CBN (2008)

Capital markets

Ghana, Nigeria and Sierra Leone have established stock exchanges. They operate within the confines of the national boundaries and have few linkages to other WAMZ member countries.

The Ghana Stock Exchange (GSE) was formed on 25 July 1989 and opened for trading on 12 November 1990 with 11 companies listed that year. Both equities and debt securities are listed on the exchange, with government bonds dominating the debt offerings. On the equities side, as at the end of December 2007 the GSE had about 34 quoted firms listed on the GSE. Expressed as a percentage of market capitalization, trade in a given year was extremely low, despite the distortion to the absolute numbers due to the inclusion of AngloGold Ashanti, which accounted for a high proportion of the market's capitalization.

Trading on the GSE occurs daily on the floor of the exchange. However, over-the-counter trading was permitted in the case of the AngloGold Ashanti shares. The GSE hitherto utilized a manual Continuous Auction Trading (CAT) system, and transited to an automated trading platform by the end of 2007. The GSE has an intra-day market cap on price movements of +/–5 per cent of previous day's close except when a transaction involves more than 100,000 shares or shares worth ¢100 million or more. Delivery is on a delivery versus payment basis with a settlement period of T+3 business days. A central depository system, initially run by the central bank but now run autonomously under Central Securities Depository Ltd (CSD), was introduced. Although CSD handles only government securities, a bill empowering it to handle equities was passed by the parliament of Ghana in February 2007.

Sierra Leone was assisted by the Commonwealth Secretariat for the establishment of a stock exchange. Trust Bank of The Gambia was listed on the GSE and has established an over-the-counter market in The Gambia to cater for investors in the equity shares of Trust Bank. Market capitalization of these stock exchanges is low compared to those of the advanced countries. There are no arrangements for cross-listing of stocks among the stock exchanges in the WAMZ.

The Nigeria Stock Exchange (NSE) was established on 15 September 1960 and commenced operations on 5 June 1961. The exchange is categorized into the first- and second-tier markets. By the first quarter of 2009, there were 213 equity and debt securities listed on the exchange, down from 228 listings in 2006, with government bonds dominating the debt offerings. According to Okereke-Onyiuke (2009), market capitalization, which stood at N10.283 trillion in January 2008, nosedived to N7.4 trillion by November 2008.[16] The banking sector is the most dominant on the market and constitutes about 60 per cent of the market capitalization of the top 20 companies.

In terms of cross-listings, the NSE had two companies cross-listed on other exchanges – Ecobank Transnational Incorporated on the Bourse Regionale des Valeurs Mobilieres (BVRM) and GSE, and Oando on the Johannesburg Stock Exchange (JSE). By the first quarter of 2009, total foreign listing on the exchange stood at 23. This cross-market linkage implies that the exchange is an important conduit for the transmission of global spill-overs.

The market is regulated by the Securities and Exchange Commission (SEC) and the NSE. The SEC is the apex government regulatory agency of the capital market while NSE is a Self Regulatory Organization (SRO) with members paying for their supervision.

In order to attain international best practice in capital market regulation, the SEC endorsed, adopted and integrated many of the international regulatory conventions and practices in its regulatory framework. In recognition of its efforts to effectively regulate the market, SEC Nigeria qualified as Appendix 'A' Signatory to the International Organization of Securities Commissions Multilateral Memorandum of Understanding (MMOU).

Trading on the NSE occurs daily and utilizes an automated real-time trading platform, with remote trading permitted by dealing members. The NSE places an intra-day cap on price movements of +/–5 per cent of previous days' close. The Central Securities Clearing System Ltd operates a computerized clearing and settlement system which acts as a depository for stock transactions with a settlement period of T+3 business days.

In an attempt to boost the growth of the capital markets in West Africa, a technical committee, made up of experts from the stock exchanges and SECs in the sub-region and WAMI staff, was set up to spearhead mechanisms for the harmonization of activities of the exchanges to ensure the operation of integrated exchanges through cross trading in the first instance, and promote cross-listing of stocks in a unified regional market.

The inter-bank and money markets

The money market is characterized by activities of the commercial banks. They purchase government debt instruments and the central banks' monetary policy management instruments with overnight or short-time maturity. Inter-bank advances are appreciable while institutional investors, such as pension funds, also participate on a limited scale. Discount houses are not major players in the money market. The instruments offered in the market transcend both short and long tenured which are either used for monetary policy or to procure government debt.

In The Gambia, activities in the inter-bank market intensified with almost all the banks actively involved, and banks use their treasury bills held at the CBG as collateral. As an evolving market, the volume of transactions grew from D575.0 million in 2007 to D1,075.5 million in 2008 reflecting an 87.04 per cent increase. This development is expected to further enhance liquidity management. However, the lucrative yield on treasury bills will challenge the deepening of inter-bank transactions. This may stifle private sector credit and undermine growth.

In Guinea, the money market consists of treasury bills of 28- to 182-days, offered through an auction mechanism. The government mainly used these instruments to finance its deficit. Government long-term bonds were also hith-erto issued.

Nigeria has a relatively robust money and inter-bank market with a wide range of instruments. The inter-bank and money market in Sierra Leone is char-acterized by four main instruments, namely, 91-day, 182-day and 364-day treas-ury bills and one-year treasury bonds. The principal investors include the commercial banks, NASSIT, discount houses, other financial institutions and individuals. The development of the inter-bank market is being hampered by the absence of clear-cut rules and regulations governing its *modus operandi*.

Insurance markets

The insurance sector in the WAMZ consists of licensed life and non-life insur-ance companies as well as licensed insurance brokers and loss adjusters. The market consists of over 150 life and non-life companies. The Gambia has nine insurance companies with a total industry gross annual premium as at end 2007 of US$7.3 million. The market share of the top three insurance companies is 57 per cent as shown in Table 8.6. At this level of operation, these insurance com-panies would find it challenging making cross-border penetration into either the Nigerian or Ghanaian markets. As shown in Tables 8.7, 8.8 and 8.9, Nigeria has the largest number with a little above 100 licensed insurance companies. The gross annual industry premiums for Nigeria in 2006 stood at US$673 million with the market share of the top ten companies around 58 per cent. In Ghana, there are around 35 life and non-life insurance companies with a total gross annual premium of US$168 million. The top ten insurance companies in Ghana make up 75 per cent of the total market share. In both Ghana and Nigeria, the life and non-life insurance companies are licensed separately.

The capital requirements for insurance companies in Nigeria differ significantly from those of The Gambia, Ghana, Guinea and Sierra Leone. The requirement for The Gambia is less than US$0.68 million. The capital is respectively US$1 million and US$2.5 million for direct insurance and re-insurance in Ghana, while for Nigeria it is around US$17 million, US$25 million and US$83 million, respectively, for life, non-life and re-insurance. In Sierra Leone, it is put at about US$80,000. This regulatory arbitrage according to a recent World Bank/WAMI study poses competitive difficulties for entry into the Nigerian and Ghanaian markets and perhaps a stumbling block to the realization of free entry and the promotion of cross-border trade in services.

Insurance laws and regulations vary greatly, with Ghana having a generally flexible framework law, the Insurance Act of 2003. The Act does not contain hard-core issues of regulation as it is in the case of Nigeria. Nigeria's Insurance Act 2003 incorporates issues of regulation in addition to the issuance of policy guidelines on a yearly basis.[17]

On the supervisory front, Ghana and Nigeria are supervised by a National Insurance Commission. The pension segment in Nigeria, since the pensions reform in 2006, is supervised by the Pensions Commission. In The Gambia and Guinea, the regulation and supervision of insurance business is the responsibility of the central banks. In a bid to improve the efficiency of the financial system in The Gambia, the central bank was empowered by the 1997 constitution to assume the regulation and supervision of insurance institutions. The Insurance Act 1974 was amended to substantially revamp its provisions, culminating in the Insurance Act 2003. The new set of regulations created under the present Act sets out the basic requirements on paid-up capital, deposits for every class of business, the amount of solvency margin and components of its calculation as well as investment requirements, among others. In Sierra Leone, the Insurance Commission regulates the insurance sector. There are nine registered insurance companies. Supervision of the sector is also carried out by the Commissioner of Insurance within the Department of Finance.

Financial integration through the Banjul Declaration benchmarks

One important feature of the Banjul Action Plan for financial integration is to promote "similarity of access, rules and treatment" to all "potential market participants"[18] as the cornerstone towards full integration of all financial instruments. The review of developments and assessment in the WAMZ provides an insight into the extent to which the Banjul Benchmarks were able to remove structural

Table 8.6 The Gambia – insurance market information (amounts in US$ millions at period exchange rates)

Item	Detail	Local currency dalasis (million)	US$ (million)
Gross annual industry premiums	For the year ended 31 December 2007	161.9	7.3
Insurance companies	Average annual premiums (in parenthesis), Top 3 insurance companies	161.9(30.9)	7.3(1.4)
	Market share of top 3 insurance companies	57.2%	57.2%
	Total number of licensed insurers: 9		
	Average annual premiums for all insurers	18.0	0.8
	Average annual premiums for all insurers outside top 3	11.6	0.52
Existing 9 insurers (2007)	Great Alliance Insurance Co.	42.1	1.9
	Gamstar Insurance Co.	29.0	1.3
	International Insurance Co.	21.6	0.97
	London Gate Insurance	15.4	0.69
	Prime	14.5	0.65
	Global Security Insurance Co.	12.7	0.57
	Gambian National Insurance Co.	10.7	0.48
	New Vision Insurance Co.	10.6	0.48
	Sunshine Insurance Co.	5.4	0.24
Minimum capital requirements	Insurance capital for all direct insurance writers, for life insurance, non life insurance and combined licences	15	0.68
	Reinsurance licence	100	4.5
	Brokers' licence		
	Loss adjusters' licence		
Regulator	Central Bank of The Gambia		
Insurance laws and regulations	Insurance Act 2003		
	Insurance Regulations 2005		
	Insurance Amendment Act 2006 – supplementary legislation that covers the operation of Islamic insurers		

Source: Central Bank of The Gambia (2007).

Table 8.7 Ghana – insurance market information (amounts in US$ millions at period exchange rates)

Item	Detail	Local currency cedi (million)	US$ (million)
Gross annual industry premiums	For the year ended 31 December 2007	210	168
Insurance companies	Average annual premiums (in parenthesis), Top 10 insurance companies	158(15.8)	126.4(12.6)
	Market share of top 10 insurance companies	75%	75%
	Total number of licensed insurers: 35		
	Average annual premiums for all insurers	6	4.8
	Average annual premiums for all insurers outside top 10	2.1	1.7
Top 10 insurers (2007 if available)	SIC Insurance Company Ghana Limited	52.8	42.2
	SIC Life	21.2	17.0
	Enterprise Insurance	16.5	13.2
	Metropolitan Insurance	12.6	10.1
	Vanguard Assurance	11.2	9.0
	GLICO Life	10.7	8.5
	Enterprise Life Insurance	10.1	8.1
	Star Assurance	10.1	8.1
	Donewell Insurance	7.2	5.8
	Star Life	5.6	4.5
Minimum capital requirements	Insurance capital for all direct insurance writers, for life insurance, non life insurance and combined licences		1.0
	Reinsurance licence		2.5
	Brokers' licence		0.025
	Loss adjusters' licence		0.025
Regulator	National Insurance Commission		
Insurance Laws and Regulations	Insurance Act 2006		

Source: NIC (2008).

Table 8.8 Nigeria – insurance market information (amounts in US$ millions at period exchange rates)

Item	Detail	Local currency (naira) (billion)	US$ (million)
Gross annual industry premiums	For the year ending 31 December 2006	80.7	673
Insurance companies	Average annual premiums, top 10 insurance companies	46.4	387
	Market share of top 10 insurance companies	57.5%	57.5%
	Total number of licensed insurers: 77		
	Average annual premiums for all insurers	1.6	14
	Average annual premiums for all insurers outside top 10	0.9	7
Top 10 insurers (2006)	Nicon Insurance Plc.	14.9	124
	Industrial & General Insurance Co.	6.6	55
	Leadway Assurance Co.	5.7	48
	Intercontinental WAPIC Insurance Plc.	3.2	26
	Niger Insurance Plc.	3.1	26
	AIICO Insurance Plc.	3.0	25
	Cornerstone Insurance Plc.	2.7	23
	Goldlink Insurance Co.	2.6	22
	Royal Exchange Assurance Nigeria Plc.	2.4	20
	A&G Insurance Co. Ltd	2.2	18
Minimum capital requirements	Life insurance licence	2	17
	Non life insurance licence	3	25
	Reinsurance licence	10	83
	Insurance brokers' licence		
	Loss adjusters' licence		
Regulator	Insurance: National Insurance Commission (NAICOM)		
	Pensions Commission (PENCOM)		
Insurance laws and regulations	Insurance Act 2003		
	Decree No. 1 of 1997 and Insurance Decree No. 2 of 1997		
	Policy guidelines produced each year (2004 to 2008)		

Source: National Insurance Commission (NAICOM) (2008).

Table 8.9 Sierra Leone – insurance market information (Amounts in US$ millions at period exchange rates)

Item	Detail	Local currency (Le billion)	US$ (million)
Gross annual industry premiums	For year ended 31 December 2007	17.6	5.92
Insurance companies	Average annual premiums	2.2	0.7
	Market share:		
	National Insurance Company (SL) Ltd	24%	
	Aureole Insurance Company (SL) Ltd	31%	
	Reliance Insurance Trust Corporation	18%	
	International Insurance Company	10%	
	Marine & General Insurance Company	1%	
	Trans-world Insurance Company	7%	
	Medical & General Insurance Company	6%	
	Sierra Leone Insurance Company	3%	
Top insurers (2007) and annual gross premiums	National Insurance Company (SL) Ltd	4.2	1.4
	Aureole Insurance Company (SL) Ltd	5.5	1.8
	Reliance Insurance Trust Corporation	3.2	1.1
	International Insurance Company	1.8	0.6
	Marine & General Insurance Company	0.2	0.1
	Trans-world Insurance Company	1.2	0.4
	Medical & General Insurance Company	1.0	0.3
	Sierra Leone Insurance Company	0.5	0.2
Minimum capital requirements	Life insurance licence (Le million)	240	80,000
	Non life insurance (Le million)	240	80,000
	Reinsurance (Le million)	2,400	800,000
	Broker's licence (Le million)	5	1,667
Regulator	Sierra Leone Insurance Commission (SLICOM) established in 2004		
Insurance laws and regulations	Insurance Act 2000		

Source: Bank of Sierra Leone (2007).

obstacles to integration in clearing and settlement systems; to prevent practices that discriminate against foreign providers of financial services; and the removal of remaining differences in national financial regulations that would engender inefficient provision of financial services. The detailed developments and assessment are carried in five main components, namely, full capital account liberalization, cross listing of stocks, regional currency convertibility, effective banking supervision and integration of payments, clearing and settlement systems.

Full capital account liberalization by country

The Gambia

The Gambia has fully liberalized its external capital account. There are no restrictions on capital transactions, foreign direct investments (FDI), real estate transactions and personal capital transactions. No controls exist on the liquidation of direct investments. The fact that investors can move funds in and out of the country as and when they wish, without hindrance, to some extent, motivates prospective investors to move resources into the country. Although, in 2003, there was a regulation restricting individuals carrying physical cash (in foreign currency) outside The Gambia exceeding US$10,000, larger amounts could be transferred abroad through the banking system or other recognized channels.

There are no restrictions on capital or stock exchange markets and derivatives as well as government and central bank securities (treasury and central bank bills) in The Gambia. Thus, no controls exist for the allocation of treasury bills to individuals and institutions, irrespective of residency or nationality status. In addition, the central bank established open foreign exchange position limits for holdings of both resident and non-resident assets and liabilities. Furthermore, there are no restrictions on the repatriation of export proceeds or other funds and no controls exist on the opening of foreign currency deposit as long as prudential regulations are respected. Withdrawal charges, however, apply as a means to limit their utilization in the domestic economy.

Ghana

Capital transactions are partially controlled in Ghana. On real estate transactions, there are no restrictions on purchases abroad or locally by residents, but the banks must submit a report to the BoG. Non-residents, on the other hand, are allowed to own leaseholds of 50 years or lower and could also carry out sale locally without restriction except that banks are under obligation to send a report to the BoG.

Dealings in capital and money market transactions are subject to some restrictions. Regarding the issue of capital market instruments, prior approval is required from the SEC and the BoG. The transfer or repatriation of proceeds from sales must be reported to the BoG. On the purchase of capital market instruments by non-residents, there are no restrictions except for the banking sector where the acquisition of any stake greater than 10 per cent requires prior approval of the BoG. Dealings in shares, bonds and other debt instruments require prior approval by the central bank. There are, however, no restrictions on the purchase and issue abroad of capital market instruments by residents, except that banks must submit such transactions to the BoG. Similarly, the purchase of locally issued securities denominated in foreign exchange is allowed.

With respect to money market instruments, regulations do not allow non-residents (except holders of domestic currency accounts) to sell or issue, locally, money market instruments. Also, sales or issues of investment instruments, locally, by non-residents are allowed in instruments of a tenor of three years or above in the case of local purchase, while in the case of local issue prior approval is required from BoG. The transfer or repatriation of proceeds from such sales must be reported to the BoG. However, regarding residents who want to purchase these instruments from abroad, there are no restrictions except that banks must submit a report on such transactions to BoG. There are no restrictions on derivatives and other instruments, but banks must submit reports to the BoG. Commercial bank lending locally in foreign exchange to both residents and non-residents also require no approval from the central bank but banks must submit reports to the BoG.

Regarding FDI, there are no restrictions on outflows but banks must submit a report to the BoG; while, although there are no restrictions on inflows, investors who want to avail themselves of a number of incentives under the Ghana Investment Promotion Centre (GIPC) Act are required to register with the GIPC. Certain areas of economic activity are not open to foreigners; otherwise, for companies not listed on the GSE, non-resident participation requires a minimum equity injection ranging between US$10,000 and US$300,000 depending on the type of business and ownership structure of the company. The GIPC Act also prohibits expropriation of the assets of foreign investors. Although there are no restrictions on the repatriation of capital dividends or profits, banks are obliged to submit a report to the BoG.

Controls also exist on personal transactions, except transfers regarding gifts, endowments, inheritances and legacies to residents from non-residents and the transfer of assets into the country by immigrants. Foreign currency deposits are subject to reserve requirement which must be held with the central bank. Assets and liabilities in foreign exchange are subject to an open exposure limit, and investment in commercial banks by non-residents requires approval from the central bank. In addition, foreign-owned banks must have a minimum capital of ¢60 million, of which 60 per cent must consist of convertible currencies brought into Ghana. However, there are no provisions specific to institutional investors and no controls are imposed by securities laws.

Guinea

The investment code (Decree No. 001/PRG/87 of January 1987 as amended by Act L/95/029/CTRN of June 1995) provides the framework for free movement of capital (i.e. freedom to transfer capital and the protection of acquired rights). However, capital transactions are subject to a wide range of controls. With regard to transactions on capital accounts and money market instruments, all capital transfers through the official foreign exchange market require a prior approval from the central bank. There are controls on all credit and guarantee operations. Although inward direct investment has been liberalized, outward direct investment require authorization by the central bank. Personal capital transactions are regulated and the authorization of the central bank is required for real estate transactions.

Commercial and other credit institutions are subject to special provisions on borrowing abroad, maintenance of accounts abroad and lending locally in foreign exchange. There are also reserve requirements, interest rate and credit controls and investment regulations for banks and non-residents.

Nigeria

Capital account transactions are largely liberalized in Nigeria. No controls exist on derivatives, direct investment and real estate transactions. In addition, there are neither specific provisions to institutional investors nor other controls imposed by securities laws. The status of capital account in Nigeria followed a systematic reduction of restrictions on capital flows into the economy. Foreign investors are allowed to invest in government bonds and securities of not less than one year maturity, subject to the issuance of a Certificate of Capital Importation (CCI) by the processing bank. Also, foreign investors are allowed to invest directly in equity as well as in the capital market through a broker but they are to obtain a CCI as evidence of such investment.

The Nigerian Investment Promotion Commission (NIPC) Act enables foreign nationals and enterprises to freely invest in the operation of any enterprise in Nigeria, except for a few enterprises such as the production and dealing in drugs, arms manufacture, etc. The foreign investor may operate alone or in joint venture with Nigerians by means of a company, which must first be registered with the Corporate Affairs Commission (CAC), a body charged with the responsibility of regulating company affairs in accordance with the Companies and Allied Matters Act of 1990. Thereafter, the foreign investor is required to also register with the NIPC. However, a foreigner not wishing to establish a business may buy shares in any Nigerian company with convertible currency. There are no restrictions in areas of foreign participation and there are statutory guarantees against nationalization and expropriation. In all this, the investor is guaranteed unrestricted repatriation of proceeds. In the case of investment in government bonds/securities, a foreign investor can divest the investment before maturity by the transfer of the underlying CCI to the new investor. In addition, investors do have unfettered access to non-government securities, such as Bankers' Acceptances.

In terms of credit operations, foreign investors are allowed to extend loans to private Nigerian entities without restrictions. Such loans could either be in the form of capital or suppliers' credit and should be evidenced by the issuance of a

CCI to facilitate repayment of principal/interest. However, such loans are without government guarantee. To enable companies to meet temporary shortages of funds, licensed banks in Nigeria may grant loans or overdrafts to non-residents.

With effect from March 2006, Nigerian residents were allowed to invest in foreign currency denominated securities, subject to the repatriation of proceeds from such investment. The repatriated proceeds must be credited to the domiciliary account of the investor for own use and/or deepening the inter-bank market while Authorized Dealers are required to render monthly returns on the transaction to CBN. Holders of both ordinary and exports proceeds domiciliary accounts are guaranteed unrestricted access to the use of their funds. They are free to sell the funds to their bankers or any party of their choice by mere transfer instructions.

There are no controls on personal capital transactions including gifts, endowments inheritances and legacies from residents to non-residents. Similarly, transfers into and out of the country are not controlled. With the exception of money laundering and investment regulations, no specific provisions apply to commercial banks and other credit institutions. Open foreign exchange limits have also been established on the assets and liabilities of banking institutions.

Sierra Leone

There are some restrictions on capital account transactions. Regarding controls on capital and money market instruments, BSL approval is required before a security registered in or outside Sierra Leone may be transferred to or purchased by a non-resident. The sale of capital market instruments locally by non-residents is not permitted; residents require permission to purchase securities abroad or to transfer funds abroad for this purpose. Capital in respect of securities registered in Sierra Leone may not be transferred abroad without the expressed permission of the BSL.

With respect to money market instruments, purchases by non-residents are not permitted and residents also are not allowed to make such purchases with domestic resources. With respect to credit operations (financial) by residents to non-residents, BSL approval is required prior to the granting of any loans, either by way of advance or bank draft, to non-resident entities. Similarly loans and advances to residents from non-residents also require approval from BSL.

Regarding controls of FDI, outward movements (outflows) are not allowed. However, there are no controls on liquidation of direct investments. Residents are prohibited from purchasing real estate abroad and non-residents may do so with funds transferred through authorized dealers with proper documentation. Commercial banks and other credit institutions are not allowed to hold more than 25 per cent of their deposit liabilities in foreign currency and the maintenance of offshore accounts is restricted. Commercial banks are not engaged in lending to non-residents or extending credits locally in foreign exchange. There are, however, no restrictions on personal capital transactions or specific provisions to institutional investors.

Capital account liberalization across the WAMZ

From the foregoing, it is evident that most countries of the WAMZ are reforming their capital accounts to attain full liberalization. With The Gambia having
fully liberalized capital accounts, other countries are at various levels of liberalization. In the case of Ghana, further efforts would have to be made to remove
restrictions on personal transactions. The restrictions on sale or issue of money
market instruments locally by non-residents have to be reviewed, while surren-
der restrictions on cocoa export proceeds would require loosening. A relaxation
of the details of reporting and approval on capital account transactions to the
central bank is pertinent. Removal of limits on the purchase of locally issued
securities denominated in foreign exchange would also be a welcome
development.

Guinea's restriction on capital account transactions are still significant and
would require substantial review to bring to the level of Ghana and Nigeria.
Some of the key areas include the requirement for approval from the central
bank on all capital accounts and money market instruments as well as all capital
transfers through the official foreign exchange market. Guinea also requires
relaxation of controls on all credit and guarantee operations. Authorization
requirements on all outward direct investment and real estate transactions as well
as regulation on personal capital transactions are constraints to full liberalization.
Commercial and other credit institutions are subject to special provisions on borrowing abroad, maintenance of accounts abroad and lending locally in foreign
exchange. There are also reserve requirements, interest rate and credit controls
and investment regulations for banks and non-residents. All these need to be
abolished to pave the way for capital account liberalization.

In Nigeria's case, administrative restrictions relating to the certification of
capital importation are an important area that requires further review.
Repatriation-of-proceeds clause on Nigerian residents, who invest in foreign currency denominated securities, can also be revisited as a step towards full liberalization of the capital account. Again, the condition that repatriated proceeds must
be credited to the domiciliary account of the investor for own-use and/or deepening the inter-bank market requires a review.

In the case of Sierra Leone, prior approval restrictions on capital and money
market instruments and credit operations from BSL has to be removed. Also,
strict restrictions especially on the sale of capital market instruments locally by
non-residents and repatriation restrictions should similarly be removed. In addition, the restrictions on money market instruments, that purchases by non-
residents are not permitted and residents also are not allowed to make such
purchases with domestic resources, have to be lifted. The ifting of prohibitions
on FDI and outward movements (outflows) would be an important liberalization
effort the country could undertake. Also, all prohibitions on purchases of real
estate abroad by residents should be removed, while the lifting of the requirement that non-residents may only do so with funds transferred through authorized dealers with proper documentation is also essential. Indeed, the prohibition

that commercial banks and other credit institutions should not hold more than 25 per cent of their deposit liabilities in foreign currency and the maintenance of offshore accounts is counter to ensuring a fully integrated financial services sector. To move forward, prohibitions such as commercial banks should not engage in lending to non-residents or extend credits locally in foreign exchange negates the objective of the entire WAMZ project.

Cross-listing of stocks

The ultimate goal of an integrated regional capital market is to enhance investment and output by removing constraints on capital account convertibility in the WAMZ. The integration process is proceeding with cautious optimism with private sector stakeholders driving the process[19] and ultimately the capital markets in The Gambia, Guinea and Sierra Leone will be developed.[20]

In The Gambia, plans are under way to establish a stock market, while equities of some companies are traded on the over-the-counter market. Newly licensed banks are being prevailed upon to sell 25 per cent of their shares to the public which should increase activity on the over-the-counter market and prepare the way for the eventual establishment of a stock exchange.

In Guinea, the Act L97/037/AM dated 25 November 1997 provided the legal framework for the establishment of the Conakry stock exchange, the SEC and a central depository system (CDS). Progress has been made towards the realization of an active capital market in Guinea.

In Sierra Leone, a legal and regulatory framework for capital market activities, including the establishment of a stock exchange, has been prepared, while a new securities law and a new companies and insolvency law are being finalized. The capital market in Sierra Leone consists of short-term government debt instruments (91-day, 182-day, 365-day treasury bills and one-year bearer bonds) and a few shares of at least six public companies. The government established the NASSIT to provide pensions for the population. The Sierra Leone Stock Exchange Technical Committee (SETC) was established in 2001 as a private sector initiative to promote the stock market and ensure firm regulation of activities. Considerable work in developing awareness of capital market participants was done by the government and the SETC. Meanwhile, the Sierra Leone Stock Exchange, which was officially inaugurated in July 2007, is equipped with the requisite enabling legal framework.

Cross-listing of stocks in the Zone is limited, with the Ecobank Transnational Incorporated listed on both the Ghana and Nigerian Stock Exchanges. Listing and regulatory requirements of stock exchanges in Ghana and Nigeria are in the process of harmonization.

Regional currency convertibility

In order to facilitate currency convertibility and to enhance efficiency in intra-regional trade financing, the WAMZ Convergence Council in May 2007 approved that commercial banks and other private sector financial entities operating within member countries of the Zone should commence the quoting of WAMZ member countries' local currencies. This implied that the currencies should be freely convertible within the WAMZ and could be used to finance goods and services in the Zone. Also it was envisaged that letters of credit could be opened in WAMZ national currencies for intra-regional imports/exports. This initiative was purely a private sector-driven activity, devoid of central bank intervention.

Quoting of the WAMZ currencies has commenced in some commercial banks but actual trading in them has been insignificant. In Ghana and Nigeria, although some banks have commenced quoting, payments for cross-border transactions to other WAMZ member countries using the local currency has not started, with the exception of the limited facility extended by one commercial bank for transactions within its regional network.

Implementation of the policy on quoting and trading in the currencies of WAMZ member countries has come about through the innovative drive of commercial banks with extensive reach of subsidiary network in the WAMZ. As competition grows, newer products are expected to be introduced to cater for the needs of more transactions in WAMZ currencies, as a means of financing intra-regional trade. Overall, progress is slowed and challenged by the absence of a central bank presence in making explicit guarantees for net positions held in their respective currencies.

Banking supervision

One important development in the area of banking supervision is the funding by FIRST Initiative for the preparation of a blueprint on the supervisory framework for the West African Financial and Supervisory Authority. The framework outlined the supervisory architecture for effective supervision. Various reforms and developments have been undertaken in the member countries towards ensuring the stability of the financial system and laying the foundations for effective harmonization in accordance with international best practice.

Member countries have adopted various strategies to implement the Basel II framework, including the establishment of committees or task forces to work on a roadmap that would inform effective implementation of the new Basel framework by 2012. This target date is relatively ahead of the Central African countries that expect to implement Basel II by 2015.

The implementation of Basel II would be challenged by a number of factors, including the complexity of Basel II which requires time to train staff to attain key understanding for effective implementation; the core principles for effective supervision are yet to be fully implemented by member countries and would require a huge amount of available resources to enhance supervisory processes; limited resources which are in competition with other development priorities could result in implementation inertia; the cost burden would also be significant owing to the small size of most banks in the Zone; and the lack of rating agencies in the Zone.

In The Gambia, as part of the financial sector reform, the CBG introduced risk-based supervision. This enables the CBG to assess the risk profile of the banks as well as the contingent liabilities they may be exposed to. Off-balance-sheet activities of the banks will be examined to safeguard prudence and responsibility in order to protect depositors. Plans are under way for The Gambia to go live on Basel II. A credit reference bureau was set up with the aim of effective credit risk management.

In Ghana, banks were insulated from the international financial crisis as the economy was quite resilient. Unlike banks in Europe, Ghanaian banks do not hold derivative instruments nor are they involved in sub-prime lending; coupled with the fact that the banks are adequately capitalized, the financial sector is quite sound and robust. The Credit Reporting Act was passed and a company was approved in principle. The Anti-Money Laundering Act was also passed and the Ministry of Finance and Economic Planning is expected to set up the Financial Intelligence Centre. The Banking Act was amended to take care of off-shore banking activities in Ghana. The minimum capital requirement for banks was raised and staggered. It was expected that domestic banks (banks with capital originating from domestic sources) would raise their capital to ¢25 million by 2009 and ¢60 million by 2012, while foreign banks had to achieve the ¢60 million target by 2009.

The BoG commenced risk-based supervision in 2007, which is a step towards full implementation of Basel II. With technical assistance from the Office of the Superintendent of Financial Institutions of Canada (OSFIC), the BoG has set up a Technical Support Unit to facilitate the implementation of Basel II. An initial readiness assessment was conducted, with the industry survey results discussed with banks. Banks should undertake a parallel run of Basel I and II prior to the effective adoption of Basel II. It is expected that the Bank will be able to achieve full implementation of Pillar II and Pillar III of Basel II. Beginning 2008, all financial institutions were required to comply with the International Financial Reporting Standards (IFRS).

In the case of Guinea, the CBG undertook a number of steps towards enhancing financial sector soundness and stability. The Banking Statute was revised and passed into law on 4 July 2005. The revisions harmonized banking supervision regulations with the Basel Core Principles including the strengthening of and increasing the frequency of on-site inspections; improving reporting standards; and maintaining closer dialogue and collaboration with commercial banks' management. Supervisory capacity, however, remains a challenge to be urgently addressed, requiring the authority's response for an effective oversight role.

In Nigeria, the role of quality data is emphasized. The country deploys an Electronic Financial Analysis and Surveillance System (e-FASS) – a web-enabled analytical tool for the supervision of banks. The e-FASS, which was designed to enhance efficient online surveillance of financial institutions, was upgraded to further improve its performance for online submission of statutory returns and to capture the requirement for Risk-Based and Consolidated Supervision. Nigeria would go live on Basel II as in the case of The Gambia.

In order to ensure full compliance with the Basel Core Principles, Nigeria has proposed to: amend the Banking and Other Financial Institutions Act (BOFIA 1991); introduce a risk-based supervisory model as well as consolidated supervision; and put in place arrangements to ensure that banks implement policies and procedures to address country risk. Against this backdrop, the CBN commenced the strengthening of its supervisory capacities through various training programmes. In adherence to its policy of the risk-based rule, the CBN requires that when it is lending to DMBs, such credit is backed by 100 per cent government securities.

Following the examination of banks in 2008 by both the CBN and the Nigerian Deposit Insurance Corporation (NDIC), examiners using a hybrid of compliance and risk-based supervision (RBS) methodology revealed that a number of strategic initiatives were put in place by some banks to adequately mitigate risks inherent in their operations.

In 2008, Nigeria was compliant in 16 of the 25 BCPs, largely compliant in eight and non-compliant in one (Principle 11 – country risk). On country risk, there are no explicit provisions requiring banks to have policies and procedures to address country risk. Seven banks have offices abroad. While the majority of exposure is through branches in major international centres, some Nigerian banks have operations in The Gambia, Ghana, Sierra Leone and Benin. Some banks do have significant placements of inter-bank funds outside Nigeria.

On the issue of credit risk management, in 2008, three credit reference bureaux operated in Nigeria. New guidelines for the licensing, operations and regulation of credit bureaux were put in place to engender their effectiveness. Operational challenges to the effectiveness of credit bureaux, however, include: poor awareness on its relevance; absence of a common infrastructural platform for information exchange between banks and the credit bureaux; problem of unique identifier and data integrity; absence of institutional mandate of the CBN to have regulatory oversight of institutions that have data exchange agreements with the credit bureaux but are outside the supervisory purview of the CBN; and the current energy crisis (*Business Day*, 20 July 2009).

The banking industry in Sierra Leone has recorded significant growth, with the addition of three new banks bringing the total number of commercial banks to 13. This enhanced the level of competition in the banking industry, which is expected to result in the introduction of new products such as the debit card by one of the leading banks. There was a high non-performing assets position of Le 88.4 billion out of a total portfolio of Le 278.4 billion, representing 32 per cent. Two banks, a development bank and the cooperative bank, were reported to be in a precarious financial position.

In order to improve on credit risk management, the BSL would need to facilitate the creation of a credit information bureau by ensuring the timely review of the existing banking laws regarding the protective customer privacy information disclosure. In addition, to strengthen the operational capacity of banks and the resilience of the sector against systemic risks, the BSL raised the minimum capital requirement of banks from Le 9 billion to Le 15 billion (equivalent to about US$5.1 million) with compliance spread over a period ending December 2009.

The Gambia has complied with 15 Basel Core Principles. The country is largely compliant with ten, materially non-compliant with one and four are non-applicable.[21] Ghana has complied with six Basel Core Principles, is largely compliant with 15, materially non-compliant with three, non-compliant with three and three are non-applicable. Guinea has complied with seven Basel Core Principles, is largely compliant with 18, materially non-compliant with one, non-compliant with none and four are non-applicable. Nigeria has complied with 16 Basel Core Principles, is largely compliant with nine, materially non-compliant with four and non-compliant with one. Sierra Leone has complied with ten Basel Core Principles, is largely compliant with 11, materially non-compliant with two, non-compliant with three and four are non-applicable.

The key areas of soundness vulnerabilities that require further action for each of the countries is indicated as follows.

The Gambia will need to intensify efforts towards ensuring appropriate loan evaluation and loss provisions procedures to mitigate risks due to bank exposures to this principle. Other areas include supervisory capacity and coverage in effective supervision to improve on the regulatory framework to strengthen institutions that will ensure full compliance with international best practice in terms of independence and resources, capital adequacy, credit policies, country risks, comprehensive risk management process, internal control and audit, money laundering, accounting and disclosure, and timely corrective action plans.

For Ghana, to ensure further compliance with the BCPs, the independence and resources of each supervisory agency should be guaranteed. Efforts also need to be focused on taming market risks, money laundering, consolidated supervision and a framework for timely corrective action.

In Guinea, the independence of the supervisory agency and resource adequacy have to be guaranteed, while a clear definition on permissible activities would have to be put in place. Other important areas requiring attention are in credit policies, loan evaluation and loss provisions, market risks, comprehensive risk management processes, supervisory framework for money laundering, validation of supervisory data, accounting disclosure and timely corrective plans.

In Nigeria, the main risks include country, market and others relating to comprehensive risk management processes. There is a need to strengthen internal control and audit mechanisms as well as the commencement of consolidated supervision.

For Sierra Leone, the key principles that require urgent action are reform of the legal framework, transfer of ownership, acquisition and investments, money laundering and remedial measures to ensure taking timely corrective action.

Cross-border payments, clearing and settlement issues in the WAMZ

The WAMZ member countries have significant differences in the delivery of payments systems, while non-cash cross-border retail payments are generally non-existent. Cash is still the main instrument utilized in making payments for small cross-border trade transactions. Payments system components in Ghana and Nigeria are being modernized, while those of The Gambia, Guinea and Sierra Leone are rudimentary and are being upgraded. For instance, the network of Automated Teller Machines (ATM) and point-of-sale services in use in Ghana and Nigeria significantly differ from the scanty fragmented systems in The Gambia, Guinea and Sierra Leone.

In addition, Ghana and Nigeria operate Real Time Gross Settlement (RTGS) systems which drive large value inter-bank payments. Assistance by the African Development Bank had been deployed to develop RTGS systems in The Gambia, Guinea and Sierra Leone. Cheque standards and other paper payment instruments are being harmonized to facilitate processing and ensuring a float-free clearing of payment instruments across the WAMZ member countries when the West African Central Bank becomes operationalized.

None of the WAMZ member countries has a legal framework and rules and procedures which reflect international best practice in technology. The most advanced in terms of the law is Ghana which has enacted a Payments Systems Act. However, the conundrum of digital signatures and bankruptcy is yet to be addressed.

Finally, it is apparent some of the countries' payments system infrastructure would not comply with the BIS Core Principles on payments systems. An important issue is that of legal certainty, which would have to be addressed urgently.

The state of financial integration in the WAMZ

Degree of integration using various measures

The level of integration in the context of the law of one price[22] is measured by the cross-country dispersions of lending and deposit rates as well as the spread that are related to the geographical location of the services. Interest rates represent the price of comparable financial products and a synthesis of financial services should lead to a higher convergence of prices and yields across countries.

Convergence of interest rates

There is some evidence of price convergence in the run-up to creating a single economic space (Figure 8.1). There is an indication of significant reduction in cross-sectional dispersion in lending rates in the region. Volatility in the interest rate differentials has also been observed to be narrowed from an average of 9.8 standard deviation units between 1990 and 2001 to 3.3 standard deviation units between 2002 and 2006.

Empirical evidence indicates a positive Beta coefficient (see Nnanna *et al.*, 2007) for the WAMZ, contrary to the *a priori* expectation of a negative Beta coefficient for a spread that has the tendency to decline rapidly over time. This means that the integration efforts are yet to produce effects that will crystallize into the law of one price when the financial sector is fully integrated. This can be ascribed to the fact that cross-border and inter-bank transactions are very weak and limited in the region.

In spite of the progress made, it is expected that the current level of savings (both personal and institutional) in the region will have to be engendered to help to narrow the margins. This can be achieved by encouraging greater use of regional retail payments as well as the diffusion of corporate risks associated with holding long liquidity positions.

Banking sector pooling of resources

Theoretically, a larger market should result in a more competitive environment, with the development of stronger credit institutions that are able to offer a wider and more complex array of financial products and services. Manna (2004) has shown that the enlargement of a market correlated with a change in the competitive advantages of the firms in initial markets, changes in equilibrium market shares are expected and more efficient banks will ultimately gain a larger equilibrium market share. Reports commissioned by the EU, for example, have stressed this relationship between market size and efficiency.

It is expected that as banking markets evolve into a single market, domestic banks begin to compete and branch network expands, the most efficient ones will gain market shares at the instance of the inefficient ones. Cross-border flows of deposits may respond in tandem with the new competitive conditions reflecting a transition from the old to the new equilibrium. Banking sector indicators for the WAMZ reveal that bank density (Figure 8.2)[23] is low at between one and three banks branches to 100,000 persons and poses a challenge for the efficient use of funds.

The Herfindahl–Hirchman (HH) Index[24] uses the relative country market shares in the total WAMZ banking assets. From Figure 8.3 it is apparent that the degree of bank concentration in the WAMZ is substantial, with Nigeria contributing an average of over 88 per cent.

Other banking sector integration indicators show interesting results. For instance, the proportion of banks assets to GDP in dollar terms has remained very low. Relative to WAEMU's 30 per cent, the EU's new member states' 77

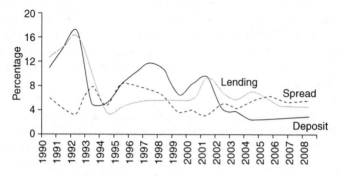

Figure 8.1 Convergence of nominal interest rates spread in the WAMZ (sources: IMF (2008) and WAMI database).

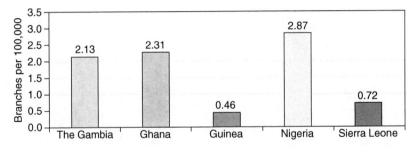

Figure 8.2 Bank branch density in the WAMZ (sources: IMF (2008) and WAMI database).

per cent and the EU-15's 280 per cent, total banking assets to GDP ratio has averaged 5.1 per cent in the last six years. It is important to note that although the WAEMU economies are at the same level with the WAMZ economies, with some countries in the WAMZ making more progress relatively than the WAEMU, the only plausible explanation for this development is the single currency and the harmonized capital market, which have contributed immensely to the relatively high (30 per cent) ratio in the WAEMU.

Capital markets integration

The Ghana Stock Exchange and the Nigeria Stock Exchange, alongside the Bourse Regionale des Valeurs Mobilieres (BRVM), have been working at modalities towards harmonization and integration of rules and procedures. In 2003, both exchanges signed a Memorandum of Understanding (MOU) covering

Table 8.10 Banks assets in percentage of GDP (US$)

	2001	*2002*	*2003*	*2004*	*2005*	*2006*	*Average*
In % of GDP (US$)							
The Gambia	0.22	6.57	9.68	12.51	8.53	10.38	**7.98**
Ghana	3.42	3.37	4.34	4.66	3.70	4.64	**4.02**
Guinea	2.21	2.31	1.89	2.99	2.69	3.65	**2.62**
Nigeria	5.66	6.84	5.63	5.10	3.92	5.10	**5.37**
Sierra Leone	2.72	2.85	3.11	3.27	4.51	5.73	**3.70**
Total	5.19	6.14	5.28	4.97	3.89	5.04	**5.09**
In % of total WAMZ bank assets							
The Gambia	0.03	0.70	0.93	1.20	0.95	0.91	**0.78**
Ghana	6.10	5.96	9.02	9.70	9.21	9.46	**8.24**
Guinea	2.30	2.12	1.86	2.61	2.13	1.92	**2.16**
Nigeria	90.83	90.46	87.36	85.67	86.48	86.47	**87.88**
Sierra Leone	0.74	0.76	0.84	0.82	1.23	1.24	**0.94**

Source: Nnanna *et al.* (2007, p. 20).

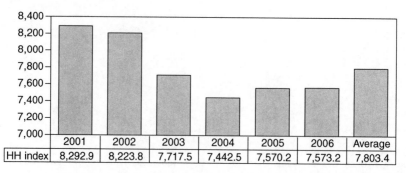

Figure 8.3 Herfindahl–Hirchman index (HHI) in the WAMZ (sources: WAMI database).

several areas of cooperation including "staff training, surveillance procedures, self-regulation and communication of information" (UNECA, 2008, p. 275). A joint Technical Committee for the Integration of the West African Securities Market[25] was instituted to consider harmonization options for integration.

The Technical Committee for the Integration of the West African Securities Markets adopted an "Eco-X model" that takes into consideration realism and practicability, having some characteristics of the Euronext Model in the interim and the BRVM Model as its ultimate. Operational integration could be achieved at the level of stock exchanges (Euronext approach) backed by parallel regulatory harmonization achieved incrementally through ECOWAS protocols/directives (Technical Committee Status Report, 2009).

The Committee identified four fundamental issues (pillars) that are critical to achieving operational integration: (1) adoption of common passport for market operators and mutual recognition issues; (2) harmonization of prospectus requirements issues; (3) facilitation of listing on West African markets issues; and (4) miscellaneous securities legislations/regulations issues. An action plan was to be produced on each of these pillars, while the constitution of a governing council that would be charged with the responsibility of making and determining policies and standardization of operational issues through protocols or signing of MOU would be an immediate step (ibid.).

Continental experience with regional capital markets integration

In Africa, various regional capital market integration efforts have been advanced. BRVM in West Africa is an example of a fully integrated regional capital market, while in Southern Africa an integrated platform of independent national exchanges had been canvassed by the Southern African Development Community's (SADC) Committee of SADC Stock Exchanges (COSSE).

The BRVM is a regional stock market for the WAEMU countries. The BRVM is located in Abidjan and it commenced as a project implemented by the Bank Centrale des Etats de l'Afrique de l'Ouest (BCEAO) under a 1993 mandate from the WAEMU Council of Ministers. By 1996, the BRVM was fully established and became autonomous with its own agencies assuming the functions hitherto performed by the BCEAO. Its central electronic platform is situated in Abidjan, while the national branch offices are located in the other WAEMU member countries. All issues relating to regulations and issuing services as well as the provisioning of securities quotations and trading are undertaken at the headquarters. Broker-dealers at the national branch offices can place orders, request information and otherwise access the central network. The BRVM was an operational success, but with few equity listings and low liquidity, efficiency in the pooling and allocation of equity capital was not remarkable.

COSSE was established in 1997 with a view to facilitating mobilization of capital and, thus, propel growth and development in the SADC region. By 2000, all SADC countries[26] with exchanges harmonized their listing requirements based on 13 principles espoused by the Johannesburg Stock Exchange (JSE). An important lesson from the integration efforts of SADC exchanges is the fact that aside from taking leadership, the JSE offered its electronic trading system to the other SADC exchanges. The widespread use of the South African rand as a convertible currency in the SADC region was a fundamental amplifying factor for the capital markets integration process.

International experience with regional capital markets integration

The Baltic nations,[27] with a strong threshold of economic growth, created platforms for an integrated capital market to optimize on scale economies and sustain liquidity creating investor confidence to attract significant amounts of foreign capital. The stock exchanges' core areas of integration hinges on: the minimization of the differences between the markets in each country; the adoption of common trading technology and systems; the harmonization of rulebooks and market practices; and introduction of common indexes. The three Baltic exchanges[28] operate a common Baltic investment market using a common trading platform within the larger Nordic Exchange.[29] Broad privatizations of state-owned enterprises (SOEs) within the larger economic liberalization programmes offer some useful insights for harmonization and integration of the WAMZ capital markets.

Insurance integration

Depth and penetration

The insurance industry in the WAMZ, although growing, is limited in its level of penetration of the insurance industry in Africa. At the ECOWAS level, in order to deepen the insurance industry, an insurance treaty, known as the Brown Card Scheme (BCS), was signed. The BCS is compulsory and is designed to cover common third-party motor insurance across the border in the region for all vehicles crossing the border. Compared to the WAEMU, the scheme was not successfully implemented in the WAMZ. Claims paid under the scheme are often delayed and vary according to significant differences in local legislation.

The Swiss Re Global Report for 2007 indicates that the Nigerian insurance industry marginally shows a presence on the continent (Obaremi, 2007; Oluba, 2008). With the rapid expansion and milestones achieved in the insurance industry in Ghana due to the existence of a flexible framework law it is expected that the country would raise its market share.

In terms of penetration at the WAMZ level, few insurance companies of Nigerian origin have made cross-border expansions in order to leverage on the huge liquidity occasioned by the increased capital adequacy requirement to benefit from the markets of the other member countries. The size of the insurance companies in The Gambia, Guinea and Sierra Leone is too small to result in any meaningful penetration and cross-border trade in insurance services. The only WAMZ member country with a presence in the African insurance market is Nigeria. Six and two Nigerian insurance companies have commenced operations respectively in Ghana and Sierra Leone, with another having a major stake in an insurance company in The Gambia. The establishment of branches under the existing laws in the member countries, however, is not sanctioned. Yet the country's share of total world premium is an insignificant 0.02 per cent. The important strategy for higher penetration is to intensify regional activity in terms of encouraging cross-border movements.

Financial integration, financial contagion and financial stability in the WAMZ

African economies are anything but insulated from the negative consequences of the global financial crisis. Some of the initial contagion effects of the financial meltdown include the approximately 30 per cent slip in the value of the rand and 27 per cent loss in the value of the South African Stock Exchange in 2008. Nigeria's stock market, one of the two WAMZ exchanges, was significantly exposed to external dynamics; consequently, the all-share index as well as market capitalization slid after the second quarter of 2007. At the local level, the market was influenced by issues relating to margin pricing and recall of loans by banks that were hitherto used for the purchase of stocks. On the global scene, the financial meltdown led to non-residents withdrawing substantially their investments. The director general of the NSE, Professor Ndidi Okereke-Onyiuke revealed in February 2009 to the Senate Committee on Capital Markets that foreign investors pulled out N812 billion from the market as a result of the global meltdown.

In contrast, Ghana's stock market experienced growth owing more to the inter-play of domestic conditions than external factors. The Nigerian stock market felt the impact of the global meltdown from the second quarter with equity market capitalization dropping from a high of N12.64 trillion on 3 May

Table 8.11 Insurance market performance in Africa in 2007

S/No.	Country	Insurance penetration (%)			Insurance density (per capita US$)			Total premium	
		Life	Non-life	Total	Life	Non-life	Total	Volume (US$)	Share of world (%)
1	South Africa	12.5	2.8	15.3	719.0	159.5	878.5	42,676	1.05
2	Tunisia	0.2	1.8	2.0	7.0	60.1	67.2	694	0.03
3	Morocco	1.1	2.2	3.4	22.9	46.0	68.9	2,153	0.05
4	Egypt	0.4	0.4	0.9	6.8	7.6	14.4	1,090	0.03
5	Nigeria	0.0	0.5	0.6	0.9	4.6	5.5	814	0.02
6	Algeria	0.0	0.5	0.5	1.3	19.7	21.0	711	0.02
7	Kenya	0.8	1.7	2.5	6.1	13.1	19.2	721	0.02
8	Angola	0.0	1.4	1.4	0.7	55.0	55.7	949	0.02

Source: Swiss Re Global (2007) Report and Oluba (2008).

to a low of N6.21 trillion on 16 December before closing at N9.56 trillion on 31 December 2008. The correction was hoisted by the tightening of liquidity in the banking sector arising from the decline in public sector spending, excess supply of stocks necessitated by profit taking by investors. Despite the declines in key market indicators, the fundamentals of the stock market remained strong as indicated by strong corporate earnings and growth potentials. Although it was observed that the stock market exhibited some signs of recovery during the last two weeks in December 2008, investors still maintained cautious optimism while studying the effect of the global financial crisis on the domestic market.

In Nigeria, the NSE All-share index dropped by 45.8 per cent. The effects of the crisis on financial sectors of the WAMZ member countries indicate that, *ex post*, a single monetary policy and one currency would pose stability concerns.

Box 8.5 Overview of the recent financial crisis, 2007–2009

The financial crisis started in the United States in 2007 following the sub-prime mortgage lending crisis leading to a credit squeeze which continued in 2008 and spread across the globe, causing significant downtown in economic activities. In September 2008 the sudden collapse of several major financial institutions in the United States produced a bout of jitters in the global financial system. Lehman Brothers and Merrill Lynch, two of Wall Street's biggest investment banks, collapsed while American officials took over American International Group to prevent the distressed insurer from failing. Bank of America was later to acquire a stake in Merrill Lynch worth about US$33 billion in stock. Other effects of the crisis included anxiety at a pending global recession, increased unemployment and inflation. The United States was officially declared to have been in recession since December 2007, while Japan and the euro area also fell into recession (applying the definition of two quarters of negative growth) during 2008.

The credit crunch persisted, compelling many governments, in particular in the United States and Europe, to provide extraordinary measures including providing substantial financial support or bailout packages to stabilize the banking system in a bid to get credit markets functioning again, while central banks took steps to boost liquidity by dropping key interest rates to near zero, lower than they have ever been. In addition, US Federal reserve implemented unusual market interventions such as buying large amounts of short-term debt issued to companies to enable day-to-day financing.

Source: Okereke-Onyiuke (2009)

The direct effect of 2008 global financial crisis on banks in the WAMZ was generally limited. The banks were relatively less coupled with the global financial architecture. Although the sector is characterized by indigenously owned banks, the cross-border establishment of subsidiaries by Nigerian banks in the WAMZ countries curiously pose challenges for financial stability. A strong bailout of problem banks with capital impaired by non-performing credits by the CBN in 2009 was very important in maintaining stability in the WAMZ financial sector. This was also complemented by subsequent visits by the CBN governor to various countries with a subsidiary presence of Nigerian banks to allay any fears that could spark-off a Zone-wide systemic failure. Other automatic stabilizers that helped in reducing the impact were the prevalence of relatively thin inter-bank markets; and the limited demand for securitized or derivative instruments.

Obstacles to financial integration in the WAMZ

Barriers to integration of the banking services

Capital adequacy requirements vary significantly and would obviously create a regulatory arbitrage that serve as an obstacle to entry into the Ghanaian and Nigerian banking industry by banks from the other member countries. Second, there are great dissimilarities in the regulatory and supervisory arrangements across the member countries. Even with the prepared uniform banking statute by WAMI, domestication in country laws would be necessary, and this has remained a challenge. There still exist dissimilarities in accounting reporting standards with only Ghana and Sierra Leone adopting the International Financial Reporting Standards (IFRS). While Nigeria has adapted the IFRS, it will take the country a few years to transition. The Gambia has commenced preparatory arrangements towards adoption, while it is uncertain if Guinea will do so. The disparity in accounting reporting standards will undermine cost efficiency of cross-border subsidiaries of banks.

A recent study by the World Bank/WAMI revealed that although quite a number of the WAMZ member countries were at various stages of improving the flow of credit information through private credit bureaux or central bank-based credit risk management systems, no legislation existed that sanctions cross-border sharing of credit information. In addition to the challenge of regional credit information sharing, although some banks with a regional outlook are able to access credit information across borders via a central data facility for their customers, this stifles inter-bank competition as they are unable to supply information on potential customers who could receive alternative banking services from other banks. Another challenge is centralization of IT systems, which raises concerns about violation of data privacy protection. The cross-border accessibility of data may not be known to the bank customers and the degree of protection of their data may be dissimilar to that in the country where they have an account.

Barriers to integration of the Ghanaian and Nigerian capital markets

Efforts must be made to remove policy barriers to integration of the Ghanaian and Nigerian capital markets, including two threshold issues – capital controls and restrictions on foreign ownership. One of the most obvious barriers to capital market integration in the West African region is the imposition of outright restrictions on foreign ownership of domestic equities. For instance, Ghana places individual and cumulative limits on foreign ownership of equities. In addition, restrictions on domestic investors' ownership of international equities adversely affect the development of a regional capital market. For instance, Nigeria's Pension Reform Act of 2004 bars pension-fund administrators from investing in private sector debt and equities securities that are not listed on a stock exchange registered under the Investments and Securities Act of 1999. This requirement effectively limits pension-fund investments in securities to those listed on the NSE.

Controls on capital mobility also constitute a significant barrier to achieving the potential that a common capital market would have on catalysing economic growth and development in WAMZ. Indeed the heads of state of the WAMZ decided that the Zone should move to capital account liberalization by 2007, in advance of the implementation of monetary union. Policy-makers in Ghana and Nigeria would, at the least, have to implement bilateral changes to capital accounts policy to accommodate cross-border capital markets activity.

From an issuer's perspective, the various differences in economic, legal and regulatory policies in Ghana and Nigeria do not constitute an absolute bar to executing cross-border capital markets transactions. For instance, Ecobank Transnational Incorporated (ETI) stock was cross-listed in 2006 on the Ghana and Nigeria stock exchanges as well as the BRVM. However, ETI had to meet the individual listing and regulatory requirements in both Ghana and Nigeria, doubling the administrative overhead. It is noteworthy that the potential deal-breaker for ETI was not the compliance requirement but the cost of listing in Nigeria. Ordinarily, the statutory cost for listing on the NSE is 18 times higher than what ETI paid in Ghana and Côte d'Ivoire. However, the Director General of the NSE secured approval from the Nigerian Securities and Exchange Commission for a waiver of most of the fees that would have been due to the exchange and regulators, matching the BVRM cost of N2 million instead of an original N36 million. This flexibility facilitated the only cross-listing of a security on both the GSE and NSE, indicating a keen understanding on the part of key stakeholders of the benefits of an integrated regional capital market. It also illustrates how competitiveness can lead to a more efficient process for raising and allocating funds within the region.

Barriers to integration of insurance markets in the WAMZ

An important obstacle to the cross-border trade in insurance services is the existence of fragmented legal framework for the practice of insurance. Most of the supervising authorities are about reviewing their various legislations. Harmonization is becoming increasingly elusive given the significant differences in capital adequacy requirements for the establishment of insurance companies. As in the case of the capital markets, restrictions and requirements on the capital accounts are also of concern for the growth of the insurance trade across borders.

Another factor would be the presence of asymmetric information that would undermine effective coordination of supervision by the regulators.

Conclusions

The important challenge for financial integration is for the member countries to create the right environment to allow business to go unhindered in the WAMZ. Restrictions on capital accounts and all house-keeping regulations that encourage regulatory arbitrages will have to be critically examined in order to provide a framework for harmonization. These will be necessary for both the banking, insurance and capital markets to build on their potentials to increase intermediation, deliver effective service at both the domestic and regional levels.

Given that reporting requirements are largely determined by regulation rather than law, the harmonization of reporting requirements could be one area where progress could be made in the short to medium term by simple agreement between the WAMZ central banks. To the extent that current laws allow it, harmonization of selected key regulations could be undertaken through customized reporting software for each country.

There is also the need for the WAMZ authorities to harmonize the fragmented approaches to and quality of supervision by concretizing a uniform MOU for use in the sharing of supervisory information. This would require identification of regulatory reporting requirements with a view to developing a single set of reports required by WAMZ bank regulators. This should be consistent with the model banking statute and transition to Basel II framework for banking supervision. Additional country-specific reports may be included if required by the existing law. Also canvassed is the institutionalization of a training programme for WAMZ supervisors to encourage the sharing of experience and further the understanding of application of regulations and supervisory practices of each regulatory agency. This will facilitate a better understanding of regulatory reports shared under a common MOU.

In the context of an integrated capital market, the key challenge would be to sell the potential benefits of the various integration options to private sector stakeholders – the exchanges, issuers, intermediaries and investors. It will be necessary to link the project activities and deliverables to the agenda of the NSE–GSE integration committee. The objective should be to understand the goals and motivations of the primary stakeholders and to provide them information to guide their action plan and if indeed it is couched in terms of the committee's priority areas.

To promote the integration of the insurance sub-sector, a closer collaboration by regulators that will support institutional sharing of regulatory information will be a welcome development. In addition, the regulatory and supervisory approaches as well as the reporting standards need to be harmonized. The creation of WAMZ committee of insurance regulators and supervisors' forum will be an effective way towards information sharing on these issues. Putting in place the terms of reference for a healthy collaboration can be done through an MOU.

190   *T.W. Oshikoya* et al.

Notes

1 Financial inclusion in this context presupposes a significant number of the WAMZ member countries' citizens have access to banking and other financial services.
2 For the purpose of this chapter, asymmetric shocks refer to the varied effect of external shocks on economies of member countries.
3 At the onset, it was thought that the financial sectors of the WAMZ and other economies of sub-Saharan Africa were decoupled from the rest of the world and, therefore, the extent of impact of the crisis on these economies was not immediately envisaged. Velde (2008) outlines some of the very important channels of impact on developing countries, which have become most apparent for the WAMZ countries. These include trade and trade prices, remittances, pressure on FDI and equity investment, inflows from donor community, slow-down in tourist visits and inflows, among others.
4 Within this framework, the Strategic Plan for financial integration has been developed to effectively anchor various aspects of market development, financial integrity, settlement infrastructure development, integration of insurance and other non-bank financial sectors as well as institutional cooperation and capacity building.
5 According to Wakeman-Linn and Wagh (2008, p. 2), these prerequisites are "currency convertibility and payment systems to reduce settlement delays; information and communication infrastructure; and the removal of legal and regulatory barriers".
6 The use of credit cards or other point-of-sale mechanisms such as mobile phones for payments across border are absent.
7 Regulatory requirements on the capital account and huge capital requirements are some of the factors inhibiting the cross listing and trading of stocks.
8 United Nations Economic Commission for Africa (UNECA) (2008). A thin financial sector is one where the markets are characterized by low liquidity, high spreads and high volatility. It is a sector that is unlikely to accommodate small adjustments of demand and supply without significant price movements resulting to a volatility that can induce risk-averse transactors who face transaction costs to desert these markets completely.
9 Information was generally obtained through WAMI staff mission visits to The Gambia.
10 Shallow in this sense implies very few banking institutions, dearth of instruments, weak inter-bank competition and generally highly regulated market with low liquidity.
11 ARB Apex Bank provides banking and non-banking support to the rural and community banks (RCBs). The ARB does not have a legal existence as bank but is used to facilitate clearing activities for rural banks as well as the provisioning of other consultancy services.
12 Ecobank Group led the way, establishing subsidiaries in virtually all the ECOWAS member countries.
13 Government debt instruments are largely at the short-end of the market. Corporate bonds and market for fixed incomes are yet to be developed. Current thinking among policy-makers is to deepen the market and extend the yield curve.
14 The banks are similarly establishing trans-Atlantic subsidiaries, especially in the UK and USA. Ecobank Transnational with Togo, a WAEMU country, as the home supervisor has established strong presence in Ghana, Guinea and Nigeria.
15 WAMZ and WAEMU. See also World Bank (2007).
16 The market crashed as a result of liquidity and confidence erosion occasioned by the bust of the market after following the aftermath of market manipulation through margin trading and capital withdrawal by foreign investors.
17 World Bank/WAMI study.

18 Sy (2006, p. 14) notes, as in Baele *et al.* (2004), that:

> a given set of financial instruments and/or services can be considered as being fully integrated if all potential market participants with the same relevant characteristics: (1) have equal access to the ... set of financial instruments and/or services; (2) face a single set of rules when they decide to deal with those financial instruments and/or services; and (3) are treated equally when they are active in the market.

19 The United States Trade and Development Agency (USTDA) provided grants for the engagement of consultants that undertook a study on how to integrate the Ghana and Nigeria Stock Exchanges – the two functional exchanges in the Zone. In order to facilitate cross-listing and trading in securities in the WAMZ and ECOWAS in general, a Technical Committee for the Integration of the West African Securities Markets was established, comprising key stakeholders: the Ghana and Nigeria Stock Exchanges, the BRVM, the respective Securities and Exchange Commissions and Central Securities Depository Systems. Others include WAMI, Operators and Shareholder Associations which could participate in meetings as observers.

20 In the case of Sierra Leone, an MOU has been signed with the SEC to complement its supervision of the non-bank financial institutions, although the Sierra Leone Stock Exchange, which was officially inaugurated in July 2007, has commenced operations with a single listing.

21 In this case, each of the six components of Principle 1 of the 25 Basel Core Principles for Effective Supervision is taken separately to bring the principles to 30.

22 According to the European Financial Integration Report (2008, p. 7), the law suggest that if markets are well integrated, financial assets with identical features should show the same price – notwithstanding their geographical location. To the extent financial products are comparable, an increase in integration should lead to a higher convergence of prices and yields across countries. Thus, an asset's price should be driven by factors other than the place where it is traded or the geographic location.

23 Defined as bank branches per 100,000 people.

24 HHI values between 1,000 and 2,000 indicate a moderate level of concentration; values above 2,000 indicate high levels of concentration. The index is calculated by summing up the squared relative market shares (in percentage points) of all the banks:

$$INDEX = \sum_{n}^{1} X_n^2$$ where X is the market share in percentage points (Saab and Vacher, 2007, p. 9).

25 The Committee comprises GSE, NSE, BRVM, SECs of the three markets and Central Securities Depositories of the three markets with the WAMI, BCEAO, Operators and Shareholder Associations as observers.

26 SADC countries with stock exchanges include Botswana, Malawi, Mauritius, Mozambique, Namibia, South Africa, Swaziland, Tanzania, Zambia and Zimbabwe. Other SADC countries include Angola, Democratic Republic of Congo, Lesotho and Madagascar.

27 The Baltic nations include Lithuania, Estonia and Latvia.

28 These include Tallinin, Vilius and Riga.

29 The Nordic market encompasses the Copenhagen, Helsinki, Stockholm and Iceland exchanges.

References

AFRINVEST West Africa (2008). "Nigerian Banking Sector Macro-economic Plays on Africa's Largest Emerging Market". Online: www.afrinvestwa.com.

Baele, L., Ferrando, A., Hordahl, P., Krylova, E. and Monnet, C. (2004). "Measuring Financial Integration in the Euro Area", *European Central Bank, Occasional Paper series*, no. 14, April.

Bank of Ghana (2007). *Annual Report.*

Bank of Ghana (2008). *Monetary Policy Committee Report.*

Bank of Sierra Leone (2007). *Annual Report.*

Bank of Sierra Leone (2008). *Banking Supervision Report.*

Bank of Sierra Leone (2006). *Financial Sector Assessment Programme.*

Brownbridge, M. and Gockel, A.F. (1996). "Impact of Financial Sector Policies on Banking in Ghana", *Institute of Development Studies (IDS) Working Paper*, no. 38.

Central Bank of The Gambia (2007). *Annual Report.*

Central Bank of The Gambia (2008). *Monetary Policy Committee Report.*

Central Bank of The Gambia (2007). *Financial Stability Report Reports.*

Central Bank of Guinea (2008). *Annual Report.*

Central Bank of Nigeria (2007). *Annual Report.*

Central Bank of Nigeria (2008). *Banking Supervision Report.*

Central Bank of Nigeria (2008). *Monetary Policy Committee Reports.*

Central Bank of Nigeria (2008). *Nigeria's Financial System Strategy 2020 Plan.*

Commission of the European Communities (2008). "European Financial Integration Report 2008", *Commission Staff Working Document*, p. 7.

De Grauwe, P. (2000). *Economics of Monetary Union*, Oxford: Oxford University Press.

Ghana (2008). "Article IV Consultation", *IMF Country Report*, no. 08/344, October.

Ghana (2008). Ministry of Finance and Economic Planning Economic Management and Capacity Building Project (EMCB–FSR), Credit No.: Cr 4124 Gh Terms of Reference for Impact Assessment of Ghana's Financial Sector Strategic Plan (FINSSP).

Guinea (1987). Investment Code, Decree No. 001/PRG/87, January IMF, 2008.

Guinea (2008). "Selected Issues and Statistical Appendix", *IMF Staff Country Report*, no. 08/20, January.

Lawfields Consulting (2009). "Lawfields Financial Sector Review for 2008 and Outlook for 2009". Online: www.lawfieldsconsulting.com/Docs/Lawfields_-Financial_Sector_Review_2008.pdf.

Manna, M. (2004). "Developing Statistical Indicators of the Integration of the Euro Area Banking System", *ECB Working Paper Series*, no. 300 (January).

Nigeria (1990). Companies and Allied Matters Act.

Nigeria (2008). Investment Code, 2008: "Nigeria: 2007 Article IV Consultation", *IMF Country Report*, no. 08/64, February.

Nnanna, O.J., Essien, E.A., Onwioduokit, E.A. and Adamgbe, E.T. (2007). "Empirical Evidence of the Benefits of Economic and Monetary Integration in the West African Monetary Zone", *West African Journal of Monetary and Economic Integration*, 7(2).

NAICOM (2008). *National Insurance Commission Nigeria Annual Report.*

NIC (2008). *National Insurance Commission Ghana Annual Report.*

Obaremi, N. (2007). "Insurance in Nigeria", *Africa Business* Special Report.

Okereke-Onyiuke, N. (2009). "The Nigerian Stock Exchange: A Review of Market Performance in 2008 and the Outlook for 2009". Online: www.scribd.com/doc/10585651/Nigerian-Stock-Exchange-Official-2008-Review-and-Outlook-for-2009.

Oluba, M. (2008). "Implicating Macroeconomic Policies in the Past and Future Performances of the Insurance Sector in Nigeria", *Economic Reflections*, B(23), September.

Samer, Y.S. and Vacher, J. (2007). "Banking Sector Integration and Competition in CEMAC", *IMF Working Paper*, no. 07/3.

Sy, A.N.R. (2006). "Financial Integration in the West African Economic and Monetary Union", *IMF Working Paper*, no. 06/214, p. 14.

Technical Committee for the Integration of the West African Securities Markets (2009). Status Report, presented at the Meeting on the Integration of the West African Securities Markets, 22 May 2009, Accra.

Thomas, H., Karl, K. and Wong, C. (2008). "Global Insurance Review 2008 and Outlook 2009: Weathering the Storm", *Swiss Re Special Report*, December 9.

UNECA (2008). "Assessing Regional Integration in Africa: Towards Monetary and Financial Integration in Africa", Chapter 7. Online: www.uneca.org/aria/aria3/index. htm.

Velde, D.W. (2008). "The Global Financial Crisis and Developing Countries: Which Countries are at Risk and What Can Be Done?", Background Note, Overseas Development Institute.

Wakemann-Linn, J. and Wagh, S. (2008). "Regional Financial Integration: Its Potential Contribution to Financial Sector Growth and Development in Sub-Saharan Africa", African Finance for the 21st Century High Level Seminar, IMF Institute and the Joint Africa Institute, Tunis, 4–5 March 2008.

WAMI (2008). *Convergence Report*. Online: www.wami-imao.org.

World Bank (2007). *Financial Sector Integration in Two Regions of Sub-Saharan Africa: How Creating Scale in Financial Markets can Support Growth and Development*, Washington, DC: World Bank.

9 Payments system infrastructure

*Chris Odiaka, Twum Ohene-Obeng and
Tajudeen Nasiru*

Introduction

A payments system, consisting of a set of rules, instructions and technical mechanisms for the transfer of money, is an integral part of the monetary system. As such, the safe and efficient operation of the payments system is of concern to both market participants and public officials, especially central bankers. Efficient domestic and cross-border payment systems are particularly essential for the smooth functioning of a single monetary zone so that citizens of the member countries can benefit fully from the principles of the free movement of goods, services, capital and people that will come with the introduction of the second monetary zone, and so that they can transfer money effectively and efficiently within the domestic system and from one part of the zone to another.

Experience indicates that the existence of a payments system that is responsive to the needs of individuals and businesses, for safe and efficient funds transfers, is an important part of the infrastructure needed to introduce a monetary union successfully. Of all the payment systems components, large-value transfer systems (Real-Time Gross Settlement – RTGS systems) are the main arteries of a nation's payment system, providing the ultimate settlement vehicle for important cross-border markets in multiple currencies, and are key infrastructural requirements for implementing a single monetary policy.

The role and importance of the payments system

Payments and settlement systems have been growing in importance over the past two decades. This is a result of an increase in both the value of transactions stemming from money and foreign exchange markets and from financial markets in general. Every central bank pays close attention to their smooth functioning, as well as to reducing the related potential risks. Smooth functioning is crucial for a sound currency, for the conduct of monetary policy, for the operations of financial markets and for the maintenance of banking and financial stability. The crucial roles of a payments system include the following features.

Foreign exchange trading

Since foreign exchange trading involves payments for currency exchanges across international borders, the payments and settlement systems of the countries whose currencies are being traded are vital to its success. For this reason, national payment and settlement systems play a key role in the day-to-day operations of the foreign exchange market.

Sound monetary policy and liquidity management

Money outside the banks cannot be subjected to regulatory and operational procedures, and the ability of monetary policy to achieve set objectives in the presence of currency outside the banking system is therefore limited. By promoting the use of the formal payments system, the ability to execute and manage monetary policy is enhanced. From a macroeconomic perspective, an automated large-value interbank payment system greatly facilitates the establishment of short-term money markets that reflect nationwide/zone-wide monetary conditions at a particular time. Such markets, in turn, provide more accurate information about the current state of nationwide/zone-wide monetary conditions.

Financial sector integration

More widespread use of the formal payments system makes it easier to pursue openness in economic and trade policies, since domestic and international payments would flow seamlessly. In a globalizing world, capital and investment would move freely and more beneficially, and the gains of economic integration would be more pronounced. One important role is the linking together of regional centres of commerce and finance, with same-day settlement finality.

Government transactions

By improving the use of the formal payments system, substantial benefits would accrue to governments, both from the point of view on enhancement to the total revenue that would be realized, as well as timeliness and improved transparency in government operations.

Given the role and importance of the payments system to economic activities, international trade as well as regional integration, and based on the experiences of other monetary unions, the main objectives of the WAMZ development programme are as follows:

1 Satisfy West African Central Bank (WACB) requirements relating to the control of reserves and current account balances;
2 Reduce float, speed up the circulation of funds and increase the efficiency of funds transmission;
3 Enhance WACB management of monetary policy by supplying timely and accurate information on fund flows and settlement account balances;

4   Expand flexibility to suit WAMZ conditions by allowing for planned expansion in terms of additional future services such as securities settlement transactions, as well as geographical expansion as appropriate;
5   Satisfy relevant international standards and principles for Systemically Important Payments Systems as promulgated by the Bank for International Settlement.

Banjul Declaration on payments system development in the WAMZ

Details of the Banjul Declaration on the regional payments system include:

1   Those member states without RTGS system should procure and implement a common RTGS system that would be adopted by the WACB;
2   Member states with RTGS system, i.e. Ghana and Nigeria, should ensure that their systems are interoperable with the common system to be implemented;
3   Those member countries without Automated Clearing House (ACH) with imaging and truncation system, should procure and implement a common system;
4   Member states with ACH, i.e. Ghana and Nigeria, should ensure that their systems are interoperable with the common system to be implemented, and that, as and when they introduce imaging and truncation, they should either adopt the common system or follow the same standards as the common system;
5   Those member states without an ACH system should procure and implement a common system;
6   Member states with an Automated Cheque Processing (ACP) system, i.e. Nigeria, should ensure its systems are interoperable with the common system to be implemented, and that, as and when it introduces enhancement, they should follow the same standards as the common system;
7   Member states without ATM/POS switches should implement such systems;
8   West African Monetary Institute (WAMI)/WACB should ensure that ATM/POS switches are interoperable internationally;
9   WACB should implement a scriptless securities settlement (SSS) system and central securities depository system (CSD) for the timely settlement of transactions in government securities from member states which will be issued in the regional currency, the eco.

Other payments system components earmarked for implementation under the Banjul Declaration include:

•   Standardized Payments Instruments for the WAMZ;
•   Harmonized Payments System Law;
•   Telecommunications infrastructure to link the WACB with the national central banks (NCBs).

State of the payments systems in the WAMZ

The state of the payment systems in the WAMZ are highlighted below. The average size of the payments handled by a system is a useful practical indicator of the system's uses.

The Gambia

Figures 9.1 and 9.2 showed the steady growth of the cheque-clearing system, reflecting the confidence of the banks and the end users in the financial market.

Ghana

The contribution of each of the components is shown in Figures 9.3 and 9.4.

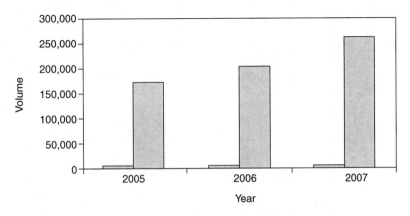

Figure 9.1 The Gambia – volume of cheques cleared, 2005–2007 (source: WAMI (2008)).

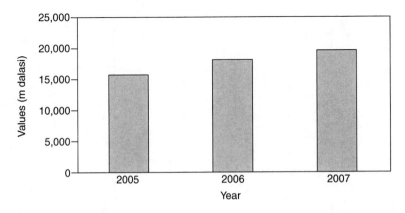

Figure 9.2 The Gambia – value of cheques cleared, 2005–2007 (source: WAMI (2008)).

Table 9.1 State of payments system in The Gambia

S/No.	Components	Level of development	Planned action	Remarks
1	Large value payments	Manual and paper-based. The primary payment instrument is cheque	Development of an RTGS system	The RTGS would be linked to the WACB central hub, when established
2	Retail payment system (cheque-clearing system)	Manual operation. The cheque-clearing cycle is D + 3 for local cheques and D + 7 for up countries' cheques	Development of an ACH	WAMZ cheque standards have been adopted
3	Securities clearing and settlement	Manual in operation	Scriptless securities and settlement (SSS)	Funds have been provided (US$0.8) has been provided by ADF for the system
4	Electronic payments (ATMS/ POS)	Switch system and card-based products		WAMZ e-banking guidelines have been adopted

Source: WAMI (2004b).

Table 9.2 State of payments system in Ghana

S/No.	Components	Level of development	Planned action	Remarks
1	Large value payments	Implemented RTGS system		Established RTGS system in 2002 to handle large value and time critical payments
2	Cheque-clearing system	Implemented automated-centralized cheque-clearing system in 1997	Decentralized automated system	Adopted the WAMZ cheque standard
3	Electronic payments (ACH, ATMs/POS)	A national switch has been implemented	An ACH under GHIPS Ltd	Adopted the WAMZ e-banking guidelines

Source: WAMI (2004).

200 *C. Odiaka* et al.

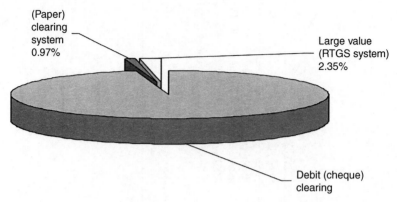

Figure 9.3 Ghana – contribution of paper and electronic modes of payments, 2007 (source: WAMI (2008)).

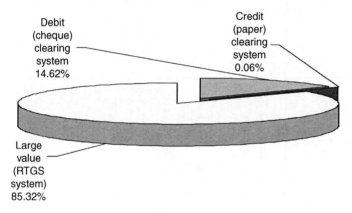

Figure 9.4 Ghana – contribution of paper and electronic modes of payment (value) GHc'm, 2007 (source: WAMI (2008)).

Large-value payments: RTGS system

Since the establishment of the RTGS, large-value and inter-bank payments have witnessed steady growth, as shown in Figures 9.5 to 9.8.

Guinea

The value of cheque transactions remained in the upward trend, reflecting the growing confidence in the use of non-cash instruments.

Nigeria

The contribution of each of the components is shown in Figures 9.10 and 9.11.

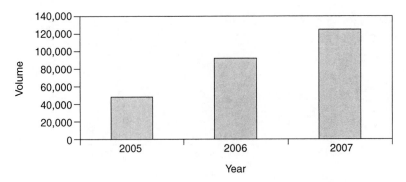

Figure 9.5 Ghana – volume of large value payments (RTGS system) (source: WAMI (2008)).

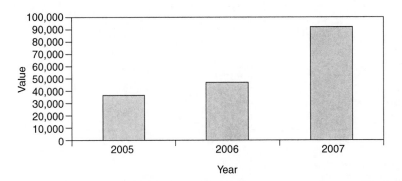

Figure 9.6 Ghana – large value payments (RTGS system) (source: WAMI (2008)).

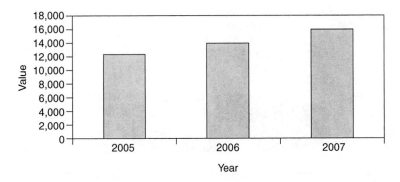

Figure 9.7 Ghana – value of cheques cleared, 2005–2007 (source: WAMI (2008)).

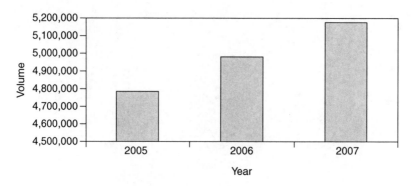

Figure 9.8 Ghana – volume of cheques cleared, 2005–2007 (source: WAMI (2008)).

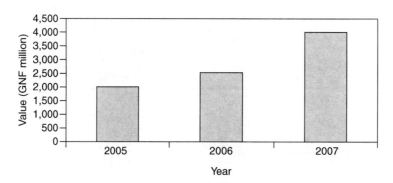

Figure 9.9 Guinea – value of cheques cleared, 2005–2007 (source: WAMI (2008)).

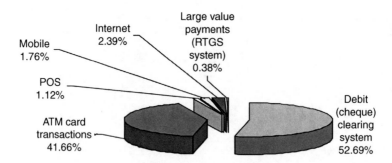

Figure 9.10 Nigeria – contribution of paper and electronic modes of payment (volume), 2007 (source: WAMI (2008)).

Table 9.3 State of payments system in Guinea

S/N	Components	Level of development	Planned action	Remarks
1	High value payments	Manual operation as banks use certified cheques for sending inter-bank payments	RTGS system	The RTGS would be linked to the WACB central hub, when established
2	Cheque-clearing system	Clearing cycle is D + 1 for certified cheques and D + 2 for ordinary cheques	Same as in The Gambia	Same as in The Gambia
3	Securities clearing and settlement system	Manual operation	SSS	Same as in The Gambia
4	Electronic payments (ATMs and POS)	There are no switching services		Adopted the WAMZ e-banking guidelines

Source: WAMI (2004).

Table 9.4 State of payments system in Nigeria

S/N	Components	Level of development	Planned action	Remarks
1	Large value payments	Implemented RTGS system		The RTGS would be linked to the WACB central hub, when established
2	Cheque-clearing system	Harmonized both up-country and local cheques to clearing cycle of D + 2	Decentralized automated system in all the clearing zones	Adopted the WAMZ cheque standard
3	ACH	Implemented an ACH		Adopted the WAMZ e-banking guidelines
4	Securities settlement system (SSS)	Scripless securities settlement system		Implemented SSS which is interfaced with the RTGS system

Source: WAMI (2004).

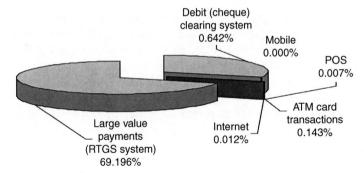

Figure 9.11 Nigeria – contribution of paper and electronic modes of payment (value), 2007 (source: WAMI (2008)).

Retail payments system: cheque-clearing system

By end June 2008, 12 cheque printers (local and foreign) were accredited by the CBN to print cheques. The volume and value of cheques trended upwards, largely due to increasing confidence in the use of cheques, arising from the reduction of the clearing cycle to T+2 and the automation of the system. The growth of the cheque usage is shown in Figures 9.12 and 9.13.

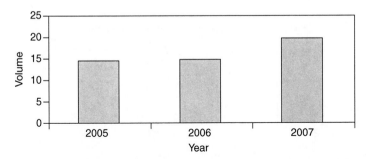

Figure 9.12 Nigeria – volume of cheques cleared, 2005–2007 (source: WAMI (2008)).

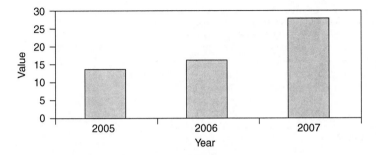

Figure 9.13 Nigeria – value of cheques cleared, 2005–2007 (source: WAMI (2008)).

Electronic payments

Electronic payments system increased during the review period. The rise in the level of transactions was largely attributable to the recognition of the need for a less cash-based society and acceptance of electronic mode of payments. Automated Teller Machine (ATMs) were the most popular means of payment due to the easy and convenient access to cash withdrawal, balance enquiries and other online transactions (Table 9.5).

The growths of electronic transactions are shown in Figures 9.14 to 9.21.

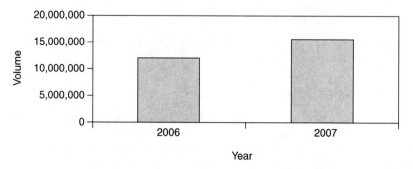

Figure 9.14 Nigeria – volume of ATM transactions, 2006–2007 (source: WAMI (2008)).

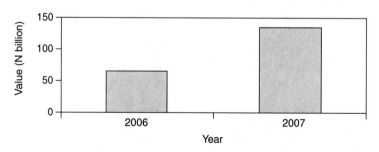

Figure 9.15 Nigeria – value of ATM transactions, 2006–2007 (source: WAMI (2008)).

Table 9.5 Breakdown of electronic payments, 2007

	Volume (%)	*Value (%)*
ATMS	88.77	88.46
Internet	5.10	7.14
POS	2.38	4.33
Mobile	3.75	0.07

Source: WAMI (2008).

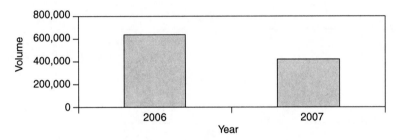

Figure 9.16 Nigeria – volume of POS transactions, 2006–2007 (source: WAMI (2008)).

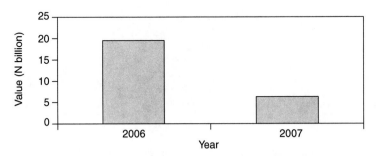

Figure 9.17 Nigeria – value of POS transactions, 2006–2007 (source: WAMI (2008)).

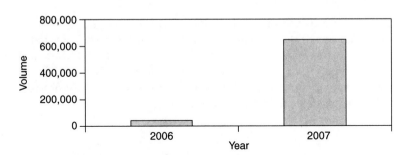

Figure 9.18 Nigeria – volume of mobile transactions, 2006–2007 (source: WAMI (2008)).

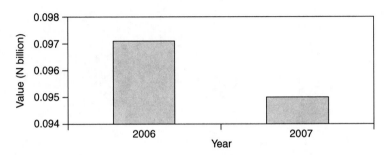

Figure 9.19 Nigeria – value of mobile transactions, 2006–2007 (source: WAMI (2008)).

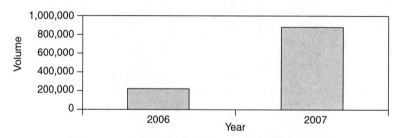

Figure 9.20 Nigeria – volume of internet transactions, 2006–2007 (source: WAMI (2008)).

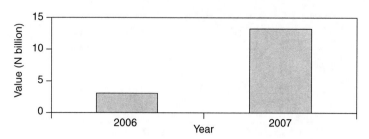

Figure 9.21 Nigeria – value of internet transactions, 2006–2007 (source: WAMI (2008)).

Wholesale payments: RTGS system

The RTGS system was operationalized in 2006, resulting in a significant growth in inter-bank funds transfers as the volume of transfers among participants of the CBN Inter-bank Funds Transfer System (CIFTS) and the CBN RTGS system increased tremendously. The growth reflected the confidence of the participants in the financial market and the stability of the CBN payments infrastructure (CIFTS and Terminos Internet Banking – TIB).

Sierra Leone

Cheque usage in Sierra Leone was stable during the period of 2005–2007, as shown in Figures 9.23 and 9.24.

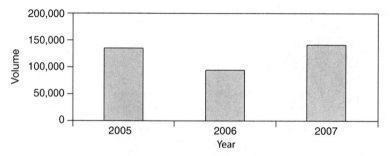

Figure 9.22 Nigeria – volume of large value payments (source: WAMI (2008)).

Table 9.6 State of payments system in Sierra Leone

S/N	Components	Level of development	Planned action	Remarks
1	Large value payments	Manual operation. Bank drafts and bankers payment are used for large value payments	Establishment of an RTGS system	The RTGS would be linked to the WACB central hub, when established
2.	Cheque-clearing system	Manual operation. Clearing cycle is D + 1 for local cheques and D + 6 for up country cheques	Establishment of an ACP and ACH	Adopted to the WAMZ cheque standard
3	Securities and settlement system (SSS)	Manual operation. The primary market for government T. bills is in book entry	Establishment of SSS	Same as in The Gambia
4	Electronic Payments (ATMS/POS)	Lack of interoperability	Implementation of an ATM switch	Adopted the WAMZ e-banking guidelines

Source: WAMI (2004).

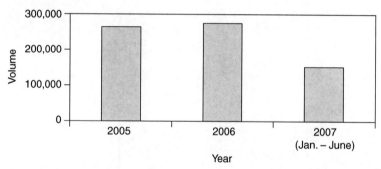

Figure 9.23 Sierra Leone – volume of cheques cleared, 2005–2007 (source: WAMI (2008)).

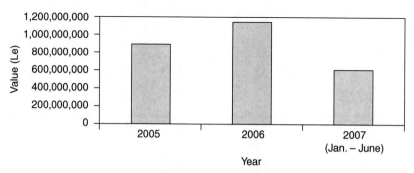

Figure 9.24 Sierra Leone – value of cheques cleared, 2005–2006 (source: WAMI (2008)).

Box 9.1 Experience of the European Union

The Trans-European Automated Real-Time Gross Settlement Express Transfer (TARGET) System

In November 1993, the working group on payment systems issued a report aimed at harmonizing payments systems in EU countries by establishing minimum common features for each constituent system (European Monetary Institute, 1993). The objectives of central banks of EU member states in promoting more unified payment arrangements were to create the technical conditions for the implementation of the single currency of the Economic and Monetary Union (EMU), and to ensure that differences between domestic payments systems would not create risks for the integrity and stability of domestic and cross-border arrangements and do not distort competition or create opportunities for regulatory arbitrage.

Ten principles were adopted, covering six areas: access conditions, risk management policies, legal issues, standards and infrastructures, pricing policies and business hours. Among the ten principles, the fourth stated that each member state should have, as soon as feasible, an RTGS system through which large-value and time-critical payments should be channelled.

The analysis (Paul Van Den Bergh) of the existing large-value payments systems in the member countries showed that more than 25 systems were dealing exclusively or in part, with large-value payments, and those systems were generally independent and not linked. The exchange of large-value payments between countries was recycling, therefore, on correspondent banking arrangements, but these arrangements were assessed to be inconsistent with the requirements for implementing a single monetary policy.

In line with the fourth principle, the central banks decided that the European large-value payment system should allow the exchange in real-time, on gross basis of payments in central bank money, based on the linkages of the RTGS that operated (or would soon operate) in EU countries.

Source: Summers (1994)

Box 9.2 African Development Bank (AfDB) support for payments system development in The Gambia, Guinea and Sierra Leone

As a pre-requisite for effective monetary integration, the WAMI undertook a payments system stock-take in 2004 in all the WAMZ member countries with a view to identifying the payments system needs of each country.

The study showed that large-value inter-bank payments were being effected by use of bank drafts in The Gambia, Guinea and Sierra Leone. Cheques were cleared and settled manually while payroll services were provided by banks through manual procedures. Similarly, the securities clearing and settlement system was manually operated in the three countries.

Given the need for an efficient system all through the Zone, WAMI sought assistance for the financing of the payments system in The Gambia, Guinea and Sierra Leone. Based on an Appraisal Report, the AfDB on 3 July 2008 approved a grant of US$23 million for payments system development in the three countries. The modernization of the payments systems to the same level as those in Ghana and Nigeria would facilitate not only the harmonization of the payment systems in all the five member countries, but also the process of launching a monetary union. The implementation of the project would also improve the efficiency of financial intermediation, liquidity management, monetary policy implementation and general deepening of the financial sector in the WAMZ.

The main components of the WAMZ Payments System Development Project include:

- Real Time Gross Settlement (RTGS) system;
- Automated Clearing House (ACH);
- Automated Cheque Processing (ACP);
- scriptless securities settlement (SSS) system;
- banking application; and
- infrastructure (telecommunications and energy) upgrade.

The assignment was to be conducted during a period of a maximum of 36 months, commencing in January 2009 and ending in December 2011.

Source: AfDB (2008)

Analysis of WAMZ payments systems

Level of development

There are variations in the level of development of the payment systems of the WAMZ member countries. The payments systems in Ghana and Nigeria were automated and have well established RTGS systems for large payments and time-critical payments, and have automated their respective cheque-clearing systems and established national switches for ATM services. However, the payment systems in The Gambia, Guinea and Sierra Leone are manual in operation, although modernization is under way (see Box 9.2).

Payments system laws, standards and guidelines

Given the need to establish an appropriate legal framework for the WAMZ payment systems, the Convergence Council approved for implementation a harmonized payments system law, common cheque standards, uniform ACP standards and electronic banking guidelines. Although these harmonized standards have been adopted by the five member countries, their implementation remains a big challenge.

Value of wholesale payments

Value of wholesale transactions carried out in the WAMZ countries each year averaged US$650 billion, representing more than four times the annual GDP of the WAMZ member countries. These transactions are usually domestic payments.

The different payment systems lack harmonization, characterized by:

1   fragmented payment system services, products, rules, regulations and procedures;
2   lack of integration of the payment systems as a result of

   • absence of RTGS system in some of the member countries,
   • absence of a central hub and relevant telecommunications network (Wide Area Network – WAN) to inter-link the RTGS systems of the member countries;

3   corresponding arrangements (limited transactions) which are inconsistent for implementing a single monetary policy;
4   high transaction costs, which also hamper or even prevent cross-border trade;
5   inefficient markets and stagnating product quality, due largely to low levels of development, automation, competition and harmonization.

Towards harmonized WAMZ payments systems

Creating a regional payments system with a view to facilitating cross-border payments between member states, promoting trade and enhancing monetary policy formulation and implementation would simultaneously enhance product quality and create a level playing field for all the member countries.

The major challenge in improving WAMZ payments systems include:

1   prompt implementation of the WAMZ payments system standards;
2   establishment of telecommunication network infrastructure, including WAN;
3   establishment of WAMZ Inter-bank Funds Transfer System (WIFTS). Upon implementation of the WIFTS, the NCBs would connect to the WACB RTGS system as direct participants and maintain settlement accounts in the common currency, when introduced. Each NCB would maintain an eco account with the WACB for settlement of cross-border payments in the common currency. Commercial banks would open eco accounts at the NCB.

The WIFTS/WACB RTGS system remained a critical infrastructural requirement for launching a monetary union. The system would enable the WACB to efficiently perform its functions, including:

*   formulating and implementing monetary policy;
*   issuing currency;
*   managing foreign reserves; and
*   providing liquidity to the financial system.

The major objectives of the WIFTS include:

*   enhance the capacity of the WACB in monetary policy management;
*   increase financial system stability in the WAMZ member countries as float will be eliminated;
*   improve the efficiency of financial intermediation throughout the WAMZ.

Establishment of WIFTS would greatly assist the monetary union in facilitating the move to a common currency, boost regional cross-border trade and regional integration as well as facilitation of an effective open market operations/banking system liquidity management system across the Zone.

Conclusions

The state of the payments systems development in the WAMZ can be summarized as follows:

1   There is a steady migration to non-cash modes of payment in the five WAMZ member countries;
2   The payments systems of the WAMZ member countries are at various levels of development;
3   Ghana and Nigeria have largely automated their payment systems, particularly the RTGS system, which is essential for cross-border funds transfers and an efficient banking system liquidity management;

4   The WACB central hub to facilitate an efficient monetary policy implementation, irrespective of the structure of the WACB to be adopted, may not be ready until 2013;

5   The connectivity of the respective domestic RTGS systems to the WACB central hub, in order to have a regional payment system for cross-border transfers and monetary policy management, is projected for 2013. In effect, the respective RTGS systems of the member countries, ACH and ATMS/national switches would remain stand-alone systems until about 2013.

References

AfDB (2008). Project Appraisal Report. Online: www.afdb.org/en/documents/project-operations/project-appraisal-reports.

Johnson, O.E., Abrams, R.K., Destresse, J., Lybek, T., Roberts, N.M. and Swinburne, M. (1998). *Payments Systems, Monetary Policy, and the Role of the Central Bank*, Washington, DC: IMF.

Summers, B.J. (1994). *The Payment System: Design, Management, and Supervision*, Washington, DC: IMF.

WAMI (2004a). *Payments System Study in WAMZ Member Countries: Stock Report*, June, Accra, Ghana: WAMI.

WAMI (2004b). *Payments System Study: Strategy and Policy Framework Report*, September, June, Accra, Ghana: WAMI.

WAMI (2008). *Convergence Report*. Online: www.wami-imao.org.

Part III

Operational and institutional framework

10 Monetary policy framework and statistical harmonization

Emmanuel Ukeje, Momodu Sissoho and Mohamed Conte

Introduction

Monetary policy as a tool of macroeconomic management is focused on several specific objectives, including enhanced growth, domestic price stability, exchange rate stability, monetary stability, maintenance of a sound financial system, balance of payments equilibrium and ensuring adequate external reserves to safeguard the international value of the domestic currency. In the literature, the major factors that have shaped the focus of monetary policy are the specific macroeconomic environment, size and structure of the financial sector, as well as the stage of the development of the economy concerned.

The primary goal of monetary policy is the attainment of price stability, to ensure predictable and conducive environment for sound economic decisions. The overriding goal of the West African Central Bank (WACB), as enshrined in its Statute, will be the maintenance of domestic price stability in the member countries. To pursue this objective successfully, the central bank should be provided with a high degree of instrumental independence, should demonstrate transparency and accountability in its operations and should abstain from financing government deficits. The Statute therefore provides that in pursuit of its primary goal of price stability, the bank shall be independent and free from the control of any government or institution and should not engage in lending to governments. The annual policy statement of the bank shall specify the inflation target. Also, the conduct of monetary policy should be based on market-based instruments and strategies.

The selection of price stability as the primary goal of monetary policy does not imply that the other potential objectives mentioned earlier are no longer relevant. If price stability becomes the ultimate goal of monetary policy, the other goals of national economic policy could be simultaneously realized, given the positive contribution of the price stability to their own sustained achievement. The price stability objective of monetary policy is therefore not inconsistent with the need to minimize fluctuations in domestic output. Further, a central bank perceived by economic agents as having a strong commitment to price stability, in both short and medium term, provides an anchor for low inflation expectations, thus facilitating the achievement of growth with price stability.

The conduct of monetary policy can be hindered by poor-quality statistics occasioned especially by different regimes of compilation methodologies. This would result in misleading signals and accompanying reactions from a supranational bank. The benchmark harmonization of statistical data on inflation and national accounts is paramount, while international best practice must be the rule for government, financial and external sector statistics.

The statistical preparations for monetary union are dictated by the requirements for the effective implementation of the common monetary policy, as well as by the need for credibility and transparency in the assessment of country compliance with the set of convergence criteria (stipulated as prerequisites for eligibility for entry into the union). The effective implementation of the common monetary policy, following the establishment of the monetary union, requires availability of statistical information of relatively good quality on the economic and financial conditions as well as the various policies and instruments. This would enable the WACB to compile monetary aggregates for the WAMZ.

Monetary policy instruments

A wide array of monetary policy instruments are used by central banks all over the world for the conduct of monetary policy. The choice of specific policy instruments depends on the particular economic environment, with particular reference to the ease with which the central bank can apply the instruments, as well as the ability of the instruments to transmit relevant impact for achieving the ultimate objective of policy and the ability to assess policy outcomes by the use of the policy instruments.

Poole (1970) defines monetary policy instruments as the policy variables that are under the control of the central bank. These are generally considered to include those items on the balance sheet of the bank, the monetary base or the bank rates at which it trades in the market. The main instrument could be the interest rate of its main lending facility or the exchange rate at which it trades in the foreign exchange market. The interest rate instrument is more conventionally preferred, especially where levels of foreign exchange reserves are not particularly high.

The monetary policy instruments proposed by WAMI to be used by the WACB are broadly the same as presently used by the national central banks (NCBs) of the WAMZ. These instruments should be structured as a package of the WACB and applied in line with the financial market environment. They include interest and exchange rates on items in the portfolios of the central banks and changes in reserve requirements. The operating frameworks include open market operations (OMO) in government and central bank securities in the secondary market, the use of repo agreements, discount window operations. Shifting government deposits between central bank and deposit money banks is also another instrument of monetary policy that could be used to influence the level of liquidity in the banking system. Essentially, improving the effectiveness of the monetary policy instruments requires the sustained development of financial markets and payments systems.

Current international practices embrace cases where the overall goal, such as the inflation target, is either defined for the central bank or else the latter determines the appropriate inflation target by itself. The emerging consensus is that democratic principles are in favour of a central bank that is goal-dependent. In other words, the government should specify the goal of the central bank backed up by a nominal anchor. It is suggested that the Authority of Heads of State and Government of the WAMZ, based on the advice of the Governing Council, should specify the goal of the WACB from time to time.

Based on the foregoing, The WACB should be goal-dependent, but instrument-independent. This means that, having been given a goal by the political authorities, the WACB should be empowered to select and use the monetary policy instruments it deems fit for achieving that goal. Instrument independence for the WACB is likely to assist the bank in applying and evaluating the effects of its policy instruments. Put differently, the WACB and its national branches will be subjected to fewer pressures when they have freedom to use the identified monetary policy instruments. This is in consonance with democratic principles which require that an independent central bank should be accountable to the public and the government. The WACB, it is proposed, should be required to present periodic reports on its operations to the authorities of the WAMZ.

The WACB must not finance governments (broadly defined) in any form. This will allow for the dominance of monetary policy and high probability of the bank achieving its overall objective of price stability. There would thus be no granting of advances, no underwriting of government securities, no foreign borrowing on behalf of the government, no financial sector restructuring which leads to the central bank taking over non-performing debt, no financing of development activities that result in injecting unproductive liquidity into the economy and no giving of overdrafts to state-owned enterprises.

The monetary policy instruments used by the national central banks of the WAMZ and which would be adopted by the WACB in its conduct of monetary policy are divided into three groups. The first group consists of the instrument variables controlled by the monetary authorities, which include changes in the balance sheet of the central bank and the domestic deposit money banks. Basically, the changes in the portfolios of the central bank affect the base or reserve money, while changes in the portfolios of the domestic deposit money banks affect their reserve balances and credit operations. This strategy of monetary control has to a large extent been efficacious in the member countries of the WAMZ.

The second group of instruments involves changes in the monetary aggregates supply, domestic credit, interest and exchange rates. The basic instrument is the conduct of open market operations involving trading in government securities in the primary market, introduction of central bank securities of short- and medium-to-long-term tenor and dealings in foreign exchange in the market. The foreign exchange operations involve swaps as well as outright sales and purchases of foreign exchange. These actions rely on influencing market-related interest rates. By definition, under a market-based monetary policy regime, the monetary authorities cannot influence these intermediate instruments except through the use of its operating policy instruments, which fall into the third category. These operating instruments can be functionally classified without giving the impression of a watertight division in their application. These operations are normally undertaken along with the use of repo agreements, discount window operations and changes in reserve requirements, liquidity ratio (prudential) and cash ratios.

Shifting of government deposits between the banks and the central bank is another form of liquidity management with the basic assumption that the central bank has the power to direct the movement of those deposits through an arrangement with the treasury. It is still the common practice in the WAMZ that government accounts are largely kept with the central bank.

In advanced countries, the interest rate is the primary tool of monetary policy with significant success achieved with this instrument, thanks to well developed financial markets. This is not the case in many developing countries. The NCBs of WAMZ favour the setting of the bank rate (minimum rediscount rate) with a defined relationship with the official rates on securities, the inter-bank funds rate and market rates. However, with developed and competitive financial markets, the central bank interest rate policy action would be promptly transmitted to the market. There is need to strengthen the financial markets and payments systems for the effectiveness of monetary policy.

The monetary policy model

Countries use different quantitative techniques to determine the critical stock of money that is consistent with the ultimate objectives of monetary policy. The quantitative techniques range from simple analytical models to sophisticated ones. Developing countries in sub-Saharan Africa have limited options because of inadequate data and the difficulty of identifying the proper transmission mechanism. While the use of sophisticated models is considered ideal by the WACB due to improvements in macroeconomic data, reliance on the simple and standard model of monetary control would be appropriate in the short run.

The model consists of several building blocks. The starting point is to determine the public's demand for money balances. Empirical estimations of the public demand for money are usually based on equations in which the independent variables are the gross domestic product (GDP), inflation, interest rates and the existing stock of money. Historical data are used in regression analysis for projecting the appropriate changes in the money demand. This method requires stability in the money demand function. The more pragmatic approach for obtaining the same information is through projection of the likely change in the ratio of money to nominal GDP or the velocity of money.[1] The next step is defining the money supply process, which is aimed at targeting the demand for money. The accounting framework consists of the monetary survey, which consolidates the accounts of the monetary authorities and the deposit money banks. By combining these accounts, money is created in two stages: the initial creation of reserve money through the increase of the liabilities of the central bank to the public and the banking system; and a secondary expansion by the domestic money banks. The money demand and supply estimates are usually undertaken within a consistent macroeconomic framework, commonly identified as the financial programming model.

Monetary policy targets and indicators

All central banks in the WAMZ except the Bank of Ghana (BOG) use the monetary targeting strategy. The central banks of the Zone target several financial variables (such as reserve money) and their counterparts in the net domestic assets in order to achieve the ultimate objective of price stability. Achieving sustained economic growth is also considered in the central banking statutes as a secondary objective of member countries provided the objective of price stability is not jeopardized. The choice of these targets depends on the structure of their economies, the availability of information technology, and the level of independence accorded the central banks. Monetary targeting based on robust liquidity forecasting technique is the preferred monetary policy framework proposed for the WACB by WAMI for monetary management. Inflation targeting would be considered when inflation forecasting techniques are well developed to a reasonable degree.

Transmission mechanism of monetary policy

The transmission mechanism of monetary policy indicates the channels through which changes in monetary policy instruments influence the ultimate objectives of inflation and output. The transmission mechanism varies from country to country, and economists hold divergent views on how it operates. Four main channels have been identified in the literature. They include the direct interest rate effect on the cost of credit and cash flow of debtors and creditors; the impact on domestic asset prices both financial and real assets; the exchange rate; and the availability of credit (see Mishkin, 1995; Bernanke and Getler, 1995; Meltzer, 1995). Given the differences in the economic environment and structure, it is important to understand within the policy design and implementation setting, since the policy instruments impact on inflation and output objectives in a complex way with long and variable lags.

The dynamics of the transmission process when quantified can help policymakers better monitor and evaluate the effectiveness of their policy actions. The channels of transmission mechanism in developed market economies is stylized to start from the policy instrument, which is a change in the official short-term interest rate affecting market interest rates, asset prices, the exchange rate and people's expectations and confidence. In economies where the financial markets are underdeveloped, the standard transmission mechanism may be weak or not as effective as in developed financial systems. Deregulation of the financial sector enhances the competitiveness of the financial markets in developed economies, but the situation is far from ideal in most developing countries. Consequently, a change in interest rates may not transmit the appropriate signals promptly and even though the signals may show in the long run, it would result in the emergence of a new set of monetary conditions.

Monetary policy actions in economies with less developed financial markets are generally transmitted to the real sector through the credit and exchange rate channels. In the credit channel, an increase in the money supply raises the stock of credit in the economy which directly influences consumers spending, resulting to increased borrowing from the banking sector. Even in the informal financial sector, a substantial amount of credit is disbursed through market associations, trade and town unions. In an open economy with a floating exchange rate regime, wealth portfolios may include domestic and foreign assets. With an increase in the money supply, for instance, a portfolio adjustment may take place resulting in higher demand for foreign assets and a depreciation of the exchange rate. The portfolio adjustment can also take place in response to changes in domestic and international interest rates. A depreciated exchange rate will increase the prices of imported goods and cost of output, while reducing the price of exports, resulting in an increase in net exports and hence output, respectively, assuming the Marshall Lerner condition holds.[2]

The transmission mechanism in the WAMZ countries

The WACB will vigorously pursue the reform of the financial sector in the WAMZ member countries to enhance the efficiency of the financial markets and the transmission mechanism of monetary policy through changes in official interest rates. This section briefly reviews the existing monetary policy frameworks. The transmission channels of monetary policy were investigated in the WAMZ countries using annual data for the period 1980–2007 and employing a Vector Auto-regression (VAR) Model.

VAR models are dynamic systems of equations in which the current level of each variable in the system depends on past movements in that variable and all other variables in the system. This methodology allows us to place minimal restrictions on how monetary shocks affect the economy – which, given the lack of analytical work on the workings of the monetary transmission mechanism – is a distinct advantage. In addition, this approach recognizes explicitly the simultaneity between monetary policy and macroeconomic developments, that is, the dependence of monetary policy on other economic variables (the policy reaction function), as well as the dependence of economic variables on monetary policy. Also, once estimated, VAR can be used to simulate the response over time of any variable in the set to either an own disturbance or a disturbance to any other variable in the system and to produce variance decomposition and impulse response of the variables.

A precondition for monetary union is a market-determined interest rate and reasonable convergence of the monetary policy transmission mechanism across the participating countries. A change in the union's common central bank instrument setting could give rise to serious strains and inefficiencies, since it has very different effects on economic and financial conditions in different parts of the union. For instance, when the central bank raises interest rates in response to a Zone-wide inflationary shock and if the consequences of this monetary contraction differ from country to country, either in terms of the timing or the impact on real variables, then the output cost of maintaining price stability will be unevenly spread across the monetary union. Convergence of the monetary transmission mechanism is therefore advantageous for the operation of a monetary union. However, it is important to emphasize that full uniformity of the monetary transmission mechanism is not required. Even within Europe's monetary union there is evidence of differences in the monetary transmission mechanism across participating countries. But if in the WAMZ, those differences were pronounced, the implications could be significant for the effectiveness of the future common monetary policy. The NCBs are given significant degrees of autonomy in their monetary policy operations which augur well for their credibility.

The Gambia

The Central Bank of The Gambia (CBG) adopted an indirect monetary policy framework in the context of the economic and financial reforms undertaken since 1986. This involves the use of OMO in government and central bank securities as well as imposition of reserve requirements in place of selective credit and interest rate controls. A treasury bills market (money market) was introduced in 1987 to facilitate the migration from direct to indirect monetary policy regime. The CBG uses weekly auctioning of treasury and central bank bills through primary dealers for both government deficit financing and control of money supply, while using reserve money as an intermediate target. The independence of the bank in the conduct of monetary policy was enhanced under the revised Statute of the Central Bank (2005), which also prescribed price stability as the overriding mandate of the bank. Recent innovations include the setting up of a Monetary Policy Committee (MPC) in 2004 to oversee monetary policy implementation and ensure that the price stability objective is given prominence in the monetary and exchange rate activities of the bank. Since its establishment, the MPC, though still defining its price objective in terms of headline inflation, also reports on core inflation as well as other indicators, as a barometer of underlining price developments.

The results of the study of the channels of monetary policy transmission in The Gambia showed that the interest rate channel was weak in influencing changes in output. The bank lending channel was more profound in channelling the effect of monetary policy on output. The result also found that money supply and exchange rate had significant effects on inflation, which confirms the exchange rate pass-through mechanism and the monetarist approach to inflation. The study also revealed that reserve money multiplier was stable and predictable indicating that the monetary aggregates are amenable to control by the central bank. This supports the appropriateness of the quantitative monetary targeting framework adopted by the authorities.

Ghana

The overriding goal of monetary policy in Ghana is price stability, which is stated explicitly in the Bank of Ghana Law (2002), Act 612. Section 3(1) of the law stipulates that "the primary objective of the Bank is to maintain stability in the general level of prices". The law thus gives a clear mandate to BOG to pursue inflation-targeting. It is envisioned that the implementation of sound monetary and financial policies aimed at price stability would create an enabling macroeconomic environment for the promotion of sustainable economic growth and poverty reduction. The BOG formally adopted an inflation-targeting framework for its monetary policy operations to track underlying inflation, using a core measure of the Consumer Price Index (CPI), which excluded energy and utility prices in May 2007. Prior to that, the strategy for monetary management was based on monetary targeting, i.e. the view that inflation is essentially a monetary phenomenon.

In the case of Ghana, the study on the transmission mechanism of monetary policy revealed an inverse relationship between real GDP and treasury bill rate and the coefficient was significant. Furthermore, a positive relationship between inflation and treasury bill rate was also evident. This result showed that monetary policy in Ghana had significant impact on both output and inflation, and the interest rate channel was effective in transmitting the impact of monetary policy on domestic output and prices. The implication of the results is that an expansionary monetary policy[3] increased both output and domestic prices channelled via the interest rate channel. The exchange rate channel revealed that the exchange rate is negatively related to treasury bill rate with a statistically significant coefficient. Concurrently, the result found a negative relationship between output and exchange rate. However, the coefficient was insignificant, indicating a weak exchange rate channel. The result nevertheless indicated a strong exchange rate pass-through to domestic prices, as evident by the positive relationship between inflation and exchange rate with a statistically significant coefficient.

Guinea

The objective of monetary policy in Guinea is to control inflation. The authorities set targets for rate of growth of reserve money and monitor its evolution through quarterly benchmarks on its counterparts: the central bank's minimum level of net foreign assets and its net credit to government position. Since 1993, indirect monetary policy instruments, or OMO, have been in use, with the application of reserve requirements.

Results of the estimation showed that in Guinea, monetary policy had significant effect on inflation and output. However, in terms of the transmission channel, the results indicated that the interest rate channel was weak, while the exchange rate pass-through to domestic prices was significant, indicating that exchange rate depreciation resulted in price increases during the review period. The credit channel (bank lending channel) was the main route through which the impact of monetary policy was transmitted to the domestic economy. Thus the coefficient of private sector credit[4] was statistically significant for both output and inflation. The results showed a positive relationship between inflation and exchange rate with a statistically significant coefficient.

Nigeria

The main monetary policy objective in Nigeria is price stability and promoting non-inflationary growth. The primary means adopted to achieve this objective is to set aggregate money supply targets[5] and to rely on OMO and other policy instruments to achieve the target. In November, 2006, the MPC of the Central Bank of Nigeria (CBN) adopted a new policy framework that introduced a new Monetary Policy Rate (MPR) to replace the Minimum Rediscount Rate (MRR). The new framework became necessary as the MRR proved not to be sufficiently responsive to CBN's policy initiatives, especially in tackling the problem of excess liquidity in the system. The MPR determines the lower and upper band of the CBN standing facility and was intended as the nominal anchor for all other rates in the market. The MPC meets every other month to review developments in the economy.

According to the findings on the monetary policy transmission mechanism in Nigeria, shocks to monetary policy affected both output and inflation. The decrease in output following the monetary shock was mostly considered to be the result of investment contractions and only to a lesser degree the result of personal consumption contraction. Also, a temporary growth of the short-run interest rate is followed by the real appreciation of the exchange rate over time. The results indicate that the dominant channel of transmitting monetary impulses to GDP is through the interest rate channel.

Sierra Leone

Monetary policy in Sierra Leone is conducted within the framework of a monetary targeting regime. Prior to 1990, monetary policy was conducted using direct instruments of monetary management. In 1990, the Bank of Sierra Leone, in a bid to address emerging economic challenges, shifted away from direct monetary controls (which was found to be financially repressive) to an indirect system of monetary management. Thus, the main instrument of monetary policy is OMO, and operations are concentrated in the primary market for government securities.

The study revealed that shocks to monetary policy affected prices and output in Sierra Leone. The study also found that the interest rate channel was not effective in the transmission of monetary policy shocks to output and inflation. This may be attributed to the relatively underdeveloped state of the money market in the country and the limited participation of the general public in securities trading. However, the results showed that shocks to monetary policy were transmitted to output and inflation through the bank lending channel. The study also found that depreciation of the exchange rate resulted in an increase in the aggregate price level, confirming the exchange rate pass-through to domestic price hypothesis.

Foreign reserve management

Foreign exchange reserves perform an important role because they increase a country's or union's overall resilience to shocks. A good example of the usefulness of an adequate level of reserves as well as effective reserve management was demonstrated in the currency or financial crises that hit a number of Asian countries in the late 1990s. What started out as a financial crisis quickly turned into a currency crisis with member countries' reserves falling to historically low levels. Effective reserve management ensures that adequate official public sector foreign assets are readily available to, and controlled by, the authorities for meeting a defined range of objectives for a country or union. The importance of sound practices were highlighted by experiences where weak or risky reserve management practices restricted the ability of the authorities to respond effectively to financial crises, which accentuated the severity of these crises.

Weak or risky reserve management practices have significant financial and reputational costs. Some countries, for example, incurred large losses that had direct or indirect fiscal consequences. Accordingly, appropriate portfolio management policies concerning the currency composition, choice of investment instruments and acceptable duration of the reserve portfolio, reflecting a country's specific policy setting and circumstances, serving to ensure that assets are safeguarded, are readily available and support market confidence. Also, through their interaction with the financial markets, reserve managers gain access to valuable information that keeps policy-makers informed of market developments and views on potential threats.

Reserve management options for WAMZ

The central banks in the Zone manage foreign exchange reserves on behalf of their governments. Following the acceptance of the obligations of Article VIII, Sections 2, 3, and 4 of the IMF Articles of Agreement on current account convertibility, in addition to the reduction of capital controls by most of the member countries, exchange rates were allowed to float within certain bounds. Under the circumstances, external reserves were maintained to ward off speculative attacks on the domestic currencies and to redeem local currencies held abroad on account of eligible current account transactions, when need arises. All the countries in the WAMZ operate flexible exchange rate systems, which make redundant the use of capital controls to defend a pegged exchange rate.

It is expected that the WACB would implement an optimal reserves management framework. The reserves to be managed by the WACB are to be pooled from member countries of the WAMZ that also belong to the WACB. The major guiding principle for foreign reserve management is the adoption of aggressive foreign reserve management while ensuring liquidity and the safety of investment. The primary concern should be a reasonable yield with manageable risks.

The maximization of income or returns on reserves entails rational portfolio management that combines safe and risky investments in such a manner that results in a positive yield. Sound reserve management policies can support, but are not a substitute for, sound macroeconomic management. Moreover, inappropriate economic policies (whether fiscal, monetary or exchange rate-focused) can pose serious risks to the ability to manage reserves.

Under the WACB, the reserves to be managed come in the form of full or partial pooling. Full pooling of reserves entails the transfer of all the reserves of the NCBs to the WACB. Under this scenario, adequate provision is made for short-term claims falling due. Also, the normal needs of the member countries is determined and provided for before reserves are transferred to the WACB. In order to eliminate any resort to the use of the reserves already transferred to the WACB by the NCBs and provision for short-term claims, reserves should be partially pooled by the WACB, in which part of the NCBs' foreign reserves are held by the WACB, while the remaining reserves are held by the respective NCBs.

Exchange rate regime

The exchange rate system is critical in the determination of the minimum quantum of reserves that a central bank should hold. In a fixed exchange rate system, the quantum of reserves should be relatively large to reflect the ability of the common central bank to defend the external value of the currency and stabilize the foreign exchange market. On the other hand, in a flexible exchange rate arrangement, reserves may not be unduly large as market forces are largely relied upon to determine the external value of the currency. Proposals by WAMI on the options of exchange rate system for the WAMZ common currency, the eco, favour a flexible exchange rate regime bordering on a managed float, with some degree of intervention through foreign reserves held by the WACB (WAMI, 2001).

The IMF classifies flexible exchange rate systems based on the degree of flexibility and the existence of formal or informal commitments to an exchange rate path. It distinguishes between more rigid forms of pegged regimes (such as currency board arrangements), other conventional pegged regimes against a single currency or a basket of currencies, exchange rate bands around a fixed peg, crawling peg arrangements and exchange rate bands in order to help assess the implications of the choice of exchange rate regime for the degree of independence of monetary policy. All the countries in the WAMZ fall under the category of those with a managed floating exchange rate without a predetermined path.

Framework for the WAMZ statistical harmonization programme

The general approach to statistical harmonization for the WAMZ monetary union is characterized by the establishment and adoption of "minimum standards" which stipulate data quality rules, compilation standards or thresholds. It is based on consensus among experts on best available practices to ensure comparability, reliability and relevance of the data from member states. The strategy therefore focuses on the principles of methodological soundness (i.e. definitions, scope and classification), accuracy and reliability (i.e. assessment of source data and statistical methodology) and serviceability (i.e. timeliness, periodicity and accessibility). The focus of the harmonization programme was to ensure that member states' statistics are comparable through the adoption of a common presentational platform and classification systems. The specific frameworks adopted by the WAMZ Statistical Harmonization Programme for the various sector statistics are discussed in the following paragraphs.

Monetary and financial statistics

For the monetary and financial statistics in the WAMZ, the major concerns are the provision of a wider coverage and classification issues in the compilation of monetary aggregates to include all the institutions that receive deposits and other repayable funds from the public and grant credit to different sectors of the economy. With respect to the minimum comparability standards that allow WAMI to monitor macroeconomic convergence in the WAMZ countries, there is need for harmonization of concepts, as well as definition and classification of main sectors and sub-sectors, based on economic objectives, functions and behaviour. Sectorization is key to the analytical aggregates on credit and broad money that form the basis of the surveys of the financial corporations sector. The categorization of financial corporation sectors as recommended in the Monetary and Financial Statistics Manual (MFSM) follows the sectorization principles in the SNA1993.[6] It is important to note that the definition of residency in this sectorization should also be consistent with the BPM5.[7]

All countries in the WAMZ are required to endeavour to apply as closely as possible the above sectoral groupings in their monetary and financial statistics, which is the primary framework for presentation of the monetary statistics. Therefore, the Depository Corporation Survey (DCS) consolidates the accounts of all depository corporations (issuers of broad money liabilities). These include the accounts of the Central Bank Survey (CBS) and the Other Depository Corporation Survey (ODCS) (referring to commercial banks within the region). The ultimate aim is to achieve the broadest coverage to the level of the ODCS to produce the Financial Corporation Survey (FCS), which consolidates the entire sector of financial corporations and enables the analysis of credit extended by the overall economy.

Government fiscal operations

Data on fiscal operations of government are essential in analysing economic and financial developments in member states as well as assessing compliance with primary and secondary criteria. The framework for fiscal data harmonization is based on the Government Finance Statistics (GFS) Manual, which sets uniform standards for the compilation and classification of the various components of budgetary operations of government. These include data on government expenditure, revenue and fiscal deficits, as well as their financing modalities. Furthermore, data on tax revenue and wages form an important variable in the determination of convergence compliance. While some countries present data for the central government, others report for all of the public sector, including state and local governments. The minimum comparability standard set for the WAMZ is to cover central government accounts. Where the financial activities of the different tiers of government are significant, however, the reliability of assessing the fiscal stance is compromised. The ultimate aim is to achieve wide coverage of the accounts to the level of general government.[8]

Balance of payments (BOP) statistics

The framework for the BOP is based on the standard concepts, definitions, classifications and conventions as provided and illustrated in the fifth edition of the BPM5 and a companion volume, the Balance of Payments Compilation Guide. According to the BPM5, the two major classifications in the BOP statement are the current account and the capital and financial account. The former shows transactions in the real economy and relates to goods, services, income and current transfers, while the latter records the transactions in the financial economy. Since the WACB operations include the pooling of reserves, as stipulated in Article 30 of the WACB statutes, it is important to have a separate statistical template (a common template for international reserves and foreign currency liquidity). The definitions of these assets are in line with definitions given under reserve assets mentioned above. Therefore the WACB's claim in foreign currency on non-residents of the single currency zone – plus gold, special drawing rights (SDRs) and the reserve position in the IMF – are the relevant BOP transactions/holdings for the WAMZ and they are the reserve assets, provided that they meet the liquidity and marketability criteria required by BPM5. However, if NCBs are to retain any part of their reserve assets, then only those effectively controlled by them are included in the national BOP reserve assets item. The balance of payments for the WAMZ comprises the transactions of residents of the Zone with countries outside the Zone and must exclude cross-border exchanges of goods, services, capital and income within the WAMZ.

Real sector statistics

The framework for the harmonization of the national accounts is based on SNA93. Member countries are required to implement programmes and projects to update their SNA methodological frameworks in line with SNA93 guidelines. These include improving transactions coverage, timeliness of reporting, quality of source data through regular surveys and frequent updating of sectoral establishment and enterprise registers. Out-of-date ratios and benchmarks also need to be revamped. Member countries should also adopt uniform nomenclature (International Standard Industrial Classification – ISIC). The exercise should include estimations of unrecorded and informal sector activity.

As regards CPI harmonization, the adopted framework is for countries to update their basket contents and base years using recent household expenditure surveys, which at the commencement of the WAMZ programme were in some cases more than ten years old and not reflective of existing consumption patterns. Other key benchmarks included the extension of coverage to national (rural and urban) in all countries and adoption of the Classification of Individual Consumption by Purpose (COICOP).

Conclusions

An assessment of the monetary policy transmission mechanism in the WAMZ countries revealed that while, on the one hand, the interest rate channel appeared to be dominant in Ghana and Nigeria, on the other hand, the bank lending channel appeared to be important in The Gambia, Guinea and Sierra Leone. This result may be due to the relatively underdeveloped nature of the financial sector in the latter countries.

The central banks in Ghana and Nigeria (and to some extent The Gambia) are better able to guide the market interest rate using monetary policy instruments. Financial institutions are in a position to make better pricing, and market participants are more sensitive to interest rate changes. This showed that the importance of the interest rate in resource allocation and in transmitting monetary policy has become more apparent in these countries.

Monetary policy instruments have witnessed further improvement over the years. A framework was set up in which a combination of open market operations and other instruments such as central bank lending and rediscount facilities, are used to adjust reserve money and to manage credit aggregates. The role of open market operations was strengthened in the daily management of liquidity. Second, the role of interest rates as an indicator of the monetary policy stance was strengthened through the MPC framework. It is therefore important that the monetary authorities in these countries institute policy measures aimed at broadening and deepening of the money market through the development of varied money market instruments and development of secondary market trading.

Although the strategy for monetary policy management in all the member countries, except Ghana, is based on monetary targeting, there are plans by the remaining countries to migrate to inflation targeting regimes. The WACB is likely to adopt an inflation-targeting framework for its monetary policy strategy by tracking headline and underlying or core inflation, using a Harmonized Index of Consumer Prices (HICP) for the Zone.

Despite the progress being made in improvement of data quality in the Zone, there is a need for further harmonization, especially in respect of the required standards for the common monetary policy of the WAMZ. There is need to continue pursuing the implementation of SNA93 so countries will reduce the lag in the compilation and publication of comprehensive (preferably quarterly and half-yearly) GDP estimates with production and expenditure approaches, and to monitor industrial and agricultural output and prices more reliably.

The adoption of common suitable software for the processing of source data is important for furthering the harmonization process, focusing on remaining deficiencies in respect of the data compilation methodologies and reporting standards. This has proven very beneficial in the area of automating customs data processing in the Economic Community of West African States (ECOWAS), which could be extended to the other data areas within the framework of the adoption of a common nomenclature and methodology for compiling the various sectoral accounts details. It must be noted that the process of improvement and harmonization of statistics would continue even after monetary union. The process will continue to pursue the strengthening of collaboration with partners, including the ECOWAS Commission, African Development Bank and the World Bank, in order to secure technical support and capacity building to the national statistics offices of member countries.

Notes

1 The velocity of money is the inverse of the rates of money to nominal GDP.
2 The Marshall Lerner condition states that depreciation will improve net export when the elasticities of demand for import and export exceeds unity.
3 Expansionary monetary policy means an increase in money supply, engendered by a fall in treasury bill rates. The fall in treasury bill rate is due to the purchase of treasury bills from the open market by the government, which subsequently results to an increase in money supply.
4 Private sector credit was the variable used to capture the bank lending channel. This channel indicated that the increase in money supply would increase bank deposits, which then result in an increase in bank lending to the private sector. The increase in private sector credit also increases investment and hence output growth, through the multiplier effect.
5 Plans are far advanced in the preparations towards the introduction of inflation targeting as the monetary policy strategy in Nigeria.
6 SNA means Systems of National Accounts.
7 BPM5 means Balance of Payments Manual, fifth edition.
8 Includes all levels of government – central, state and local government.

References

Al-Mansouri, A.K.L. and Dziobeck, C.C. (2006). "Providing Official Statistics for the Common Market and Monetary Union in Gulf Cooperation Council (GCC) Countries: A Case for 'Gulfstat' ", *IMF Working Paper*, WP/06/38 correction.

Batini, N. and Laxton, D. (2006). "Under What Condition Can Inflation Targeting Be Adopted? The Experience of Emerging Markets", *Central Bank of Chile Working Paper*, no. 406.

Bénassy-Quéré, A. and Coupet, M. (2003). "On the Adequacy of Monetary Arrangements in Sub-Saharan Africa", Working paper release by CEPII (Centre d'Etudes Prospectives et d'Informations Internationales), August.

Bernanke, B.S., and Gertler, M. (1995). "Inside the Black Box: The Credit Channel of Monetary Policy Transmission", *Journal of Economic Perspectives*, 9(4), 27–48.

Bull, P. (2004). *The Development of Statistics for Economic and Monetary Union*, Frankfurt am Maim: ECB, January.

Central Bank of Nigeria (2006). *Monetary Policy Committee Report.*

ECB (1998). *The Single Monetary Policy in Stage Three: General Documentation on ESCB Monetary Policy Instruments and Procedures*, Frankfurt am Maim: ECB.

ECB (1999). "The Stability-oriented Monetary Policy Strategy of the Eurosystem", *ECB Monthly Bulletin*, January, 39–50.

ECB (2003). "Concerning Certain Statistical Reporting Requirements of the European Central Bank and the Procedures for Reporting by the National Central Bank", ECB/2003/2.

EMI (1997). *The Single Monetary Policy in Stage Three: Specification of the Operational Framework*, Frankfurt am Maim: EMI.

Gambia (2005). Central Bank of The Gambia Act.

Ghana (2002). Bank of Ghana Act.

IMF (1993). *Government Finance Statistics Manual* [GFSM], Washington, DC: IMF.

IMF (1993). *Balance of Payments Manual*, 5th edn [BPM5], Washington, DC: IMF.

IMF (2000). *Monetary and Financial Statistics Manual* [MFSM], Washington, DC: IMF.

IFC (2006). "Central Bank Statistics", *IFC Bulletin*, 24, August.

Lee, J. and Crowley, P.M. (2009). "Evaluating the Stresses from ECB Monetary Policy in the Euro Area", *Bank of Finland Research Discussion Papers*, 11 April.

Manna, M.H.P. and Quiros, G. (2000). "The Eurosystem's Operational Framework in the Context of its Monetary Policy Strategy", paper presented at the Conference on the Operational Framework of the Eurosystem and Financial Markets, ECB, 5–6 May.

Meltzer, A.H. (1995). "Monetary, Credit and (Other) Transmission Processes: A Monetarist Perspective", *Journal of Economic Perspectives*, 9(4), 49–72.

Mishkin, F.S. (1995). "Symposium on the Monetary Transmission Mechanism", *Journal of Economic Perspectives*, 9(4), 3–10.

Poole, W. (1970). "Optimal Choice of Monetary Policy Instruments in a Simple Stochastic Macro Model", *Quarterly Journal of Economics*, 84(2), 197–216.

United Nations (1993). *System of National Accounts*, New York: UNSTA.

WAMI (2001). *Proposals on a Framework of Monetary Policy for the West African Central Bank* [WACB], Accra, Ghana: WAMI.

WAMI (2002). *Proposals for the Introduction of the Eco Unit of Account*, Accra, Ghana: WAMI.

WAMI (2004). *Data Inadequacies in the WAMZ: An Analysis of Problems, Solutions and Prospects*, Accra, Ghana: WAMI.

WAMI (2004). *Monetary Policy Instruments and Procedures for the West African Central Bank* [WACB], Accra, Ghana: WAMI.

11 Legal and institutional framework

Hussein Thomasi, Adeniyi Karunwi,
Linda Omolehinwa and Gladys Kufuor

Introduction

Legal and institutional frameworks form the bedrock of any monetary union and are the fundamental building blocks for the efficient operation of a system of monetary union. The European Monetary Union, for example, was established by the Treaty of the European Union[1] which places the responsibility for defining and implementing the monetary policy of the single currency firmly in the hands of the European System of Central Banking.[2] The embryonic stage for the creation of a second monetary union of the WAMZ is rooted in Article 54 of the revised Treaty of Economic Community of West African States where it was envisaged that member states of the Economic Community of West African States (ECOWAS) would attain "the status of an economic union within a period of fifteen years".[3] Following the decision of the Authority to fast-track the programme of monetary integration as set out in Chapter 2, the Agreement of the West African Monetary Zone (WAMZ) establishing the second monetary zone of West African states was signed.

This chapter will give a brief overview of various legal instruments which encompass the legal framework of the WAMZ and the institutions established by some of these instruments for the operation of the second monetary union.

Legal and institutional frameworks

The legal and institutional frameworks of the WAMZ were designed to reflect the specific requirements and cultural peculiarities of the Zone.[4] Whereas the European Union adopted a federal or decentralized system of central banking Barnard, 2002, p. 553) the WAMZ has adopted a unitary system of central banking and a single regulator for the supervision and regulation of financial institutions in the Zone. The strategy adopted of maximum harmonization of legal instruments in the Zone and common or unitary institutions is reflected in the legal instruments prepared so far. The linchpin in the establishment of the union is the West African Monetary Institute (WAMI)[5] which has been mandated to undertake all preparations necessary for the take-off of the West African Central Bank (WACB).[6] A list of all the legal instruments is presented in Table 11.1.

Table 11.1 WAMZ legal instruments

No.	Legal instrument
1	Agreement of the West African Monetary Zone
2	Stabilization and Cooperation Fund
3	West African Monetary Institute Statute
4	The West African Central Bank Statute
5	The West African Financial and Supervisory Authority Act
6	The Statute of the WAMZ Secretariat
7	Banking Statute of the WAMZ
8	Non-Bank Financial Institution Statute of the WAMZ
9	Payments System Statute of the WAMZ
10	Single Economic Space and Prosperity Agreement
11	Fiscal Responsibility Act

Source: Author's compilation.

The agreement of the WAMZ

The Agreement establishing the WAMZ was signed in 2000 by The Gambia, Ghana, Guinea, Nigeria and Sierra Leone. The objectives of the WAMZ, as stated under Article 13 of the Agreement of the WAMZ, were the attainment of stable prices, sound fiscal and monetary policies, exchange rate stability and a sustainable balance of payments for member states of the WAMZ. In addition, under the Agreement of the WAMZ, the Statute establishing the WACB was also signed,[7] in order to reinforce commitment as well as pave the way for the eventual domestication into national laws.

The Agreement of the WAMZ places particular importance on the convergence of economic policies and strong economic performance of member states. Good governance provisions were articulated under this Agreement. For instance, Article 16.1 prohibits any "institution or body of the WAMZ, a central government, regional, local or other public authority or any other body governed by public law to apply for or receive credit facility from the WACB". Further, Article 16.2 prohibits the offering for sale of debt instruments belonging to any of the institutions referred to above to the WACB. Article 16.4 prohibits any measure that may establish privileged access to financial institutions in favour of governments and their institutions or bodies or WAMZ institutions. Article 16.6 forbids the placing of restrictions on payments in respect of current account transactions between member states and third countries.

While it is the responsibility of member states to manage the convergence process, the Agreement of the WAMZ recognizes the need for regional support for countries that may experience temporary economic imbalances, hindering the integration process. Consequently, in accordance with the Agreement, a Stabilization and Cooperation Fund (SCF) was established to provide financial assistance to member states that may experience temporary disequilibria in their balance of payments.

Stabilization and Cooperation Fund

The SCF is a specialized mechanism operated under the authority of the Convergence Council. It is established to provide financial assistance for the correction of temporary disequilibria in the balance of payments of member states. The fund is a specialized mechanism operated under the authority of the WAMZ. By Article 2 of its provisions member states and donors would contribute to the SCF.[8] The SCF is disbursed either as short-term stabilization loans to correct temporary distortions in the external payments position or medium-term stabilization loans to correct balance of payments distortions caused by extraordinary and unforeseen situations. Member states seeking such loans are required to adopt policies to correct their economic imbalances.

The West African Monetary Institute (WAMI) Statute

The establishment, general principles, objectives and functions of WAMI are set out in the WAMI Statute. WAMI is a warehousing institute responsible for carrying out all the functions leading to the establishment of the WACB and the introduction of a single currency for the WAMZ. The functions of WAMI are summarized as follows:

1 monitoring and assessing compliance with the convergence criteria;
2 adopting price stability as its central objective and strengthening the coordination of monetary policies in order to achieve that objective;
3 making the necessary preparations for the conduct of a common monetary policy;
4 making preparations for the issue of a common currency;
5 supervising the development of an Exchange Rate Mechanism and a West African Monetary Unit for settlements in the Zone.

The West African Central Bank (WACB) Statute

The common central bank for the Zone is designated the West African Central Bank (WACB) by the Statute of Agreement of Authority of Heads of State and Government of the WAMZ.[9] The primary objective of the WACB is to ensure price stability in the Zone. Other functions include the issuance of the Zone's common currency, the eco, as well as the formulating and implementing of a common monetary policy for countries in the Zone, who are the sole subscribers to and holders of the capital of the WACB.

The West African Financial Supervisory Authority Act

In recognition of the importance of banking supervision in ensuring financial sector soundness in the proposed monetary union, the Authorities of the WAMZ at the seventh meeting of the Convergence Council adopted the West African Financial Supervisory Authority (WAFSA) as a centralized supervisory institution to undertake supervision and regulation of banks and non-banking financial institutions in the member states.

The objective of the instrument is to provide an effective legal and regulatory framework for the licensing and supervision of banks and non-bank financial institutions with a view to ensuring the soundness, safety and stability of banks and non-bank financial institutions as well as a stable macroeconomic environment.

It is apparent from the foregoing that the WAFSA and the WACB are Siamese twins whose functions are inexorably complementary to ensure a safe and sound financial sector as well as achieving and sustaining the objective of price stability in the member countries. The aim of the centralized approach to banking supervision is to relieve the common central bank of moral hazard problems and facilitate full concentration on the primary objective of price stability. Another reason is to create a harmonious front for a relatively symmetrical fusion of the WAMZ and the West African Economic and Monetary Union (WAEMU) within the framework of the ECOWAS Monetary Cooperation Programme.

The Statute of the WAMZ Secretariat

The Statute of the WAMZ Secretariat was signed by the Authority on 3 September 2004 in Conakry, Guinea. The Statute establishes the WAMZ Secretariat to take over the functions of WAMI following the establishment of the WACB. The WAMZ Secretariat will undertake statistical harmonization, development of a macroeconomic database, monitoring and development of fiscal and trade policies multilateral surveillance within the monetary union. The focus of these responsibilities is to ensure sustainability of the convergence process in the Zone, in line with best practice, that would promote the objectives of the WAMZ.

Like the WAFSA, the Secretariat is not a revenue-generating institution. The Secretariat, which mimics those of the European Union and the WAEMU, is an executive arm of the integration and a focal point for the harmonization of economic, statistical and trade policies of member states.

Banking Statute of the WAMZ

The objective of the Banking Statute of the WAMZ is to provide an effective legal and regulatory framework for the supervision of banks and non-bank financial institutions in the Zone in order to ensure the safety and stability of banks and non-bank financial institutions and also ensure a stable macroeconomic environment. The Statute was approved by the Convergence Council in Banjul, The Gambia, on 7 November 2008.

The Non-Bank Financial Institutions Statute of the WAMZ

The Non-Bank Financial Institutions Statute provides the legal framework for the licensing, regulation and supervision of non-bank financial institutions in the WAMZ by the WAFSA. The Statute was approved by the Convergence Council at their twenty-second meeting in Freetown, Sierra Leone, on 19 June 2008.

Payment Systems Statute of the WAMZ

This Statute establishes an appropriate legal framework for the supervision and regulation of clearing and settlement systems as a means of promoting efficiency and stability in the financial system in the WAMZ. The Statute was approved by the Convergence Council in Freetown, Sierra Leone, on 19 June 2008.

Single Economic Space and Prosperity Agreement

The main objective of this Agreement is to create a homogeneous economic area for the promotion of trade and economic relations between the member states by the removal of barriers which impede trade and other economic activity in order to raise the living standards of its citizens. The Statute was approved by the Convergence Council in Freetown, Sierra Leone, on 19 June 2008.

The Fiscal Responsibility Act

The Fiscal Responsibility Act seeks to provide an appropriate legal framework to promote fiscal discipline in member states. It establishes a Fiscal Responsibility Council with oversight responsibility over fiscal policies formulation and implementation.

A major activity for member countries under the WAMZ legal agenda is the ratification and domestication of the key legal instruments.[10] A checklist of a minimum number of legal instruments for a successful union is provided in Table 11.1.

Status of ratification and incorporation into national law

Agreements or treaties between states, in principle, require ratification, which is the act of giving official sanction or approval to the Agreement by the national assembly or parliament of a member state. The Agreement, however, may not have any effect in national law unless it is incorporated. In international law, incorporation is the process by which countries pass domestic legislation to give effect to international Agreements. Incorporation is necessary for countries which follow the Dualist system[11] such as the Commonwealth countries, including The Gambia, Ghana, Nigeria and Sierra Leone. Some countries, however, adopt the Monist system. France and its former colonies are examples of countries which adopt the Monist system[12] where international Agreements, once ratified by the legislature (the national assembly or parliament), become legally binding in domestic law. Under such a system, international agreements are considered self-executing. The Republic of Guinea adopts the Monist system and by its constitution a treaty once ratified takes precedence over domestic law, upon publication.

For the commencement of a monetary union in the WAMZ, it is obligatory that member states ratify all the relevant legal instruments which must thereafter be incorporated into national law. The status of the ratification of the legal instruments in WAMZ member countries are summarized as follows.

The Gambia

The Gambia has ratified the Agreement of the WAMZ and the WACB Statute, which must then be incorporated into national law.

Ghana

Ghana has not ratified the Agreement of the WAMZ, the WACB Statute and the Statute of the WAMZ Secretariat.

Guinea

The WACB Statute and the Agreement of the WAMZ have been ratified by the National Assembly and are legally binding in domestic law in accordance with the Monist system used in Guinea.

Nigeria

The WAMZ Agreement, the WACB Statute and the WAMZ Secretariat Statute have not been ratified by the national assembly.

Sierra Leone

The WAMZ Agreement and the previous WACB Statute were ratified in 2003, but never passed into national law.

Constitutional implications

Constitutional implications arise from the ratification of the WACB Statute. The loss of sovereignty in respect of national currencies to a supra-national body, that is, the WACB, is expected to create conflict in respect of the provisions of some constitutions in member countries. For example, by Article 183 of the Constitution of Ghana, the Bank of Ghana is the sole authority to issue the currency of Ghana. Further in Article 184, the Bank of Ghana is directed to submit to the Auditor General for audit a statement of its foreign exchange receipts and payments or transfers in and out of Ghana.

The Constitution of the Republic of The Gambia in Article 161 also grants sole authority to the Central Bank of The Gambia to issue its currency. It continues in Article 161 (3) to appoint the central bank as the sole banker to the government and the principal depository bank for all funds raised for or on behalf of the government. There are provisions for appointment of the Board of Directors among others.

The Nigerian Constitution (1999) makes no reference to central banking issues and no amendment is therefore needed.[13] The process for amendment of the constitution differs from country to country and in some countries may require a referendum.

Institutional framework

Following the postponement of the take-off date for monetary union to on or before January 2015, the final structure and the system of central banking for the WACB and other WAMZ institutions are being reviewed and streamlined for the adoption by the Convergence Council and Authority of Heads of State and Government of the WAMZ.[14]

Conclusions

According to the Banjul Action Plan and Decision of WAMZ Authorities, the following WAMZ Statutes should have been ratified by member states:

- The Agreement of the WAMZ;
- The WACB Statute;
- The Statute of the WAMZ Secretariat;
- The WAFSA Act;
- Banking Statute of the WAMZ;
- Non-Bank Financial Institutions Statute of the WAMZ.

The WAMZ legal instruments already signed by the Authorities must be ratified by the member states who have so far failed to do so, as a matter of urgency. Non-ratification of the above legal instruments not only poses problems of legality in member states but also questions the willingness and commitment to the project. It is therefore recommended that member states endeavour to ratify and incorporate all the necessary WAMZ legal instruments into national law for the successful launching of the monetary union.

The independence of WAFSA was originally deemed to satisfy the Basel Core Principles. Questions were raised as to the relevance of the Basel Core Principles in the light of developments in the global financial sector. This aspect requires rethinking in order to determine the necessary measures that should be put in place to guard against financial failures where the Basel Core Principles are no longer relevant.

Notes

1 Hereafter referred to as the EC Treaty.
2 Barnard (2002, p. 539) – Article 105(2) EC Treaty: The ESCB is established by the Protocol on the Statute of the ESCB and the ECB.
3 See Article 54.1 of the ECOWAS Treaty.
4 The Zone comprises developing countries which lack adequate infrastructure, legal framework and systems which can be harmonized to support the operation of a monetary zone.

5 An organization akin to the European Monetary Institution which was mandated to establish the European System of Central Banking. See www.ecb.int/ecb/history/emu/html/index.en.html.
6 Article 4 of the Statute of the WAMI.
7 Agreements are usually signed by the respective heads of government or their designated representatives
8 The size of the SCF was conceived to be US$50 million but was increased to US$100 million. All contributions by member countries are in accordance with the ECOWAS budgetary contribution formula. In the case of the WAMZ, the contributions are as follows: The Gambia (6.9 per cent), Ghana (16.9 per cent), Guinea (10.9 per cent), Nigeria (60.4 per cent) and Sierra Leone (4.9 per cent).
9 WACB headquarters is in Ghana.
10 The WAMZ legal instruments are to be ratified by all member countries and incorporated into national law, where applicable, before the commencement of the monetary union.
11 Dualists emphasize the difference between national and international law, and require the translation of the international law into national law. If a state accepts a treaty but does not adapt its national law in order to conform to the treaty or does not create a national law explicitly incorporating the treaty, then it violates international law. According to dualists, national judges never apply international law, only international law that has been translated into national law (Malenovský, 1993).
12 Monists assume that the internal and international legal systems form a unity. International law does not need to be translated into national law. The act of ratifying the international law immediately incorporates the law into national law. International law can be directly applied by a national judge, and can be directly invoked by citizens, just as if it were national law (Dixon, 1996).
13 Amendment to certain acts of parliament such as the CBN Act may, however, be necessary.
14 The report of the consultant on the study on the structure and type of central bank for the WAMZ is being reviewed.

References

Bernard, C. (2002). *The Substantive Law of the EU*, 2nd edn, Oxford: Oxford University Press.

Dixon, M. (1996). *Textbook on International Law*, 3rd edn, London, Chapter 4.

ECOWAS (1993). Revised Treaty. Published by the Executive Secretariat, Abuja, Nigeria. Online: www.worldtradelaw.net/fta/agreements/ecowasfta.pdf.

Gambia (2002). Constitution of the Republic of Gambia. Online: www.ncce.gm/files/constitution.

Ghana (1992). Constitution of the Republic of Ghana. Online: www.parliament.gh/constitution_republic_ghana.html.

Malenovský, J. (1993). *Mezinárodní právo verejné*, Brno, Chapter 5.

Nigeria (1999). Constitution of the Federal Republic Nigeria. Online: www.nigeria.congress.org/resources/constitution.

WAMI (2000). *Agreement, Statutes and other Provisions of the West African Monetary Zone*, ECW/AGR/WAMZ/1, December.

WAMI (2001). *Decisions of the Authority of Heads of State and Government of the West African Monetary Zone*, Accra, Ghana: WAMI.

Part IV
The way forward

12 A comparative analysis

Temitope W. Oshikoya, John H. Tei Kitcher and Emmanuel Onwioduokit

Introduction

The lessons of experience suggest that the establishment of any properly functioning monetary union is a feat requiring, above all, time for full preparation. The experience of other monetary unions, especially the European Monetary Union and the Gulf Cooperation Council (GCC), vividly highlights the fact that formation of a monetary union is a long-term process, requiring both political will and culture of regionalism. In view of these all-important realities, this chapter provides a comparative analysis between the WAMZ and other monetary unions, with specific reference to the GCC and the West African Economic and Monetary Union (WAEMU).

The WAMZ and GCC compared

The Authorities of the GCC countries decided in 2001 to establish a monetary union by 2010, about the same time the WAMZ Authorities decided to have monetary union. However, unlike the WAMZ authorities that envisaged a monetary union in just 18 months, the GCC gave themselves a nine-year period.

The GCC states have several distinct socio-economic characteristics that make them more homogeneous and less likely to suffer asymmetric shocks. They are also culturally and historically the same people, with the same language, religion and geographical proximity. Using the principles of the Optimum Currency Area (OCA), the GCC made progress with respect to economic structure, real and nominal convergence, a customs union, labour mobility and financial integration. Comparable selected macroeconomic statistics for the two monetary unions are given below.

The GCC countries are relatively wealthier than the WAMZ countries. They have vast oil and gas reserves (the world's largest if measured in barrels of oil per capita), yet unlike many other oil-rich states have very small populations. The total population of the GCC is about 36.5 million compared to WAMZ population of about 189.2 million. While the population of the GCC is one-fifth that of WAMZ, the total nominal gross domestic product (GDP) of the GCC is more than triple that of the WAMZ. Average per capita income in the GCC is thus 20 times that of the WAMZ. The GCC has a combined GDP of US$774.4 billion as at 2007 against the WAMZ's US$214.5 billion during the same period. Thus the average per capita income for the GCC stood at US$23,548.2 against WAMZ per capita income of US$1,286.8.

Relative to the WAMZ, there is also less heterogeneity and more symmetry in the economic structure of the GCC, although diversification has increased among the countries. Unlike the WAMZ, where there is only one major oil producer, the GCC countries are all oil-producing, although the level of production varies from country to country. The contribution of agriculture to the GDP in the GCC is insignificant, and the country with the highest contribution is Saudi Arabia (3 per cent). In the case of the WAMZ, the smallest contribution to GDP by agriculture is 22.3 per cent (that of Guinea). On average, agriculture contributes about 37 per cent to the WAMZ's GDP, compared to about 0.8 per cent in the GCC. Also compared to the WAMZ countries, where the structure of production has remained basically static over the last three decades, the GCC countries have achieved rapid progress in the past three decades, leading to a 30 to 35 per cent decline in oil's contribution to GDP, from 65 to 70 per cent in the mid-1970s. In terms of relative size, Saudi Arabia constitutes about half the GDP of GCC, while the largest WAMZ economy, Nigeria, represents about four-fifths of the GDP of the Zone.

The GCC agreed on five convergence criteria, which mimic those applied by the EU member states for the euro. In addition, all members have their currencies pegged to the US dollar, except for Kuwait, which moved to a peg of baskets of currency. The inflation rate in the GCC as at 2007 ranged between 3 per cent (Saudi Arabia) and 12 per cent (Qatar). Comparative figures for the WAMZ were 6.2 per cent (The Gambia) and 12.5 per cent (Ghana). Foreign exchange reserves for the GCC countries ranged from four months of import equivalent for Bahrain to 13.8 months for Kuwait. In the WAMZ, comparable months of import cover ranged from one month (Guinea) to 13 months (Nigeria).

The GCC adopted a common external customs tariff in 2003. In early 2008, the common market initiative for the GCC countries was launched and implementation is underway through the adaptation of national legislation and regulations. Currently, about 75 per cent of the needed harmonization has already been achieved. Labour mobility is quite high within the GCC. Unlike in the WAMZ, infrastructure in the GCC is well-developed, comparable to that of Europe, education for nationals is free, including at the tertiary level, and there is access to a universal healthcare system. Public sector workers are among the best paid in the world.

In September 2008, the GCC central bank governors approved the charter for a monetary council (equivalent of the European Monetary Institute and the West African Monetary Institute), a precursor to a regional central bank. In September 2008, the governors of the GCC countries indicated that there are three important policy issues that need to be addressed before the commencement of the monetary union. These are: inflation needs to be reduced to lower single-digit figures rather than at low levels; the statistical base needs to be harmonized to provide comparable economic and financial data; and the Gulf Monetary Union needs to be supported by investments in financial infrastructure (including legal and regulatory), payments systems and developments and linkage of money markets and capital markets. However, a recent review by the authorities indicates that the realization of the target date of 2010 for a monetary union is unlikely, given the outstanding challenges, which include: agreement on the nature and scope of the GCC monetary authority and the introduction of a common currency; harmonization of key regulatory and supervisory frameworks, especially for the financial sector, and statistical methodologies for key financial and economic indicators; and agreement on the customs union and the issues outstanding with regard to the sharing of customs revenue.

GCC central bank governors have recently signalled that the new common currency would not be in circulation by the agreed 2010 target.

In essence, the challenges faced by the WAMZ countries on the road to monetary union are not unique, as even the GCC that is comparatively more homogeneous in population, economic structure and even culture and religion is also facing similar challenges. Recently, Oman has opted not to join the single currency if the 2010 deadline is maintained. While reiterating a full commitment to monetary union, Saudi Arabia, the largest economy in the GCC, indicated that the 2010 target was "very ambitious", leaving the door open for a postponement, thus effectively calling for the launch of the single currency to be delayed, but certainly not cancelled. In comparing the progress of the GCC to that of the WAMZ, it becomes clear that, while the GCC has had a long-term view of monetary union, the WAMZ has been somewhat over-ambitious in the target dates it has set for achieving monetary union.

The WAMZ and the WAEMU compared

The West African Monetary and Economic Union (WAEMU/UEMOA) was established in 1994, comprising countries that already shared a single currency in the form of the CFA franc. The longstanding prior existence of the CFA franc and Central Bank of West African States (BCEAO) helped WAEMU to take the lead in the monetary and economic integration processes in West Africa and it now includes eight countries (Guinea-Bissau joined in 1997). The second monetary zone, the WAMZ was set up in 2001, comprising five member countries with the objective of establishing a common central bank as well as introducing a common currency, to be called the eco. Both WAEMU and WAMZ are sub-regional institutions within the Economic Community of West African States (ECOWAS) and are expected to work towards establishing a single currency for the whole of ECOWAS.

While the WAMZ adopted a macroeconomic convergence framework as the basis for forming economic and monetary union, the WAEMU monetary union essentially emerged out of the historical relations between France and its former colonies. It was only in 1994, following the devaluation of the CFA, that the pre-existing monetary union was extended to include aspects of economic integration, with WAEMU adopting a set of macroeconomic convergence criteria.

There are strong cultural, historical, social and economic ties between the peoples of the WAEMU and WAMZ. Aside from the geographic proximity of the two blocs there is greater similarity in the structure of the economies of the two groupings. Agriculture is the largest employer in most of the countries in both, with the primary sector accounting for the largest share of GDP. Nigeria is so far the only major oil-exporting country in the WAMZ while all the countries in the WAEMU are oil-importing, with the exception of Côte d'Ivoire. Both zones are potentially rich in mineral resources. Apart from Nigeria and Côte d'Ivoire, most of countries in ECOWAS are small open economies. All the countries are, however, susceptible to exogenous shocks.

Although WAMZ has fewer member countries, it has a relatively larger population than WAEMU. WAMZ is home to 189.2 million inhabitants (2007 estimate), of which 78.2 per cent reside in Nigeria. WAEMU has a combined population of 87.3 million, or around half of the total population of the WAMZ. The combined estimated GDP of WAMZ at US$214.5 billion is four times larger than that of WAEMU, which stood at US$57.2 billion. Of the total GDP of WAMZ, Nigeria accounts for 86.1 per cent, while Côte d'Ivoire accounts for 34.6 per cent of WAEMU's GDP. While the relative proportionate share of the total GDP of WAEMU is broadly dispersed, the proportionate share of the combined GDP in WAMZ is largely dominated by Nigeria.

Average per capita income (purchasing power parity in US$) is slightly higher in the WAMZ (US$1,286.8) than in WAEMU (US$1,147.38), and weighted average inflation is relatively lower in the WAEMU (3.7 per cent) than in the WAMZ (10.1 per cent). The average reserve position, expressed in months of imports, is slightly higher in WAEMU (6) than in WAMZ (5.6).

There are disparities between the member countries in both zones in respect of the achievement of sustainable macroeconomic convergence. However, there is some evidence of the convergence of macroeconomic stability indicators, in particular inflation and fiscal balance, in WAEMU. In the WAMZ, harmonized policy coordination through observance of prescribed macroeconomic convergence criteria is progressing steadily.

As regards the ECOWAS common market programme, countries in both zones have adopted the ECOWAS common external tariff and are participating in the ECOWAS Trade Liberalization Scheme (ETLS). The protocol on free movement of goods and services is also being widely observed. However, the objective of labour mobility, although entrenched in the ECOWAS protocol, is not being fully complied with in either of the two zones.

The overall picture indicates that, while there is relative macroeconomic stability in the WAEMU zone (due mainly to the lower rate of inflation), the levels of competitiveness as well as economic growth are generally higher in the WAMZ.

Conclusions

The challenges faced by the WAMZ countries on the road to monetary union are not unique, as is well illustrated by the fact the GCC, with its comparatively more homogeneous population, economic structure and even culture and religion, is also facing similar challenges. A credible monetary union is usually premised on the achievement of specific criteria by its candidate member countries and in the European case it took half a century to introduce the euro (in 1999, after postponements and shifts in dates along the way). These examples demonstrate the need for sufficient time to build a durable union that will be credible. The overriding concern of the WAMZ monetary union at this point should not necessarily be that of any damage to its credibility arising from further postponement, but the long-term sustainability and viability of such a union. Overall, it is clear that, the establishment of a sustainable and efficient monetary union in the WAMZ is not just an imperative but an ultimatum. The key to success will be found in doing the right thing at the right time, with the help of appropriate durable and sustainable infrastructure and economic fundamentals.

References

Backe, P. and Wojcik, C. (2002). "Alternative Options for the Monetary Integration of Central and Eastern European EU Accession Countries", *Occasional Paper*, 3, Institute for Economic Research (Ljubljana).

Bayoumi, T. (1997). *Financial Integration and Real Activity*, Manchester: Manchester University Press.

Breuss, F. Fink, G. and Haiss, P. (2004). "How Well Prepared Are the New Member States for the European Monetary Union?", *Journal of Policy Modeling* (Special Issue on "Englargement of the European Monetary Union").

Buiter, W.H. (2007). "Economic, Political and Institutional Prerequisites for Monetary Union among the Members of the Gulf Cooperation Council", paper prepared for the seminar "Preparing for GCC Currency Union: Institutional Framework and Policy Options", 20–21 November 2007, Dubai.

Buiter, W.H. and Sibert, A.C. (2006). "When Will the New EU Members from the Eastern Europe Join the Euro Zone?", provisional paper (May).

Coe, D. and Helpman, E. (1995). "International Research and Development Spill Overs", *European Economic Review*, 39, 859–87.

De Grauwe, P. (2000). *Economics of Monetary Union*, 4th edn, Oxford: Oxford University Press.

Eichengreen, B. (2004). "Real and Pseudo Preconditions for an Asian Monetary Union", paper presented to the Asian Development Bank High-Level Conference on Asia's Economic Cooperation and Integration, Manila (July).

Gros, D.T.N. (1998). *European Monetary Integration*, Harlow: Addison Wesley Longman.

Hebous, S. (2006). "On the Monetary Union of the Gulf States", *Working Paper*, 431, Kiel Institute for the World Economy, Dusternbrooker Weg 120 D 24105, Kiel, February.

Helliwell, J.F. (1998). *How Much Do National Borders Matter?* Washington, DC: Brookings Institution Press.

Ibrahim, B.A. (2004). "Do the AGCC Economies need a Single Currency? Some Potential

Costs and Benefits of a Monetary Union for the Member States of the Arab Gulf Cooperation Council (AGCC)", *Economic Research Forum*, conference proceedings.

Jikang, Z. and Yin, L. (2005). "Is East Asia Suitable for a Monetary Union? Experience from EU and Evidence from China, Japan and South Korea", draft paper submitted to First Consortium Meeting EU–NESCA (November).

Laabas, B. and Limam, I. (2002). *Are GCC Countries Ready for Currency Union?* Kuwait: Arab Planning Institute.

McCallum, J. (1995). National Borders Matter: Canada–US Regional Trade Patterns, *American Economic Review*, 85, 615–23.

Robson, P. (1984). *The Economics of International Integration*, London: George Allen and Unwin.

Walter, N., Becker, W. and Muhlberger, M. (2006). *Estonia, Lithuania, Slovenia: Poised to Adopt the Euro (Views on Long-term Convergence)*, Frankfurt: Deutsche Bank Research.

WAMI (2008). *Convergence Report*. Online: www.wami-imao.org.

World Bank (2008). *World Economic Outlook*, Washington, DC: World Bank.

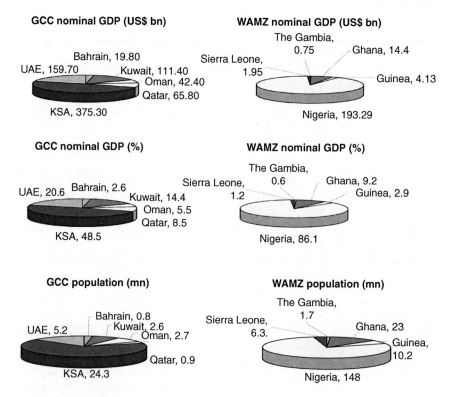

Figure 12.1 Production and income in the GCC and the WAMZ (2007) (source: World Bank (2008) and WAMI (2008)). *continued*

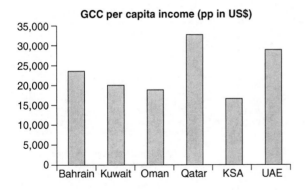

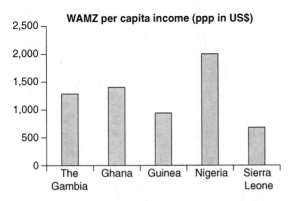

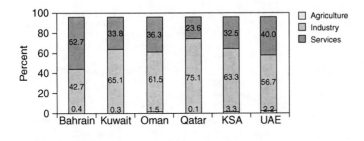

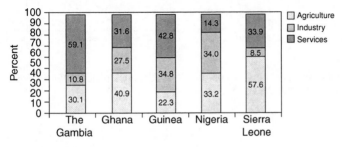

Figure 12.1 continued.

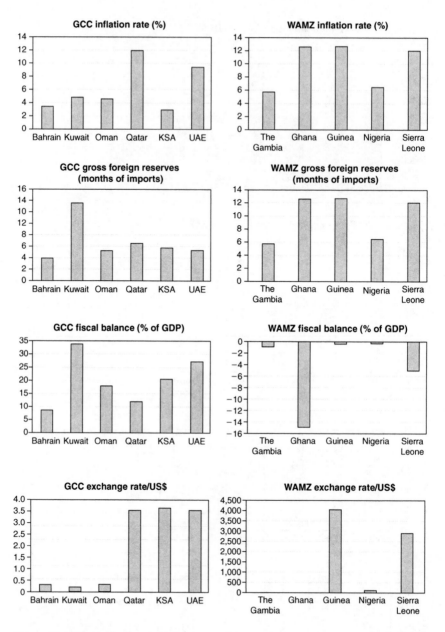

Figure 12.2 Key indicators in the GCC and the WAMZ (2007) (source: World Bank (2008) and WAMI (2008)).

WAMZ nominal GDP (US\$ bn)

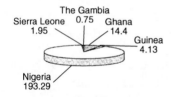

The Gambia
0.75
Sierra Leone
1.95
Ghana
14.4
Guinea
4.13
Nigeria
193.29

UEMOA nominal GDP (US\$ bn)

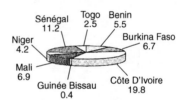

Sénégal
11.2
Togo
2.5
Benin
5.5
Niger
4.2
Burkina Faso
6.7
Mali
6.9
Guinée Bissau
0.4
Côte D'Ivoire
19.8

WAMZ share of GDP (%)

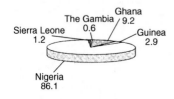

Ghana
9.2
The Gambia
0.6
Sierra Leone
1.2
Guinea
2.9
Nigeria
86.1

UEMOA share of GDP (%)

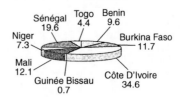

Sénégal
19.6
Togo
4.4
Benin
9.6
Niger
7.3
Burkina Faso
11.7
Mali
12.1
Guinée Bissau
0.7
Côte D'Ivoire
34.6

WAMZ population (mn)

The Gambia
1.7
Sierra Leone
6.3
Ghana
23
Guinea
10.2
Nigeria
148

UEMOA population (mn)

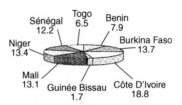

Sénégal
12.2
Togo
6.5
Benin
7.9
Niger
13.4
Burkina Faso
13.7
Mali
13.1
Guinée Bissau
1.7
Côte D'Ivoire
18.8

WAMZ per capita income (PPP in US\$)

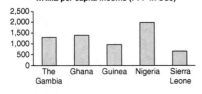

UEMOA per capita income (PPP in US\$)

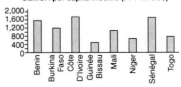

WAMZ inflation rate (%) end period

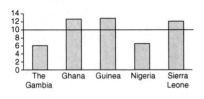

UEMOA inflation rate (%) end period

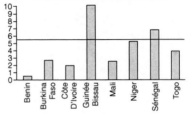

Figure 12.3 Key indicators in the WAMZ and the WAEMU/UEMOA (2007) (source: World Bank (2008) and WAMI (2008)).

WAMZ gross foreign reserves (months of import)

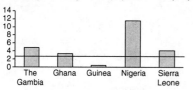

UEMOA gross foreign reserves (months of imports)

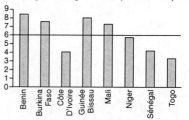

WAMZ fiscal balance (% of GDP) excluding grants

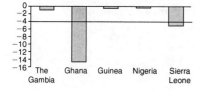

UEMOA fiscal balance (% of GDP) excluding grants

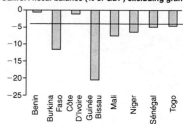

Figure 12.3 continued.

Index